SOLICITORS' ACCOUNTS — A PRACTICAL GUIDE

SOLICITORS' ACCOUNTS — A PRACTICAL GUIDE

Dale Kay
Solicitor (Hons)

and

Janet Baker
LLB (Hons), Solicitor

Published by
Blackstone Press Limited
Aldine Place
London
W12 8AA
United Kingdom

Sales enquiries and orders
Telephone +44-(0)-20-8740-2277
Facsimile +44-(0)-20-8743-2292
e-mail: sales@blackstone.demon.co.uk
website: www.blackstonepress.com

ISBN 1-84174-238-4
© Dale Kay and Janet Baker 2001
First edition 1997
Second edition 1998
Third edition 1999
Fourth edition 2000
Fifth edition 2001

Some material contained in this manual was originally published by Blackstone Press in 1992 under the title *Solicitors' Accounts: A Student's Guide*

British Library Cataloguing in Publication Data
A catalogue record for this book is available from the British Library

This publication is protected by international copyright law. All rights reserved. No part of this publication may be reproduced, stored in a retrieval system, or transmitted in any form or by any means, electronic, mechanical, photocopying, recording or otherwise, without the prior permission of the publisher.

Typeset in 10/12 Palatino by Montage Studios Ltd, Tonbridge, Kent
Printed and bound in Great Britain by Antony Rowe Limited, Chippenham and Reading

CONTENTS

Preface vii

1 Introduction to Solicitors' Accounts 1

1.1 The purpose of keeping accounts — 1.2 An introduction to double-entry bookkeeping — 1.3 Classification of accounts — 1.4 Worked example on double entry — 1.5 The trial balance — 1.6 Exercises on double-entry bookkeeping and trial balance — 1.7 Suggested answers to exercises on double-entry bookkeeping and trial balance — 1.8 Exercise on double-entry bookkeeping and trial balance — 1.9 Suggested answers to exercise on double-entry bookkeeping and trial balance

2 Final Accounts and Adjustments 29

2.1 Introduction — 2.2 Closing the accounts — 2.3 Presentation of final accounts — 2.4 The balance sheet — 2.5 Exercise on basic final accounts — 2.6 Suggested answer to exercise on basic final accounts — 2.7 The need for adjustments — 2.8 Outstanding expenses adjustment — 2.9 Summary — 2.10 Payment in advance — 2.11 Summary — 2.12 Closing stocks — 2.13 Summary — 2.14 Work in progress (or work in hand) — 2.15 Summary — 2.16 Bad debts and doubtful debts adjustments — 2.17 Summary — 2.18 Depreciation — 2.19 Sale of assets — 2.20 Exercises on adjustments and final accounts — 2.21 Suggested answers to exercises on adjustments and final accounts

3 Partnership Accounts 71

3.1 The accounts kept by a partnership — 3.2 Final accounts — 3.3 Drawings — 3.4 Partnership changes — 3.5 Exercises on partnership final accounts — 3.6 Suggested answers to exercises on partnership final accounts — 3.7 Test on partnership final accounts — 3.8 Suggested answers to test on partnership final accounts

4 Basic Accounting Concepts and Manufacturing and Trading Accounts 103

4.1 Financial accounting concepts — 4.2 Accounting bases and policies — 4.3 Manufacturing and trading accounts — 4.4 Practice exercise — 4.5 Suggested answer to practice exercise

5 Company Accounts and Consolidated Group Accounts 113

5.1 Accounts of limited companies — 5.2 Limited companies' profit and loss accounts — 5.3 Reports and records required under the Companies Acts — 5.4 Practice exercises — 5.5 Suggested answers to practice exercises — 5.6 Group companies and consolidated accounts — 5.7 Practice exercises — 5.8 Suggested answers to practice exercises

CONTENTS

6 Interpretation of Accounts and Accounting Ratios — 157

6.1 Introduction — 6.2 Check factors outside the accounts — 6.3 General areas to look at — 6.4 Trends — 6.5 Ratios — 6.6 Example — 6.7 Exercise — 6.8 Suggested answer to exercise

7 Basic Solicitors' Accounts — 175

7.1 Introduction — 7.2 The Solicitors' Accounts Rules 1998 (SAR) — 7.3 Basic entries — 7.4 Payments out of petty cash – office account — 7.5 Profit costs — 7.6 Transfers — 7.7 Exercises on basic ledger entries — 7.8 Suggested answers to exercises on basic ledger entries — 7.9 Value Added Tax — 7.10 Exercises on ledger accounts including VAT — 7.11 Suggested answers to exercises on ledger accounts including VAT

8 Financial Statements and Conveyancing Transactions — 207

8.1 Financial statements to clients — 8.2 Conveyancing transactions — 8.3 Receipt of deposit on exchange of contracts — 8.4 Mortgage advances — 8.5 Mortgage redemption — 8.6 Completion — 8.7 Exercises on conveyancing transactions — 8.8 Suggested answers to exercises on conveyancing transactions

9 Deposit Interest and Probate Transactions — 241

9.1 Paying interest to the client — 9.2 Earning interest on clients' money — 9.3 Example on deposit interest — 9.4 Suggested answer to example on deposit interest — 9.5 Probate transactions — 9.6 Exercises on probate transactions — 9.7 Suggested answers to exercises on probate transactions — 9.8 Test 1 on probate transactions — 9.9 Suggested answer to test 1 on probate transactions — 9.10 Test 2 on probate transactions — 9.11 Suggested answer to test 2 on probate transactions

10 Further Transactions — 261

10.1 Commissions — 10.2 Agency — 10.3 Abatements — 10.4 Dishonoured cheques — 10.5 Small transactions — 10.6 Bad debts — 10.7 Exercises on further transactions — 10.8 Suggested answers to exercises on further transactions — 10.9 Test on further transactions — 10.10 Suggested answer to test on further transactions — 10.11 Test on ledger accounts including VAT — 10.12 Suggested answer to test on ledger accounts including VAT — 10.13 Revision questions — 10.14 Suggested answers to revision questions — 10.15 Self assessment questions on the Solicitors' Accounts Rules 1998 (SAR) — 10.16 Suggested answers to self assessment questions

Index — 295

PREFACE

Accounts is regarded as a pervasive subject, although separately assessed. A word of encouragement. Most students do well and even manage to enjoy the time they spend on accounts. Do not worry if you did not enjoy GCSE maths; the only maths involved here is very basic arithmetic. You should find that an understanding of the principles and format of accounts will help you with your business law and in understanding the operation of a solicitor's own practice. You will appreciate the line drawn between money belonging to the solicitor's own practice and the money belonging to clients. Do use the exercises in the book and those given to you in your course; this is the best way to come to grips with the subject.

I would like to thank Janet Baker, whose original book still forms the basis of this Guide. My thanks also go to my family, to all my students, my colleagues and ex-colleagues and to everyone at Blackstone.

Dale Kay
May 2001
Manchester

ONE

INTRODUCTION TO SOLICITORS' ACCOUNTS

1.1 The Purpose of Keeping Accounts

All businesses must keep a day-to-day record of their financial transactions, from which they will be able to prepare a set of final accounts.

These fall into two main sections:

(a) *The profit and loss account* — a record of income and expenses for the period in question, showing the net profit or loss made by the business.

(b) *The balance sheet* — a list of the assets and liabilities of the business, showing what the business owns and what it owes.

From these not only will it be possible to see the profit, or loss made, but a comparison may be made between the profit for this period and the profit made in previous periods. The size of the profit may be compared with other, similar, businesses. Profit made should be checked in relation to the assets held by the business, for example, if the business has assets worth £2m and is making a profit of £25,000 this is clearly unsatisfactory. The balance sheet also shows whether the business can pay what is due in the short- or long-term.

The information provided by the accounts will be used not only by the owners or managers of the business, who will need to know what has happened or is happening financially, but will need to be revealed to the Inland Revenue or Customs and Excise to agree tax liabilities, or to the bank who may be lending money to the business. If the business is to be sold, then the buyer will require financial information, as will a new partner joining the business.

1.1.1 TYPES OF ACCOUNTS KEPT BY A BUSINESS

A business must keep separate accounts for:

(a) *Personal accounts*. Each person, firm or company with whom the solicitor has business dealings, for example, the solicitor will open an account in the name of Office Supplies Ltd to record the solicitor's indebtedness to that company.

(b) *Income accounts (nominal)*. Each source of income, for example, an account called the 'costs account' will be opened to record costs charged to the solicitor's clients.

(c) *Expense accounts (nominal)*. Each type of business expenditure, for example, if the solicitor pays rent for the office a rent account will be opened.

(d) *Asset/Real accounts*. Each type of asset, for example, a motor cars account will be opened to record the purchase of cars for use by the firm.

(e) For solicitors, each client on whose behalf money is handled. These are personal accounts.

1.1.2 THE LAYOUT OF AN ACCOUNT

There are several methods of drawing an account. The method adopted in this book is as follows.

NAME OF ACCOUNT

Date	Details	Dr	Cr	Balance

The following points should be noted:

(a) This layout has five columns.

(b) There is one column each for date and details. Note that the details column must indicate clearly the name of the account which forms the other part of the double entry.

(c) The column headed 'Dr' (abbreviation of debit) is always on the left. Debit entries, the meaning of which will be explained later in the chapter, are made in this column.

(d) The column headed 'Cr' (abbreviation of credit) is always on the right. Credit entries are made in this column.

(e) There is a balance column which gives a running balance on the account after each transaction is completed. The balance is the difference between the debit and credit entries.

Note that Rule 32(5) of the Solicitors' Accounts Rules 1998 also imposes an obligation to show the current balance on each client's ledger, or the balance must be readily ascertainable from the records kept.

1.2 An Introduction to Double-entry Bookkeeping

A basic account is a record or a history of financial transactions.

To record monies received and monies paid out, a simple single entry cash account could be drawn up as follows:

INTRODUCTION TO SOLICITORS' ACCOUNTS

Example Roger receives £500 salary (income) during the week and pays out £200 rent (expense) and £100 on food (expense).

CASH ACCOUNT

	Received	Paid	Balance
	£	£	£
Wages (Income)	500		500
Rent (expense)		200	300
Food (expense)		100	200

Although this may appear to be an adequate record, it would not show, for example, any goods or services received or supplied on credit, nor how much food was left in the cupboard and it would be difficult to extract information on the breakdown of expenses and income if many entries were made.

To maintain a complete and accurate record of financial transactions, the double-entry system of bookkeeping is used.

1.2.1 THE PRINCIPLE

The principle of double-entry bookkeeping is that there are two aspects to every single financial transaction:

(a) The benefit received.

(b) The consideration given.

Thus two entries are made for each single transaction.

In the example above Roger received £500 cash, but £500 worth of work was given by him in return for this cash.

Thus the entries would be:

CASH ACCOUNT

	Benefit received	Consideration given	Balance
	£	£	£
Salary	500		500

INCOME EARNED ACCOUNT
(Value of work done — names the source of the income)

	Benefit received	Consideration given	Balance
	£	£	£
Cash		500	500

When Roger paid for the rent he received the benefit of £200 worth of accommodation, and £200 cash was given by him.

3

INTRODUCTION TO SOLICITORS' ACCOUNTS

Thus the entries would be:

RENT ACCOUNT
(names the source of the loss)

	Benefit received	Consideration given	Balance
Cash	£ 200	£	£ 200

CASH ACCOUNT

	Benefit received	Consideration given	Balance
Balance Rent paid	£	£ 200	£ 500 300

When Roger paid for the food the entries would be:

FOOD ACCOUNT

	Benefit received	Consideration given	Balance
Cash	£ 100	£	£ 100

CASH ACCOUNT

	Benefit received	Consideration given	Balance
Balance Food	£	£ 100	£ 300 200

The benefit received is shown on the left hand side of the account and called the **DEBIT** entry, the consideration given is shown on the right hand side of the account, and called the **CREDIT** entry.

DEBIT   CREDIT
BENEFIT RECEIVED   CONSIDERATION GIVEN

This may seem strange or wrong at this stage, as many people associate credit with receipts, and debit with payments out, usually based on an individual's bank statement sent out from the bank, where payments out are shown as debit entries and receipts are shown as credit entries.

Example Jane pays £1,000 into her bank account with the Northern Bank PLC. The Northern Bank will draw up its accounts as follows:

NORTHERN BANK PLC
CASH ACCOUNT

	Benefit received Debit	Consideration given Credit	Balance
Jane	£ 1,000	£	£ 1,000 Dr

JANE ACCOUNT

	Benefit received Debit	Consideration given Credit	Balance
Cash	£	£ 1,000	£ 1,000 Cr

The bank has followed the rules given above, but all Jane sees is one part of the double entry. From Jane's point of view the credit entry records a receipt. From the Bank's point of view the receipt was recorded on the Bank's cash account and Jane's account shows that Jane has given the cash. Jane is a creditor of the Bank — see later.

Remember that the two entries made *do* record the same *single* transaction.

The following is of vital importance and must be committed to memory:

A debit represents:

In real accounts
An increase in the value of an asset.

In personal accounts
A reduction in the amount of a liability.

In nominal accounts
An item of expenditure.

A credit represents:

A reduction in the value of an asset.

An increase in the amount of a liability.

An item of income.

The principle of double-entry bookkeeping is therefore: *for every debit entry in one account there must be a corresponding credit entry in another account.*

1.2.2 THE CASH ACCOUNT IN THE DOUBLE-ENTRY SYSTEM

The cash account records all money, cash and cheques paid into the firm's bank account and all payments made by cheque (NB: a separate account is kept to record cash payments — the petty cash account). So in all transactions involving the receipt of money/cheques paid into the bank or payments by cheque the cash account will be one account of double entry.

INTRODUCTION TO SOLICITORS' ACCOUNTS

Example Jack Jones starts up in business as a painter and decorator. He borrows £1,000 from his brother Fred Jones and spends £300 on wallpaper and paint and £600 on a second-hand van. He does a job for £125 and pays the cheque he receives in payment into the bank.

At this stage Jack's cash account will look like this:

CASH ACCOUNT

Date	Details	Dr	Cr	Balance
		(Received) £	(Paid) £	£
	Fred Jones' loan	1,000		1,000 Dr
	Decorating materials		300	700 Dr
	Motor van		600	100 Dr
	Income	125		225 Dr

The cash account tells Jack how much money he has in the bank but it does not tell him the whole story about his business:

(a) It does not show that he owes Fred £1,000.

(b) It does not show that he has spent his money on decorating materials which he will use to earn his income.

(c) It does not show that he has acquired an asset, the van.

(d) It does not show that he has earned income of £125.00.

To complete the picture, Jack will have to open the accounts to show the other side of each transaction:

FRED JONES: LOAN ACCOUNT
(Personal account)

Date	Details	Dr	Cr	Balance
	Cash loan	£	£ 1,000	£ 1,000 Cr

DECORATING MATERIALS ACCOUNT
(Expense account)

Date	Details	Dr	Cr	Balance
	Cash — wallpaper and paint	£ 300	£	£ 300 Dr

MOTOR CARS ACCOUNT
(Asset/real account)

Date	Details	Dr	Cr	Balance
	Cash — van	£ 600	£	£ 600 Dr

INTRODUCTION TO SOLICITORS' ACCOUNTS

INCOME ACCOUNT

Date	Details	Dr	Cr	Balance
		£	£	£
	Cash		125	125 Cr

Of course not all transactions will involve money being paid into or out of the bank, i.e., where the firm buys or sells goods on credit. By looking at the cash account Jack will not be able to tell how much he owes to others (his creditors) or how much is owed to him (his debtors). To record credit transactions two accounts other than the cash account will be used.

Suppose in the above example the following had occurred:

(a) Instead of paying £600 cash for the van Jack bought it on credit from Kwiksales. He will still use the motor cars account to show that he owns a van value £600 but now, instead of the double entry being in the cash account, he will open an account to show that he owes £600 to Kwiksales (a creditors account).

MOTOR CARS ACCOUNT
(Asset)

Date	Details	Dr	Cr	Balance
		£	£	£
	Kwiksales — van bought on credit	600		600 Dr

KWIKSALES ACCOUNT
(Personal account)

Date	Details	Dr	Cr	Balance
		£	£	£
	Motor vehicles — van on credit		600	600 Cr

(b) As well as receiving a cheque for £125 for work done, Jack did £250 worth of work for Brown and agreed with Brown that he could pay at the end of the month. Jack needs to show in his income account that he has earned £250, but as he has not been paid yet, the double entry will not be in the cash account. He must open another account in the name of Brown to show that Brown is indebted to him to the tune of £250 (a debtors account).

PROFIT COSTS RE WORK DONE
INCOME ACCOUNT

Date	Details	Dr	Cr	Balance
		£	£	£
	Cash		125	
	Brown		250	375 Cr

BROWN ACCOUNT
(Personal account)

Date	Details	Dr	Cr	Balance
		£	£	£
	Profit Costs Income — work done on credit	250		250 Dr

1.3 Classification of Accounts

All financial transactions will therefore be recorded by double entry in the ledger accounts of a business. These ledger accounts can be divided into three types:

(a) *Personal accounts* These will be debited when the individual, firm or company dealing with the business receives goods, cash or services from the business, and credited when the individual, firm or company gives goods, cash or services to the business.

(b) *Real accounts* These will be debited when the business receives an asset, or assets are increased and credited when the business disposes of an asset, or assets are reduced.

(c) *Nominal accounts* Nominal expense accounts are debited with the loss/money paid out — they name the source of the loss by showing nominally what the business has received in return for its loss.

Nominal income accounts are credited with the gain/money received — they name the source of the gain by showing nominally what the business has given in return for the gain.

NB: each account drawn up will have a balance column which will show the difference between all the debit entries made and all the credit entries made. For example, if an account has debit entries totalling £10,000 and credit entries totalling £8,000 it will have a debit balance of £2,000.

1.3.1 PERSONAL ACCOUNTS

The following should be noted with regard to personal accounts:

(a) They record transactions involving individuals, firms or companies.

(b) A separate account must be kept for each person, firm or company with which the firm has dealings, for example, each debtor and creditor.

The rule for making entries in a personal account is:

Debit the account of the person, firm or company which receives value from the transaction.

Thus in the example above Brown's personal account is debited with £250 because he has received work/value from the firm.

Credit the account of the person, firm or company giving value to the firm.

Thus in the example above (involving Kwiksales) their personal account is credited because they have given value to the firm.

INTRODUCTION TO SOLICITORS' ACCOUNTS

1.3.2 THE PERSONAL ACCOUNTS OF THE BUSINESS PROPRIETOR

The accounts look at a transaction from the point of view of the business. For accounting purposes the business and its owner are treated as separate entities. This principle holds good for a solicitor's practice. The accounts which record transactions between the business and its owner are personal accounts. These accounts are:

1.3.2.1 Capital account

When a solicitor sets up in practice he will introduce assets, e.g., money, premises, car and equipment. When this happens:

(a) The business receives assets, the value of which must be recorded in the appropriate account.

(b) The business incurs a liability to the owner for the assets introduced — this is the owner's capital and is shown in his capital account.

Example On 1 January Harry starts up in practice as a sole practitioner. He introduces £8,000 cash, a car valued at £5,000 and office equipment worth £2,000. These opening entries will be recorded as follows:

CASH ACCOUNT

Date	Details	Dr (Received) £	Cr (Paid) £	Balance £
Jan 1	Capital introduced by Harry	8,000		8,000 Dr

MOTOR CARS ACCOUNT

Date	Details	Dr £	Cr £	Balance £
Jan 1	Capital introduced by Harry	5,000		5,000 Dr

OFFICE EQUIPMENT ACCOUNT

Date	Details	Dr £	Cr £	Balance £
Jan 1	Capital introduced by Harry	2,000		2,000 Dr

CAPITAL ACCOUNT

Date	Details	Dr £	Cr £	Balance £
Jan 1	Cash and assets introduced		15,000	15,000 Cr

1.3.2.2 Drawings account

From time to time the proprietor will take money out of the business either in cash or by paying private expenses, for example, a home gas bill. These are called drawings and are usually recorded in a personal account, the drawings account.

INTRODUCTION TO SOLICITORS' ACCOUNTS

Example On 31 January Harry draws £1,000 out of the firm's bank account for his own use and pays his personal tax of £500. The entries to record these transactions are as follows:

DRAWINGS ACCOUNT

Date	Details	Dr	Cr	Balance
		£	£	£
Jan 31	Cash — drawings	1,000		
Jan 31	Cash — personal tax	500		1,500 Dr

CASH ACCOUNT

Date	Details	Dr	Cr	Balance
		£	£	£
	Balance			8,000 Dr
Jan 31	Drawings — cash		1,000	7,000 Dr
	Drawings — personal tax		500	6,500 Dr

The credit balance on the capital account shows the amount which the business owes to its proprietor, i.e., the amount he has invested. The debit balance on the drawings account shows the amount the proprietor owes the business. You will see later that, when the final accounts are prepared, the firm's profit is calculated in the profit and loss account and, where the business is run by a sole proprietor, this profit belongs to him. The amount which the proprietor has invested in the business (i.e., the amount which the business owes to him) is calculated by taking the drawings from the profit and adding the resulting figure to the balance on the capital account.

1.3.3 REAL ACCOUNTS

The following should be noted with regard to real accounts:

(a) They record the cost price of the firm's assets.

(b) To decide whether a purchase is an asset, consider its degree of permanence. A typewriter, for example, has a relatively long working life and its purchase is the acquisition of an asset. A ball-point pen, however, has a relatively short working life and its purchase is a business expense recorded in a nominal expense account, not in a real account.

(c) The cash account is a real account as it records the value of money in the bank. The cash account is also sometimes treated as the personal account of the banker.

(d) Real accounts usually have a debit balance. An exception to this general rule is the cash account which will have a credit balance if the firm has a bank overdraft, as this is not just a real account but a personal account with the bank.

(e) The rule for making entries in real accounts is:

Debit a real account with the value of an asset acquired by the practice.

Thus, in the example about Jack Jones, the decorator, his motor vehicles account was debited with £600 when he purchased the van.

Credit an asset account when the stock of assets is reduced

Note that a credit entry will be made in the cash account when cheques are drawn against the firm's bank account.

Example *Real accounts*

Assume that a firm has £10,000 cash in the bank.

The firm purchases office furniture for £2,000.

DEBIT the increase on the office furniture account

CREDIT the decrease on the Cash Account

OFFICE FURNITURE ACCOUNT

Date	Details	Dr	Cr	Balance
	Cash	£ 2,000	£	£ 2,000 Dr

CASH ACCOUNT

Date	Details	Dr	Cr	Balance
	Balance Office Furniture	£	£ 2,000	£ 10,000 Dr 8,000 Dr

The balances on the accounts show the shift from cash to computer; at first the firm had £10,000 cash, now it has £8,000 cash and a computer worth £2,000.

1.3.4 NOMINAL ACCOUNTS

The following should be noted with regard to nominal accounts:

(a) Some nominal accounts are income accounts. Nominal income accounts record the receipt of income by the firm. The following are examples of nominal income accounts kept by a solicitor:

   (i) Profit costs account. This account records details of profit costs charged to clients. It is based on the bills sent to clients.

   (ii) Interest receivable account. This account records interest received by the firm on money held in a deposit account.

   (iii) Rent received account. This account records rent received by the firm if it leases off its surplus office accommodation.

Nominal income accounts are credited with income received and will therefore always have credit balances.

INTRODUCTION TO SOLICITORS' ACCOUNTS

Example A firm lets its surplus office premises for which it receives rent of £800 per month. On 1 January the firm receives the first month's rent.

RENT RECEIVED ACCOUNT

Date	Details	Dr	Cr	Balance
		£	£	£
Jan 1	Cash		800	800 Cr

CASH ACCOUNT

Date	Details	Dr	Cr	Balance
		£	£	£
Jan 1	Rent received	800		800 Dr

Example The firm renders services to Basil, for which the charge is £500. When the bill is sent to Basil, the income (work done) account will be credited; it shows what the business has given in return for the gain. Note that in solicitors' firms the income account based on the bills sent out is usually called the profit costs account. Basil's personal account will be debited, showing that Basil has received £500 worth of services. The debit balance will show that Basil is a debtor of the firm; he owes £500.

PROFIT COSTS ACCOUNT (Work done account)

Income account

Date	Details	Dr	Cr	Balance
		£	£	£
	Basil — bill		500	500 Cr

BASIL ACCOUNT (Personal account)

Date	Details	Dr	Cr	Balance
		£	£	£
	Profit costs — bill	500		500 Dr

When Basil pays the bill, the entries will be:

Debit the cash account (real account) and credit Basil's account.

CASH ACCOUNT

Date	Details	Dr	Cr	Balance
	Balance say Basil	£ 500	£	£ 8,000 Dr 8,500 Dr

BASIL ACCOUNT

Date	Details	Dr	Cr	Balance
	Balance Cash	£	£ 500	£ 500 Dr —

The debt of £500 due from Basil has been paid and converted into cash.

Note: the balance on Basil's account was £500 debit, the balance is now nil as the amount owed has been paid.

(b) Some nominal accounts are expense accounts. Nominal expense accounts record the payment of business expenses.

(c) A separate nominal expense account is opened for each type of expense which the firm has; for example, most firms will have rent, council tax, electricity, telephone and salaries accounts.

(d) A nominal expense account is debited each time the firm pays a business expense.

Example On 30 November the firm pays an office electricity bill of £500.

ELECTRICITY ACCOUNT

Date	Details	Dr	Cr	Balance
Nov 30	Cash	£ 500	£	£ 500 Dr

CASH ACCOUNT

Date	Details	Dr	Cr	Balance
Nov 30	Electricity	£ (Received)	£ (Paid out) 500	£ 500 Cr

INTRODUCTION TO SOLICITORS' ACCOUNTS

(e) If goods are acquired under leasing or rental agreements under which the firm does not acquire ownership of the goods, the goods are not assets and their acquisition will not be recorded in a real account. Payments made under the leasing or rental agreement are business expenses and are recorded in a nominal expense account.

Example A firm leases a word processor from Computer Supplies Ltd. The quarterly rental is £100. On 1 April the first instalment is paid. Assume the firm has a cash balance of £5,000 at the bank.

RENTALS ACCOUNT

Date	Details	Dr	Cr	Balance
		£	£	£
Apr 1	Cash (word processor)	100		100 Dr

CASH ACCOUNT

Date	Details	Dr	Cr	Balance
		£	£	£
Apr 1	Balance Rentals (word processor)		100	5,000 Dr 4,900 Dr

Nominal expense accounts will always have debit balances.

Manufacturing and trading accounts are dealt with in more detail in **Chapter 4**, where the same principles apply. Where goods are purchased as part of the trading cycle, e.g., goods are purchased for £6,500 cash, the entries would be:

Credit the cash book £6,500

Debit the purchases (expense account) £6,500

On the assumption that the firm starts with £16,500 cash then the accounts would be as follows:

CASH BOOK

Date	Details	Dr	Cr	Balance
		£	£	£
	Balance Purchases		6,500	16,500 Dr 10,000 Dr

PURCHASES ACCOUNT

Date	Details	Dr	Cr	Balance
		£	£	£
	Cash	6,500		6,500 Dr

When the goods are sold then the entries would be as follows:-

Example Goods are sold for £9,000 cash.

The cash book will be debited with the receipt of £9,000

The sales account (an income account) credited with £9,000

CASH BOOK

Date	Details	Dr	Cr	Balance
		£	£	£
	Balance			10,000 Dr
	Sales	9,000		19,000 Dr

SALES ACCOUNT

(Nominal income account)

Date	Details	Dr	Cr	Balance
		£	£	£
	Cash		9,000	9,000 Cr

1.4 Worked Example on Double Entry

Fiona, a sole practitioner, sets up her practice on 1 February with £10,000 cash, office equipment worth £1,000 and premises valued at £140,000.

During the month of February the practice engages in the following transactions:

(a) It buys a copier costing £2,000 on credit from Office Assistance Ltd.

(b) It pays her home telephone bill of £80.

(c) It pays her secretary's salary of £1,300.

(d) It receives one month's rent from the tenant occupying part of the office premises — £800.

(e) It buys a desk for £500 in cash.

(f) It buys a car on credit from Karsales Ltd for £9,000.

(g) It pays the first instalment of £250 to Karsales Ltd under the credit agreement.

(h) Fiona draws £1,000 out of the bank for her own use.

(i) It buys a bookcase for £200 cash.

(j) The firm sends a bill to Jim for £500, re profit costs for work done.

(k) Jim pays the bill of £500.

INTRODUCTION TO SOLICITORS' ACCOUNTS

OFFICE EQUIPMENT ACCOUNT

Date	Details	Dr	Cr	Balance
		£	£	£
Feb 1	Capital introduced	1,000		
	Office Assistance Ltd (copier)	2,000		3,000 Dr

A real account.

PREMISES ACCOUNT

Date	Details	Dr	Cr	Balance
		£	£	£
Feb 1	Capital introduced	140,000		140,000 Dr

A real account.

OFFICE ASSISTANCE LTD ACCOUNT

Date	Details	Dr	Cr	Balance
		£	£	£
Feb	Office equipment		2,000	2,000 Cr

A personal account.

DRAWINGS ACCOUNT

Date	Details	Dr	Cr	Balance
		£	£	£
Feb	Cash (home telephone bill)	80		80 Dr
	Cash (drawings)	1,000		1,080 Dr

A personal account.

SALARIES ACCOUNT

Date	Details	Dr	Cr	Balance
		£	£	£
Feb	Cash (secretary)	1,300		1,300 Dr

A nominal expense account.

RENT RECEIVED ACCOUNT

Date	Details	Dr	Cr	Balance
		£	£	£
Feb	Cash		800	800 Cr

A nominal income account.

OFFICE FURNITURE ACCOUNT

Date	Details	Dr	Cr	Balance
		£	£	£
Feb	Cash (desk)	500		500 Dr
	Cash (bookcase)	200		700 Dr

A real account.

MOTOR VEHICLES ACCOUNT

Date	Details	Dr	Cr	Balance
		£	£	£
Feb	Karsales Ltd (car)	9,000		9,000 Dr

A real account.

KARSALES LTD ACCOUNT

Date	Details	Dr	Cr	Balance
		£	£	£
Feb	Motor vehicles (car)		9,000	9,000 Cr
	Cash (HP instalment)	250		8,750 Cr

A personal account.

CAPITAL ACCOUNT

Date	Details	Dr	Cr	Balance
		£	£	£
Feb	Cash and assets introduced		151,000	151,000 Cr

A personal account.

PROFIT COSTS INCOME ACCOUNT

Date	Details	Dr	Cr	Balance
		£	£	£
	Jim — bill		500	500 Cr

A nominal income account.

JIM

Date	Details	Dr	Cr	Balance
		£	£	£
	Profit Costs — bill	500		500 Dr
	Cash — you		500	—

A personal account.

INTRODUCTION TO SOLICITORS' ACCOUNTS

CASH ACCOUNT

Date	Details	Dr	Cr	Balance
		£	£	£
Feb	Capital introduced	10,000		10,000 Dr
	Drawings (telephone)		80	9,920 Dr
	Salaries		1,300	8,620 Dr
	Rent received	800		9,420 Dr
	Office furniture		500	8,920 Dr
	Karsales Ltd		250	8,670 Dr
	Drawings (cash)		1,000	7,670 Dr
	Office furniture (bookcase)		200	7,470 Dr
	Jim	500		7,970 Dr

A real account/personal account with the bank.

1.5 The Trial Balance

1.5.1 PURPOSE OF THE TRIAL BALANCE

The trial balance is a technique for ensuring the accuracy of the double-entry system and for assembling the balances on the accounts in a form convenient for the preparation of final accounts.

1.5.2 PREPARATION OF THE TRIAL BALANCE

We have seen earlier in this chapter that every transaction is recorded by means of two entries in the accounts, a debit entry in one account and a credit entry in another. It follows therefore that, at any given time, the total of the debit balances and the total of the credit balances should agree.

The trial balance is prepared by listing all the debit balances in one column and all the credit balances in another column. The two columns are totalled and should agree. *NB:* the trial balance is merely a list of all the balances, it is not an account.

Example On 31 October the bookkeeper extracts the following balances from the accounts of A. Solicitor:

	£
Capital account	15,000
Motor cars account	20,000
Office furniture account	5,000
Rent paid account	1,300
General expenses account	200
Council tax account	1,250
Postage account	100
Stationery account	80
Salaries account	1,600
Drawings account	800
Cash account	4,500 Dr
Petty cash account	170
Loan account	20,000

The following trial balance is then prepared.

INTRODUCTION TO SOLICITORS' ACCOUNTS

A. SOLICITOR: TRIAL BALANCE AS AT 31 OCTOBER

Name of account	Dr	Cr
	£	£
Capital amount due to owner		15,000
Motor cars — asset/real account	20,000	
Office furniture — asset/real	5,000	
Rent — expense	1,300	
General expenses — expense	200	
Council tax — expense	1,250	
Postage — expense	100	
Stationery — expense	80	
Salaries — expense	1,600	
Drawings — amount taken out by owner — personal	800	
Cash — asset/real	4,500	
Petty cash — asset/real	170	
Loan — liabiity		20,000
	35,000	35,000

Note that the debit balances will either be in respect of real/asset accounts or expense accounts. The credit balances will either be in respect of liabilities (e.g., to the owner of the business or creditors) or income accounts.

1.5.3 ERRORS NOT REVEALED BY THE TRIAL BALANCE

The fact that the total debit and total credit balances agree does not mean that the bookkeeper has not made any mistakes. There are some errors which will not be revealed by the trial balance, for example:

(a) Errors of entry — the same incorrect entry is made in both accounts used to record the transaction.

> **Example** The firm buys a typewriter for £500. The bookkeeper inadvertently makes a debit entry in the office equipment account of £50 and a credit entry of £50 in the cash account.

(b) Compensating errors — the bookkeeper makes two separate errors which cancel each other out.

> **Example** The bookkeeper incorrectly totals one account by £100 too much on the credit side and another by £100 too much on the debit side.

(c) Errors of omission — the bookkeeper omits both parts of the double entry from the accounts.

(d) Errors of commission — the bookkeeper makes the correct entry but in the wrong account.

INTRODUCTION TO SOLICITORS' ACCOUNTS

> **Example** The firm buys office equipment costing £1,000. Instead of debiting the office equipment account with £1,000 the bookkeeper debits the office furniture account.

(e) Errors of principle — the bookkeeper makes an entry in the wrong type of account.

> **Example** The purchase of office equipment is shown in the general expenses account, i.e., a nominal instead of a real account. If this error remains undetected at the time the firm's final accounts are prepared the business expenses will be overstated in the profit and loss account and the value of the assets will be understated in the balance sheet.

1.6 Exercises on Double-entry Bookkeeping and Trial Balance

1 Complete the following:

	Account to be debited	Account to be credited

(a) Buys office equipment for cash.

(b) Buys office equipment on credit from Brown.

(c) Buys a new car for use by the firm and pays cash.

(d) Pays an employee's salary.

(e) Buys stationery for cash.

(f) Pays insurance premium.

(g) Draws cash for own use.

(h) Pays office telephone bill.

(i) Pays private electricity bill.

2 Paula starts in practice as a solicitor on 1 July with cash of £10,000, a car worth £16,000 and premises worth £128,000. During the month of July the following transactions occur:

1 July   Pays council tax £900.
3 July   Buys office furniture £1,800. Pays by cheque.
8 July   Pays secretary's salary £1,500.
10 July   Receives £12,500 as a loan from her brother-in-law Ted, to be repaid in three years without interest.
12 July   Pays home telephone bill £80.
13 July   Pays office cleaner £100.
14 July   Draws £2,500 for her own use.
15 July   Pays assistant solicitor's salary £2,000.
17 July   Buys stationery £500.

20

INTRODUCTION TO SOLICITORS' ACCOUNTS

19 July   Leases a photocopier from Supplies Ltd for £50 per month and pays the first month's instalment.
20 July   Buys a computer on credit from Supplies Ltd for £800.
21 July   Pays office electricity bill £175.
27 July   Pays instalment of £80 to Supplies Ltd.

Prepare accounts to record the above transactions and prepare a trial balance as at 31 July.

3   The bookkeeper has extracted the following balances from the accounts of Sam, a sole practitioner, on 30 September. From the balances you are asked to prepare a trial balance.

	£
Salaries	1,000
Travelling expenses	400
Furniture	600
Leasehold property	15,000
Capital	36,000
Drawings	2,000
Loan account	1,000
Petty cash	100
Council tax	150
Rent	750
Administration expenses	4,000
Motor cars	12,500
Cash account	500 Dr

4   The bookkeeper has extracted the following balances from the accounts of Sally Jones, a sole practitioner, on 31 January. From the balances you are asked to prepare a trial balance.

	£
Salaries	3,000
Office equipment	15,000
Freehold property	235,000
Capital	220,000
Drawings	13,200
Midshire Bank — loan account	20,000
Cash — office account	1,000 Dr
Cash — client account	125,000 Dr
Council tax	900
General expenses	1,400
Debtors	2,000
Creditors	1,500
Rent received	2,000
Costs	30,000
Due to clients	125,000
Bank interest paid	2,000

5   From the following information, extracted as at 30 June, prepare a trial balance for Timothy, a sole practitioner.

	£
General expenses	200
Salaries	1,200
Drawings	4,000
Rent	1,250
Council tax	150

Electricity	800
Creditors	2,500
Office furniture	7,000
Bank overdraft	2,300
Loan account	9,000
Car	7,700
Capital	8,500

1.7 Suggested Answers to Exercises on Double-entry Bookkeeping and Trial Balance

1

		Account to be debited	Account to be credited
(a)	Buys office equipment for cash	Office equipment account (real account)	Cash account (real account)
(b)	Buys office equipment on credit from Brown	Office equipment account	Brown's account (personal account)
(c)	Buys a new car for use by the firm and pays cash	Cars account (real account)	Cash account
(d)	Pays an employee's salary	Salaries account (nominal expense account)	Cash account
(e)	Buys stationery for cash	Stationery account (nominal expense account)	Cash account
(f)	Pays insurance premium	Insurance account (nominal expense account)	Cash account
(g)	Draws cash for own use	Drawings account (personal account)	Cash account
(h)	Pays office telephone bill	Telephone account (nominal expense account)	Cash account
(i)	Pays private electricity bill	Drawings account	Cash account

2 CAPITAL ACCOUNT

Date	Details	Dr £	Cr £	Balance £
July 1	Sundry assets and cash introduced		154,000	154,000 Cr

MOTOR CARS ACCOUNT

Date	Details	Dr	Cr	Balance
		£	£	£
July 1	Capital	16,000		16,000 Dr

PREMISES ACCOUNT

Date	Details	Dr	Cr	Balance
		£	£	£
July 1	Capital	128,000		128,000 Dr

COUNCIL TAX ACCOUNT

Date	Details	Dr	Cr	Balance
		£	£	£
July 1	Cash	900		900 Dr

OFFICE FURNITURE ACCOUNT

Date	Details	Dr	Cr	Balance
		£	£	£
July 3	Cash	1,800		1,800 Dr

SALARIES ACCOUNT

Date	Details	Dr	Cr	Balance
		£	£	£
July 8	Cash (secretary)	1,500		1,500 Dr
July 13	Cash (office cleaner)	100		1,600 Dr
July 15	Cash (assistant solicitor)	2,000		3,600 Dr

LOAN ACCOUNT: TED

Date	Details	Dr	Cr	Balance
		£	£	£
July 10	Cash		12,500	12,500 Cr

DRAWINGS ACCOUNT

Date	Details	Dr	Cr	Balance
		£	£	£
July 12	Cash (telephone bill)	80		80 Dr
July 14	Cash	2,500		2,580 Dr

INTRODUCTION TO SOLICITORS' ACCOUNTS

STATIONERY ACCOUNT

Date	Details	Dr	Cr	Balance
		£	£	£
July 17	Cash	500		500 Dr

RENTAL ACCOUNT
PHOTOCOPIER

Date	Details	Dr	Cr	Balance
		£	£	£
July 19	Cash (photocopier)	50		50 Dr

OFFICE EQUIPMENT ACCOUNT

Date	Details	Dr	Cr	Balance
		£	£	£
July 20	Supplies Ltd (computer)	800		800 Dr

SUPPLIES LTD

Date	Details	Dr	Cr	Balance
		£	£	£
July 20	Office equipment (computer)		800	800 Cr
July 27	Cash	80		720 Cr

ELECTRICITY ACCOUNT

Date	Details	Dr	Cr	Balance
		£	£	£
July 21	Cash	175		175 Dr

CASH ACCOUNT

Date	Details	Dr	Cr	Balance
		£	£	£
July 1	Capital	10,000		10,000 Dr
	Council tax		900	9,100 Dr
July 3	Office furniture		1,800	7,300 Dr
July 8	Salary		1,500	5,800 Dr
July 10	Loan: Ted	12,500		18,300 Dr
July 12	Drawings		80	18,220 Dr
July 13	Salary		100	18,120 Dr
July 14	Drawings		2,500	15,620 Dr
July 15	Salary		2,000	13,620 Dr
July 17	Stationery		500	13,120 Dr
July 19	Rentals		50	13,070 Dr
July 21	Electricity		175	12,895 Dr
July 27	Supplies Ltd		80	12,815 Dr

PAULA: TRIAL BALANCE AS AT 31 JULY

Name of account	Dr	Cr
	£	£
Capital		154,000
Motor cars	16,000	
Premises	128,000	
Council tax	900	
Office furniture	1,800	
Salaries	3,600	
Loan accounts		12,500
Drawings	2,580	
Stationery	500	
Rentals	50	
Office equipment	800	
Supplies Ltd		720
Electricity	175	
Cash	12,815	
	167,220	167,220

3 SAM: TRIAL BALANCE AS AT 30 SEPTEMBER

Name of account	Dr	Cr
	£	£
Salaries	1,000	
Travelling expenses	400	
Furniture	600	
Leasehold property	15,000	
Capital		36,000
Drawings	2,000	
Loan account		1,000
Petty cash	100	
Council tax	150	
Rent	750	
Administration expenses	4,000	
Motor cars	12,500	
Cash account	500	
	37,000	37,000

4 SALLY JONES: TRIAL BALANCE AS AT 31 JANUARY

Name of account	Dr	Cr
	£	£
Salaries	3,000	
Office equipment	15,000	
Freehold property	235,000	
Capital		220,000
Drawings	13,200	
Loan account		20,000
Cash (office)	1,000	
Cash (client)	125,000	
Council tax	900	
General expenses	1,400	
Debtors	2,000	
Creditors		1,500
Rent receivable		2,000
Costs		30,000
Due to clients		125,000
Bank interest paid	2,000	
	398,500	398,500

5   TIMOTHY: TRIAL BALANCE AS AT 31 JUNE

Name of account	Dr	Cr
	£	£
General expenses	200	
Salaries	1,200	
Drawings	4,000	
Rent	1,250	
Council tax	150	
Electricity	800	
Creditors		2,500
Office furniture	7,000	
Cash		2,300
Loan account		9,000
Car	7,700	
Capital		8,500
	22,300	22,300

1.8 Exercise on Double-entry Bookkeeping and Trial Balance

Allow around 45 minutes to complete this exercise.

Jane starts in practice as a solicitor on 1 January. She introduces £15,000 into the firm's bank account and a car worth £8,200. She leases her office premises and pays rent of £1,000 per month. During the month of January the following transactions take place:

4 January	Pays first month's rent.
5 January	Pays salary £1,200 to secretary.
6 January	Buys a second-hand computer costing £650 on credit from Wylie Ltd.
9 January	Pays office telephone bill £25.
11 January	Pays council tax £150.
18 January	Pays legal executive's salary £1,500.
19 January	Pays home electricity bill £200.
21 January	Buys car on credit from Motors Ltd. The car costs £14,000.
22 January	Buys stationery for £80.
23 January	Pays office electricity bill £45.
24 January	Pays instalment of £65 to Wylie Ltd.
25 January	Draws £1,600 for her own use.

Prepare accounts to record the above transactions, and prepare a trial balance as at 31 January.

1.9 Suggested Answers to Exercise on Double-entry Bookkeeping and Trial Balance

CAPITAL ACCOUNT

Date	Details	Dr	Cr	Balance
		£	£	£
Jan 1	Sundry assets and cash introduced		23,200	23,200 Cr

MOTOR CARS ACCOUNT

Date	Details	Dr	Cr	Balance
		£	£	£
Jan 1	Capital	8,200		8,200 Dr
Jan 21	Motors Ltd	14,000		22,200 Dr

RENT ACCOUNT

Date	Details	Dr	Cr	Balance
		£	£	£
Jan 4	Cash	1,000		1,000 Dr

SALARIES ACCOUNT

Date	Details	Dr	Cr	Balance
		£	£	£
Jan 5	Cash (secretary)	1,200		1,200 Dr
Jan 18	Cash (legal executive)	1,500		2,700 Dr

OFFICE EQUIPMENT ACCOUNT

Date	Details	Dr	Cr	Balance
		£	£	£
Jan 6	Wylie Ltd (computer)	650		650 Dr

WYLIE LTD

Date	Details	Dr	Cr	Balance
		£	£	£
Jan 6	Office equipment		650	650 Cr
Jan 24	Cash	65		585 Cr

TELEPHONE ACCOUNT

Date	Details	Dr	Cr	Balance
		£	£	£
Jan 9	Cash	25		25 Dr

COUNCIL TAX ACCOUNT

Date	Details	Dr	Cr	Balance
		£	£	£
Jan 11	Cash	150		150 Dr

DRAWINGS ACCOUNT

Date	Details	Dr	Cr	Balance
		£	£	£
Jan 19	Cash (electricity bill)	200		200 Dr
Jan 25	Cash	1,600		1,800 Dr

MOTORS LTD ACCOUNT

Date	Details	Dr	Cr	Balance
		£	£	£
Jan 21	Motor cars		14,000	14,000 Cr

STATIONERY ACCOUNT

Date	Details	Dr	Cr	Balance
		£	£	£
Jan 22	Cash	80		80 Dr

ELECTRICITY ACCOUNT

Date	Details	Dr	Cr	Balance
		£	£	£
Jan 23	Cash	45		45 Dr

CASH ACCOUNT

Date	Details	Dr	Cr	Balance
		£	£	£
Jan 1	Capital	15,000		15,000 Dr
Jan 4	Rent		1,000	14,000 Dr
Jan 5	Salaries		1,200	12,800 Dr
Jan 9	Telephones		25	12,775 Dr
Jan 11	Council tax		150	12,625 Dr
Jan 18	Salaries		1,500	11,125 Dr
Jan 19	Drawings		200	10,925 Dr
Jan 22	Stationery		80	10,845 Dr
Jan 23	Electricity		45	10,800 Dr
Jan 24	Wylie Ltd		65	10,735 Dr
Jan 25	Drawings		1,600	9,135 Dr

JANE: TRIAL BALANCE AS AT 31 JANUARY

Name of account	Dr	Cr
	£	£
Capital		23,200
Motor cars	22,200	
Rent	1,000	
Salaries	2,700	
Office equipment	650	
Wylie Ltd		585
Telephones	25	
Council tax	150	
Drawings	1,800	
Motors Ltd		14,000
Stationery	80	
Electricity	45	
Cash	9,135	
	37,785	37,785

TWO

FINAL ACCOUNTS AND ADJUSTMENTS

2.1 Introduction

Basic final accounts consist of:

(a) profit and loss account; and

(b) balance sheet.

Final accounts are prepared annually at the end of the firm's financial year.

Immediately before the final accounts are prepared a trial balance is drawn up to assemble the balances on the accounts. Each balance shown on the trial balance will either be:

(a) transferred to the profit and loss account; or

(b) shown on the balance sheet.

2.1.1 PROFIT AND LOSS ACCOUNT

The following points should be noted with regard to the profit and loss account:

(a) It is a double-entry account, i.e., it is part of the double-entry system.

(b) Its function is to calculate the net profit or loss made by the practice during the financial year.

(c) The practitioner can use the information in the profit and loss account to calculate the percentage of gross income used in overheads. A comparison can be made with previous years' accounts to see whether this percentage is increasing. The information thus obtained may be used to reorganise the practice; for example, it may become necessary to make staff redundant or to investigate means of cutting overheads.

(d) A detailed breakdown of the costs figure in the profit and loss account will tell the solicitor whether the income is narrowly or broadly based. For example, it may be that the bulk of the income comes from conveyancing work and that the firm's main conveyancing client is a developer. It may be necessary to consider whether the practice can diversify, as reliance on one main source of work can be dangerous.

FINAL ACCOUNTS AND ADJUSTMENTS

2.1.2 BALANCE SHEET

The following points should be noted with regard to the balance sheet:

(a) The balance sheet is a statement of the firm's assets and liabilities on a given date, usually the last day of the financial year.

(b) The balance sheet is not an account and is therefore not part of the double-entry system. It is a list of the balances on the asset and liability accounts.

(c) At any time the assets of the practice should equal its liabilities. This is because each time the practice acquires something of value it gives consideration.

Example X, a solicitor, commences in practice with £2,000 in cash which is placed in the firm's bank account. Immediately X has a balance sheet; it is:

Liability		Asset	
Capital	£2,000	Cash at bank	£2,000

X's practice is thus shown to own £2,000 cash (an asset) all of which is owed to X, the owner of the practice (a liability).

(d) An analysis of the information in the balance sheet will tell the proprietor whether the practice is solvent and whether too much of the proprietor's capital is tied up in fixed assets which will be difficult to realise.

2.2 Closing the Accounts

(a) Immediately prior to preparing the final accounts the nominal income and expense accounts are closed by transferring the balance on each account to the profit and loss account.

(b) Nominal expense accounts have debit balances and so to effect a transfer from a nominal expense account to the profit and loss account, the bookkeeping entries are:

(i) Credit the nominal expense account.

(ii) Debit the profit and loss account.

Example At the end of the year the firm's salaries account has a debit balance of £15,000. The balance is transferred to the profit and loss account on 31 December.

SALARIES ACCOUNT

Date	Details	Dr	Cr	Balance
		£	£	£
	Balance			15,000 Dr
Dec 31	Profit and loss account: transfer		15,000	

FINAL ACCOUNTS AND ADJUSTMENTS

(c) Nominal income accounts have credit balances and so to effect a transfer from a nominal income account to the profit and loss account, the bookkeeping entries are:

   (i) Debit the nominal income account.

   (ii) Credit the profit and loss account.

Example At the end of the year the firm's costs account has a credit balance of £300,000. On 31 December the balance is transferred to the profit and loss account.

COSTS ACCOUNT

Date	Details	Dr	Cr	Balance
		£	£	£
	Balance			300,000 Cr
Dec 31	Profit and loss account: transfer	300,000		———

(d) When the transfer entries have been made, the nominal income and expense accounts are closed.

(e) The balance sheet, unlike the profit and loss account, is not an account on double entry and so the balances on the asset and liability accounts are not transferred to the balance sheet. They are merely listed on the balance sheet. The asset and liability accounts are ongoing and will be kept open for as long as the asset is owned by the firm or for as long as the liability remains unsettled.

2.3 Presentation of Final Accounts

2.3.1 VERTICAL FORMAT: PROFIT AND LOSS ACCOUNT

There are two methods of presenting final accounts: the horizontal format and the vertical format. In this book, as in the examination, the vertical format will be used. A basic vertical format profit and loss account is shown in the following example:

SALLY JONES: PROFIT AND LOSS ACCOUNT FOR THE YEAR ENDED 31 JANUARY 2000

	£	£
INCOME		
Profit costs	300,000	
ADD rent received	20,000	
	———	320,000
LESS EXPENDITURE		
Salaries	60,000	
Rates	9,000	
General expenses	14,000	
Bank interest charged	2,000	85,000
		———
NET PROFIT		235,000

This is a very simple example of a profit and loss account. You will see later in the chapter when we have dealt with adjustments that a third column is used in the profit and loss account to adjust the nominal income and expense account balances, to show, as accurately as possible, the profit or loss.

FINAL ACCOUNTS AND ADJUSTMENTS

2.3.2 COMMENTS ON THE PROFIT AND LOSS ACCOUNT

(a) Be able to identify the nominal income and expense accounts which make up the profit and loss account.

(b) At the end of the financial year the nominal accounts are closed. The credit balances from the nominal income accounts are transferred to the income side of the profit and loss account. The debit balances from the nominal expense accounts are transferred to the expenditure side of the profit and loss account.

(c) The balance left after deducting total expenditure from total income is net profit (or loss). If a profit is made this is credited to the capital account in the case of a sole practitioner. If a loss is made this is debited to the capital account. For the position in the case of a partnership see **Chapter 4**.

(d) Note that drawings made by the proprietor are appropriations of profit, not business expenses. Thus the balance on the drawings account is not transferred to the profit and loss account, but will be shown on the balance sheet.

2.4 The Balance Sheet

2.4.1 DEFINITIONS

2.4.1.1 Assets

These consist of property of all kinds owned by the business, such as freehold or leasehold premises, stocks of goods, e.g., stationery, cars, cash at the bank, petty cash, debts owed by customers (who will pay — converting the debt into cash), work in progress (work done, which will eventually be billed and cash received in payment) or goodwill (an intangible asset).

Assets are split into two groups:

(a) Fixed assets

(b) Current assets.

Fixed assets
These are items of property of long life, i.e., relatively permanent, they are held to be used in the business and not primarily for resale or conversion into cash. They are fixed in the sense that to dispose of them would usually damage the business, e.g., buildings (freehold or leasehold), machinery, office equipment, library, fixtures and fittings, furniture, motor vehicles, goodwill.

Current assets
Also known as circulating assets. These arise from the day-to-day trading or working cycle of the business, they represent cash, or are primarily intended for conversion into cash, or they have a short life, e.g., stationery. They include: cash at the bank, petty cash, debtors, work in progress and payments in advance (see later). If the firm is a trading one, then goods (stock) intended for resale will be a current asset.

Note: those assets which are cash, or assets which can be easily converted into cash, e.g., debtors, are known as liquid assets.

2.4.1.2 Liabilities

Money owed by the business in respect of loans to the business, e.g., capital, bank loans, mortgages, or money owed for goods or services supplied to the firm, i.e., creditors.

Like assets liabilities can be broken down into groups:

(a) Capital.

(b) Long term liabilities.

(c) Current liabilities.

Capital
This represents the proprietor's stake in the business — the value of what he or she has introduced into the business, either in the form of cash or assets introduced. The firm owes the proprietor the amount standing on the capital account. The proprietor is effectively a long-term creditor of the business. Note also that any profit made by the business will be owed to the proprietor as well. The amount the proprietor has taken out of the business over the year (drawings) will reduce the amount due to him or her.

This will be shown as follows:

CAPITAL

PLUS PROFIT

LESS DRAWINGS

The Drawings account is a personal account, showing that the proprietor is a debtor of the business. *NB:* It is not an expense account and should never be shown on the profit and loss account. Think of it as a personal account which will reduce the amount due to the proprietor.

Long-term liabilities
Usually some formal loan from an individual, bank or other financial institution, repayable over, or after, a stated number of years. These would include long term bank loans (not usually overdrafts), private loans, mortgages.

Current liabilities
If the liability has to be settled in the short term, in the next accounting period, i.e., it is repayable at short notice, then it is a current liability. These include: creditors, bank overdrafts, outstanding expenses.

The form of balance sheet more commonly used now is the vertical form.

The starting point would be to list all assets first, then list all liabilities underneath. The total assets should equal the total liabilities.

FINAL ACCOUNTS AND ADJUSTMENTS

Example

Name of business

Balance Sheet as at 31 August 2001

ASSETS

Fixed Assets

ADD

Current Assets

TOTAL ASSETS

LIABILITIES

Capital
Plus Profit
less Drawings

ADD

Long Term Liabilities

EQUAL

ADD

Current Liabilities

TOTAL LIABILITIES

2.4.2 LISTING ASSETS AND LIABIILTIES ON THE BALANCE SHEET

There is a common set order in listing the assets and liabilities on the balance sheet.

Assets
Fixed assets are shown first and then current assets. The general rule is that you start at the top with the most permanent asset and work down to the least permanent. The top asset on the list will be the most difficult to turn into cash, the bottom will be the most liquid asset, e.g., cash itself. (The order of liquidity is reversed.)

For example, fixed assets may start with premises, which are usually the most permanent fixed asset belonging to the firm, and end with motor cars which are usually the least permanent fixed asset. Current assets start with work in progress which is the least liquid current asset, as it needs two stages to be converted into cash; first it would have to be billed, then the debtors will have to pay.

There are then two changes to the vertical form shown previously.

Current liabilities are not shown under the liabilities section, they are instead deducted from the current assets, to give a figure known as net current assets, or working capital, being that portion of the capital invested in the business which is left to run the business after providing the fixed assets. This figure is then added to the fixed assets.

FINAL ACCOUNTS AND ADJUSTMENTS

Long-term liabilities will then be deducted from this total.

The total achieved should equal the capital due to the proprietor/owner of the business.

The vertical form balance sheet will look as follows:

NAME OF BUSINESS

BALANCE SHEET as at 31 December 2001

FIXED ASSETS

ADD

NET CURRENT ASSETS

(BEING CURRENT ASSETS
LESS CURRENT LIABILITIES)

TOTAL

LESS LONG-TERM LIABILITIES

FINAL TOTAL, i.e., NET ASSETS

CAPITAL EMPLOYED

CAPITAL

PLUS PROFIT

SUB TOTAL

LESS DRAWINGS

FINAL TOTAL — AMOUNT DUE TO OWNER(S)

2.4.3 THE SOLICITOR AND CLIENT MONEY

When a solicitor handles money on behalf of his/her clients, it is the client's money and not the solicitor's. The Solicitors Accounts Rules 1998 say that a solicitor must keep the records showing dealings with this money totally separate from the solicitor's own money. To do this the solicitor must have a separate bank account (or accounts) for clients' money called the Client Account. The money held in the client bank account(s) must always equal the amount that is shown due to clients.

This can be shown at the end of the balance sheet.

FINAL ACCOUNTS AND ADJUSTMENTS

2.4.4 VERTICAL FORMAT: BALANCE SHEET

SALLY JONES: BALANCE SHEET AS AT 31 JANUARY 2001

	£	£	£	
FIXED ASSETS				
Freehold property	235,000			
Office equipment	15,000			
			250,000	
CURRENT ASSETS				
Debtors	20,000			
Cash (office bank account)	10,000			
		30,000		
LESS CURRENT LIABILITIES				
Creditors		15,000		
NET CURRENT ASSETS			15,000	
			265,000	
Less long-term liabilities				
Midshire Bank loan			40,000	
TOTAL			225,000	(Net Assets)
CAPITAL EMPLOYED				
Capital at start of year	200,000			
Add net profit	64,000			
		264,000		
Less drawings		39,000		
TOTAL			225,000	(Amount due to owner)
CLIENT ACCOUNT				
Cash at bank client current account	300,000			
deposit account	200,000	500,000		
Due to clients		500,000		

2.5 Exercise on Basic Final Accounts

From the following balances extracted from the accounts of Alexandra on 30 November 2001 prepare:

(a) A trial balance.

(b) A profit and loss account.

(c) A balance sheet.

FINAL ACCOUNTS AND ADJUSTMENTS

	£
Profit costs	130,000
Light and heat	3,600
Drawings	55,000
Creditors	4,969
Cash at bank (office)	19,230 Dr
Cash at bank (client)	750,000 Dr
Premises	220,000
Insurance commission received	3,000
Council tax	1,700
Salaries	48,000
Stationery	2,000
Capital	100,400
Bank loan	120,000
Debtors	7,960
Petty cash	879
Due to clients	750,000

2.6 Suggested Answer to Exercise on Basic Final Accounts

ALEXANDRA: TRIAL BALANCE AS AT 30 NOVEMBER 2001

Name of account	Dr	Cr
	£	£
Profit costs		130,000
Light and heat	3,600	
Drawings	55,000	
Creditors		4,969
Cash at bank (office)	19,230	
Cash at bank (client)	750,000	
Premises	220,000	
Insurance commission received		3,000
Council tax	1,700	
Salaries	48,000	
Stationery	2,000	
Capital		100,400
Loan		120,000
Debtors	7,960	
Petty cash	879	
Due to clients		750,000
	1,108,369	1,108,369

PROFIT AND LOSS ACCOUNT FOR THE YEAR ENDED 30 NOVEMBER 2001

	£	£
INCOME		
Profit costs	130,000	
ADDITIONAL INCOME insurance commission received	3,000	133,000
LESS EXPENDITURE		
Light and heat	3,600	
Council tax	1,700	
Salaries	48,000	
Stationery	2,000	55,300
NET PROFIT		77,700

FINAL ACCOUNTS AND ADJUSTMENTS

ALEXANDRA: BALANCE SHEET AS AT 30 NOVEMBER 2001

	£	£	£
FIXED ASSETS			
Premises			220,000
CURRENT ASSETS			
Debtors	7,960		
Cash (office bank account)	19,230		
Petty cash	879		
		28,069	
LESS CURRENT LIABILITIES			
Creditors		4,969	
NET CURRENT ASSETS			23,100
TOTAL ASSETS LESS CURRENT LIABILITIES			243,100
Less long-term liabilities			
Bank loan			120,000
TOTAL			123,100
CAPITAL EMPLOYED			
Capital at start of year	100,400		
Add net profit	77,700		
		178,100	
Less drawings		55,000	
TOTAL			123,100
CLIENT ACCOUNT			
Client bank balance	750,000		
Less: due to clients	750,000		

2.7 The Need for Adjustments

The balances on the nominal income and expense accounts do not show all income earned or all expenditure incurred during the year. Adjustments are made to ensure that income includes all work done during the current year even though it has not yet been billed. They are also made to ensure that expenditure includes expenses incurred in the current year, in respect of which bills have not yet been paid, and does not include expenses which, although paid in the current year, relate to the next financial year.

The adjustments which will be made immediately before the final accounts are prepared are detailed below. Note that all the adjustments made after the trial balance will be shown twice, once on the profit and loss account and once on the balance sheet.

2.8 Outstanding Expenses Adjustment

There are expenses incurred during the current financial year in respect of which payment is not made until the next financial year, for example, gas, electricity and telephone charges.

FINAL ACCOUNTS AND ADJUSTMENTS

At the end of the financial year, provision is made for the expense incurred but not paid during the current year. If a bill has not already been received the provision will be an estimate.

The adjustment is shown by making a debit entry in the appropriate nominal expense account. The double entry is a credit in the same nominal expense account at the start of the next financial year.

Effectively the entries shown will shift the expense from the next year into the current year.

Example A solicitor prepares final accounts on 31 October. At that date the telephone account has a debit balance of £600. It is decided to make provision of £200 for telephone charges due but unpaid. The telephone account will appear as follows:

TELEPHONE ACCOUNT

Date	Details	Dr	Cr	Balance
		£	£	£
Oct 31	Balance Provision c/d	200		600 Dr 800 Dr

The balance on the expense account, including the provision made at the end of the financial year, is transferred to the profit and loss account and the nominal expense account is closed. Continuing the example:

TELEPHONE ACCOUNT

Date	Details	Dr	Cr	Balance
		£	£	£
Oct 31	Balance Provision c/d Profit and loss account: transfer	200	800	600 Dr 800 Dr ——

The provision is carried down as a credit entry in the expense account at the start of the next financial year. The provision will be set off against payment of the bill in the next financial year. Continuing the example, on 10 November the bill of £200 is paid.

TELEPHONE ACCOUNT

Date	Details	Dr	Cr	Balance
		£	£	£
Oct 31	Balance Provision c/d Profit and loss account: transfer	200	800	600 Dr 800 Dr ——
Nov 1 Nov 10	Provision b/d Cash	200	200	200 Cr ——

The provision for outstanding expenses is shown on the balance sheet as a current liability because on the date on which the balance sheet is prepared, it is expenditure incurred but not yet paid. Continuing the example:

FINAL ACCOUNTS AND ADJUSTMENTS

```
                    BALANCE SHEET AS AT 31 OCTOBER
                                                                    £
    FIXED ASSETS                                                   XX
    CURRENT ASSETS                          XX
    LESS CURRENT LIABILITIES
    Outstanding expenses — telephone       200
                                          ―――
                                                                   XX
                                                                 ―――
                                                                   XX
    CAPITAL EMPLOYED
                                                                   XX
```

2.9 Summary

Outstanding expense.
On the profit and loss account.
Increase expenses (Dr).
On the balance sheet.
Show as a current liability (Cr).

This credit balance will reduce expenses in the next year.

2.10 Payment in Advance

If a payment is made in the current financial year for a service which will not be used until the next financial year, for example, council tax, then, at the end of the financial year, the appropriate expense account is credited with the amount paid in advance. This has the effect of reducing the expenditure and increasing the profit. The corresponding debit entry is made in the same account at the start of the next financial year. This time the double entry shifts the expense out of the current year into the next year.

> **Example** A solicitor pays council tax of £4,000 per annum by two equal instalments, in advance, on 31 March and 30 September each year. Final accounts are prepared on 31 December each year. Thus a payment in advance of £1,000 for council tax is being made because the £2,000 paid on 30 September is for council tax from 1 October to 31 March.
>
> COUNCIL TAX ACCOUNT
>
> | Date | Details | Dr | Cr | Balance |
> |------|---------|----|----|---------|
> | | | £ | £ | £ |
> | Mar 31 | Cash | 2,000 | | 2,000 Dr |
> | Sept 30 | Cash | 2,000 | | 4,000 Dr |
> | Dec 31 | Payment in advance c/d | | 1,000 | 3,000 Dr |

The balance on the expense account is transferred to the profit and loss account at the end of the year. Continuing the example:

FINAL ACCOUNTS AND ADJUSTMENTS

COUNCIL TAX ACCOUNT

Date	Details	Dr	Cr	Balance
		£	£	£
Mar 31	Cash	2,000		2,000 Dr
Sept 30	Cash	2,000		4,000 Dr
Dec 31	Payment in advance c/d		1,000	3,000 Dr
	Profit and loss account: transfer		3,000	———

Note that the firm is charging to the profit and loss account as a business expense only the amount spent on council tax from 1 January to 31 December, i.e., in the current financial year.

The payment in advance is brought down as a debit entry on the expense account at the start of the next financial year, which is when the service that has been paid for in the current financial year will be used. Continuing the example:

COUNCIL TAX ACCOUNT

Date	Details	Dr	Cr	Balance
		£	£	£
Mar 31	Cash	2,000		2,000 Dr
Sept 30	Cash	2,000		4,000 Dr
Dec 31	Payment in advance c/d		1,000	3,000 Dr
	Profit and loss account: transfer		3,000	———
Jan 1	Payment in advance b/d	1,000		1,000 Dr

The payment in advance is shown on the balance sheet as a current asset. In theory the person to whom the payment has been made is a debtor of the firm for the service which is to be supplied. Continuing the example:

BALANCE SHEET AS AT 31 OCTOBER

FIXED ASSETS		XX
CURRENT ASSETS		
Payments in advance		
Council tax	1,000	
		XX
LESS CURRENT LIABILITIES		
		XX
		XX
CAPITAL EMPLOYED		
		XX

FINAL ACCOUNTS AND ADJUSTMENTS

2.11 Summary

Payment in advance.
On the profit and loss account.
Reduce expenses (Cr).
On the balance sheet.
Show as a current asset (Dr).

This debit balance will increase expenses in the next year.

2.12 Closing Stocks

The same principle as for payments in advance applies where the expense was incurred for something tangible such as stationery, stamps, pens, etc. Only the cost of the stationery, etc., actually used during the year should be transferred to the profit and loss account as an expense. When the stationery, etc., was paid for, a debit entry would have been made in the appropriate expense account. At the end of the financial year the stock left over will be valued and the value of this closing stock will be credited to the appropriate expense account. The corresponding debit entry is made in the same account at the start of the next financial year when the closing stock is brought down as opening stock.

Example During the year the firm pays the following amounts for stationery:

31 March	£40
16 October	£25
8 December	£35

Final accounts are prepared on 31 December. On 31 December the firm has a stock of stationery paid for but unused, valued at £30.

STATIONERY ACCOUNT

Date	Details	Dr	Cr	Balance
		£	£	£
Mar 31	Cash	40		40 Dr
Oct 16	Cash	25		65 Dr
Dec 8	Cash	35		100 Dr
Dec 31	Closing stock c/d		30	70 Dr

At the end of the year the nominal expense account is closed and the balance on it is transferred to the profit and loss account. Continuing the example:

STATIONERY ACCOUNT

Date	Details	Dr	Cr	Balance
		£	£	£
Mar 31	Cash	40		40 Dr
Oct 16	Cash	25		65 Dr
Dec 8	Cash	35		100 Dr
Dec 31	Closing stock c/d		30	70 Dr
	Profit and loss account: transfer balance		70	———

Note that only the cost of stationery used during the current financial year is transferred to the profit and loss account as a business expense.

The value of the closing stock is brought down as a debit entry in the expense account at the start of the next financial year. Continuing the example:

STATIONERY ACCOUNT

Date	Details	Dr	Cr	Balance
		£	£	£
Mar 31	Cash	40		40 Dr
Oct 16	Cash	25		65 Dr
Dec 8	Cash	35		100 Dr
Dec 31	Closing stock c/d		30	70 Dr
	Profit and loss account: transfer		70	—
Jan 1	Opening stock b/d	30		30 Dr

Note that at the start of the next financial year the closing stock from the previous year becomes opening stock.

On the balance sheet the value of the closing stock is shown as a current asset. Continuing the example:

BALANCE SHEET AS AT 31 OCTOBER

FIXED ASSETS		XX
CURRENT ASSETS		
Closing stock of stationery	30	
	—	
		XX
LESS CURRENT LIABILITIES		
		XX
		——
		XX
CAPITAL EMPLOYED		
		XX

2.13 Summary

Closing stock.
On the profit and loss.
Reduce expenses (Cr).
On the balance sheet.
Show as a current asset (Dr).

This debit balance will increase expenses next year.

FINAL ACCOUNTS AND ADJUSTMENTS

2.14 Work in Progress (or Work in Hand)

Work in progress is work done on behalf of clients during the financial year to which the final accounts relate but in respect of which bills have not been delivered to clients.

If the profit and loss account is to show income earned during the year, the value of the work in progress, which must be estimated, must be added to the profit costs figure. Profit costs are based on the bills delivered during the year.

An adjustment is made on the profit costs account at the end of the financial year to record the value of work in progress. This is known as the closing work in progress. The adjustment is made by crediting the profit costs account with the value of closing work in progress. The corresponding debit entry is made in the same account at the start of the next financial year by bringing the old closing work in progress down as opening work in progress. The effect is that this year's profit costs will be increased, the next year's profit costs will be reduced.

Example The firm prepares its final accounts on 31 October each year. On 31 October the profit costs account has a credit balance of £30,000. Work in progress is valued at £5,000.

PROFIT COSTS ACCOUNT

Date	Details	Dr	Cr	Balance
		£	£	£
Oct 31	Balance			30,000 Cr
	Closing work in progress c/d		5,000	35,000 Cr

At the end of the financial year the profit costs account is closed and the balance on the account is transferred to the profit and loss account. At the start of the new financial year the closing work in progress is brought down on the Dr side as opening work in progress. Continuing the example:

PROFIT COSTS ACCOUNT

Date	Details	Dr	Cr	Balance
		£	£	£
Oct 31	Balance			30,000 Cr
	Closing work in progress c/d		5,000	35,000 Cr
	Profit and loss account: transfer	35,000		—
Nov 1	Opening work in progress b/d	5,000		5,000 Dr

The value of the closing work in progress is shown on the balance sheet as a current asset. Continuing the example:

FINAL ACCOUNTS AND ADJUSTMENTS

```
                BALANCE SHEET AS AT 31 OCTOBER

FIXED ASSETS                                                XX
CURRENT ASSETS
Closing work in progress              5,000
                                      ─────
                                                    XX
LESS CURRENT LIABILITIES
                                                    XX
                                                    ──
                                                    XX
CAPITAL EMPLOYED
                                                    XX
```

In the following year the profit costs account begins with the debit entry for opening work in progress. This reduces the income from profit costs in that year (as the profit costs figure includes bills delivered which include costs for work carried out in the previous year). The movement on the profit costs account will be shown in the profit and loss account.

Example Work in progress at 1 January 2001   £ 15,000
Profit costs as at 31 December 2001   £125,000
Work in progress at 31 December 2001   £ 20,000

PROFIT AND LOSS ACCOUNT FOR THE YEAR ENDED
31 DECEMBER 2001

	£	£	£
INCOME			
Profit costs (based on bills delivered)	125,000		
Add closing work in progress	20,000	145,000	
Deduct opening work in progress		15,000	
VALUE OF WORK DONE DURING THE YEAR			130,000

Note: only the closing work in progress figure is shown in the balance sheet.

Note: you should show each subtotal after adding the closing work in progress and then deducting the opening work in progress. Any additional income, e.g., rent received, interest received, insurance commission received, should be shown after the work in progress adjustments have been made.

2.14.1 WORKED EXAMPLE ON CLOSING WORK IN PROGRESS ADJUSTMENT

A firm of solicitors prepares its final accounts on 30 June each year. The firm's profit costs account shows an opening debit balance on 1 July 2000 of £35,000. During the year ending 30 June 2001 bills have been delivered to clients totalling £175,000. The firm estimates that the value of work done during the year ending 30 June 2001, in respect of which bills have not yet been delivered, is £45,000. The accounts to record the above will appear as follows:

FINAL ACCOUNTS AND ADJUSTMENTS

PROFIT COSTS ACCOUNT

Date	Details	Dr	Cr	Balance
2000		£	£	£
July 1	Opening work in progress b/d	35,000		35,000 Dr
2001				
June 30	Sundry profit costs		175,000	140,000 Cr
	Closing work in progress c/d		45,000	185,000 Cr
	Profit and loss account: transfer	185,000		
July 1	Opening work in progress b/d	45,000		45,000 Dr

PROFIT AND LOSS ACCOUNT FOR THE YEAR ENDED
30 JUNE 2001

	£	£
INCOME		
Profit costs	175,000	
Add: Closing work in progress	45,000	
	220,000	
Less: Opening work in progress	35,000	
Value of work done during the year		185,000

Note: by convention the detailed movement on the profit costs account is shown on the profit and loss account.

BALANCE SHEET AS AT 30 JUNE 2001

FIXED ASSETS		XX
CURRENT ASSETS		
Closing work in progress	45,000	
		XX
LESS CURRENT LIABILITIES		XX
		XX
CAPITAL EMPLOYED		
		XX

2.15 Summary

Work in progress.
On the Profit and loss account.
Add work in progress at the end of the year to profit costs.
Deduct work in progress at the beginning of the year from profit costs.
On the Balance sheet.
Show work in progress at the end of the year as a current asset.

2.16 Bad Debts and Doubtful Debts Adjustments

2.16.1 WRITING OFF BAD DEBTS

Debts owed to the practice are an asset but it is unlikely that all debts will be recovered. It follows therefore that all income shown in the costs account is unlikely to be actually received.

FINAL ACCOUNTS AND ADJUSTMENTS

To avoid profit and the asset of debtors being overstated, an adjustment should be made for debts which are known to be bad and those which are considered doubtful.

To write off a debt of a particular client which is known to be irrecoverable, make the following entries:

(a) Credit the client's ledger account.

(b) Debit bad debts account.

Example A bill delivered to Jack for £235 (including £35 VAT) has not been paid. At the end of the financial year 31 October 2000 the debt was written off.

JACK'S ACCOUNT

Date	Details	Dr	Cr	Balance
2000 Oct 31	Balance Bad debt: written off	£	£ 235	£ 235 Dr ——

Note that the section of Jack's account shown in the example is the office account. Jack's account will also have a separate identical section for recording dealings with clients' money. This will be explained fully in later chapters and you need not be concerned with it at this stage.

BAD DEBTS ACCOUNT

Date	Details	Dr	Cr	Balance
2000 Oct 31	Jack: debt written off	£ 235	£	£ 235 Dr

2.16.2 VAT RELIEF FOR BAD DEBTS

If the debt is written off in circumstances where the client is bankrupt or a company is in liquidation or the debt has not been paid for at least six months from the date that payment was due, Customs and Excise will allow the practice to claim credit for the VAT element of the debt. The entries to write off a bad debt where VAT is recoverable are:

(a) Credit the client's ledger account with the profit costs and VAT written off (shown as separate entries).

(b) Debit the Customs and Excise account with VAT.

(c) Debit the bad debts account with the profit costs written off.

FINAL ACCOUNTS AND ADJUSTMENTS

> **Example** Continuing the above example, assume that Jack has been adjudicated bankrupt and that therefore the £35 VAT can be recovered from Customs and Excise.
>
> ### JACK'S ACCOUNT
>
> | Date | Details | Dr | Cr | Balance |
> |---|---|---|---|---|
> | 2000 Oct 31 | Balance
Bad debt: written off
Customs and Excise: VAT | £ | £

200
35 | £
235 Dr

—— |
>
> ### CUSTOMS AND EXCISE ACCOUNT
>
> | Date | Details | Dr | Cr | Balance |
> |---|---|---|---|---|
> | 2000 Oct 31 | Jack: VAT written off | £
35 | £ | £
35 Dr |
>
> ### BAD DEBTS ACCOUNT
>
> | Date | Details | Dr | Cr | Balance |
> |---|---|---|---|---|
> | 2000 Oct 31 | Jack: debt written off | £
200 | £ | £
200 Dr |

The debit entry on Customs and Excise will reduce the amount of VAT owed to Customs and Excise.

2.16.3 RECOVERY OF A DEBT THAT HAS BEEN WRITTEN OFF

When a debt that has previously been written off as a bad debt is recovered, the following entries will be made in the account:

(a) Debit cash account (office).

(b) Credit bad debts account.

Continuing the example, assume that in the year after the debt has been written off, Jack pays his bill.

> ### OFFICE CASH ACCOUNT
>
> | Date | Details | Dr | Cr | Balance |
> |---|---|---|---|---|
> | 2001 Jan 15 | Bad debts (recovered from Jack) | £

235 | £ | £

235 Dr |
>
> ### BAD DEBTS ACCOUNT
>
> | Date | Details | Dr | Cr | Balance |
> |---|---|---|---|---|
> | 2001 Jan 15 | Cash (debt recovered from Jack) | £ | £

235 | £

235 Cr |
>
> No entry is made in Jack's account, although a note that he has paid could be made.

FINAL ACCOUNTS AND ADJUSTMENTS

2.16.4 MAKING A PROVISION FOR DOUBTFUL DEBTS

In addition to writing off debts which are known to be bad the firm may also wish to provide for debts which it anticipates will be irrecoverable. This is done by making an adjustment to the debtors' figure, immediately prior to the preparation of the final accounts. The provision for doubtful debts is usually expressed as a percentage of total debts outstanding at the end of the year. To calculate the provision for doubtful debts, the following steps should be taken:

(a) Total the balances on the debtors' accounts.

(b) Deduct from the total any debts which are written off as bad after the balances on the debtors' accounts have been extracted. Note that any written off before would have already reduced the debtors' figure.

(c) Calculate the appropriate percentage of remaining debtors. The percentage of debts provided for as doubtful will vary from firm to firm and will depend on the debt recovery rate in previous years.

The provision for doubtful debts is like the provision for outstanding expenses. When the amount of the provision has been calculated it will be entered in the accounts at the end of the financial year as follows:

(a) Debit the bad debts account with the provision at the end of the current financial year.

(b) Credit the bad debts account with the provision at the start of the next financial year.

Example A. Solicitor prepares final accounts on 31 October. On that date the bad debts account has a debit balance of £1,500 in respect of bad debts written off during the year. Total debts owed to the practice amount to £20,000 and A. Solicitor decides to make a provision for doubtful debts of 5% of the total.

BAD DEBTS ACCOUNT

Date	Details	Dr	Cr	Balance
		£	£	£
Oct 31	Balance — bad debts previously written off Provision: doubtful debt c/d	1,000		1,500 Dr 2,500 Dr

2.16.5 EFFECT OF BAD DEBTS ON FINAL ACCOUNTS

At the end of the financial year the bad debts account will be closed and the balance will be transferred to the profit and loss account. If, at the end of the financial year, the bad debts account has a debit balance this will be transferred to the profit and loss account as an expense by making the following entries in the accounts:

(a) Credit the bad debts account.

(b) Debit the profit and loss account.

FINAL ACCOUNTS AND ADJUSTMENTS

Continuing the example of A. Solicitor:

BAD DEBTS ACCOUNT

Date	Details	Dr	Cr	Balance
Oct 31	Balance Provision: doubtful debts c/d Profit and loss account: transfer	£ 1,000	£ 2,500	£ 1,500 Dr 2,500 Dr ———

PROFIT AND LOSS ACCOUNT FOR THE YEAR ENDED 31 OCTOBER 2001

INCOME £
—

EXPENDITURE
Bad debts 1,500
Provision for doubtful debts 1,000
———
2,500

At the start of the next financial year the provision will be carried down as a credit entry on the bad debts account. Continuing the example of A. Solicitor:

BAD DEBTS ACCOUNT

Date	Details	Dr	Cr	Balance
2001 Oct 31	Balance Provision: doubtful debts c/d Profit and loss account: transfer	£ 1,000	£ 2,500	£ 1,500 Dr 2,500 Dr ———
Nov 1	Provision for doubtful debts b/d		1,000	1,000 Cr

The provision for doubtful debts made at the end of the financial year is shown as a deduction from the debtors figure on the current assets part of the balance sheet. The provision for doubtful debts is strictly a current liability but by convention is not shown as such on the balance sheet. Continuing the example of A. Solicitor:

BALANCE SHEET AS AT 31 OCTOBER 2001

FIXED ASSETS XX
CURRENT ASSETS
Debtors 20,000
Less: Provision for doubtful debts 1,000
———
19,000
XX
LESS CURRENT LIABILITIES
XX
———
XX
CAPITAL EMPLOYED
XX

FINAL ACCOUNTS AND ADJUSTMENTS

If the bad debts account has a credit balance at the end of the year because the firm has overestimated its provision for doubtful debts in previous years, the credit balance is transferred to the profit and loss account as income by making the following entries:

(a) Debit bad debts account.

(b) Credit profit and loss account.

> **Example** At the start of the financial year, 1 November 2000, a provision of £3,000 is brought down from the previous year. During the year bad debts of £5,000 are written off. At the end of the financial year, 31 October 2001, total debtors amount to £40,000. It is decided to make a provision for doubtful debts of 10%.
>
> ## BAD DEBTS ACCOUNT
>
> | Date | Details | Dr | Cr | Balance |
> |---|---|---|---|---|
> | | | £ | £ | £ |
> | 2000 Nov 1 | Last year's Provision bad debts | | 3,000 | 3,000 Cr |
> | | Written off | 5,000 | | 2,000 Dr |
> | 2001 Oct 31 | This year's Provision c/d | 4,000 | | 6,000 Dr |
> | | Profit and loss account: transfer | | 6,000 | — |
>
> ## PROFIT AND LOSS ACCOUNT FOR THE YEAR ENDED 31 OCTOBER 2001
>
> | EXPENSES | £ | £ | £ |
> |---|---|---|---|
> | Bad debts | 5,000 | | |
> | Add: this year's provision | 4,000 | | |
> | | 9,000 | | |
> | Less: last year's provision | 3,000 | | 6,000 |

Only one method of providing for bad debts and doubtful debts has been shown in this book. There are other, equally acceptable methods in use.

2.17 Summary

Bad debts
If bad debts are shown on the trial balance, then the debtors figure needs no adjustment as the bad debts have already been written off.
On the profit and loss account: show bad debts as an expense (Dr).
On the balance sheet: show the debtors figure as a current asset.

If further bad debts are to be written off after the trial balance then:

On the profit and loss account: show bad debts plus further bad debts as an expense (Dr).
On the balance sheet: show the debtors figure as a current asset, reduced by any further bad debts written off.

FINAL ACCOUNTS AND ADJUSTMENTS

Provision for doubtful debts:

Profit and loss account: show any bad debts plus this year's provision for doubtful debts as an expense (less last year's provision, if any).
Balance sheet: show the debtors figure as a current asset less this year's provision for doubtful debts.

Note: last year's provision for doubtful debts will be credited to the profit and loss account only — it will not affect the balance sheet, only this year's provision will be shown as the deduction from debtors.

2.18 Depreciation

2.18.1 INTRODUCTION

The real accounts show the cost price of fixed assets. The cost price of an asset is not its true value as most assets will decrease in value through wear and tear or obsolescence. Allowance should be made for this reduction in value of the practice's assets by reducing the profits each year. (The purchase of new assets is thereby provided for.)

2.18.2 CALCULATING DEPRECIATION

To record the reduction in value of an asset, a provision is made for depreciation at the end of each financial year. Depreciation of an asset cannot be assessed accurately until the asset is sold and therefore on the sale of an asset the firm may have to provide for a loss if the provision for depreciation has been underestimated, or a profit if the provision has been overestimated.

There are several ways of calculating depreciation. The simplest is the straight-line method. The formula for calculating depreciation by the straight-line method is:

$$\frac{\text{Cost of asset} - \text{value of asset at end of its life}}{\text{life expectancy of asset}}$$

> **Example** A firm buys a car for £5,500. The car has an estimated life of five years, at the end of which its sale value will be £500. The annual provision for depreciation using the straight-line method of calculating depreciation will be:
>
> $$\frac{£5,500 - £500}{5} = £1,000 \text{ p.a.}$$

A separate depreciation account is opened for each class of fixed assets to be depreciated.

Alternatively, still using the straight-line method, depreciation may be calculated as a percentage of the cost price of the asset.

> **Example** A firm buys a car for £16,000. Depreciation is calculated at 15% per annum on the cost price. Thus each year the depreciation will be £2,400.

FINAL ACCOUNTS AND ADJUSTMENTS

A further alternative is to depreciate on the reducing balance of the asset rather than the cost price. This is more likely to be used in practice.

Example A firm buys a car for £16,000. Depreciation is calculated at 15% per annum on the reducing balance of the car. Thus in year 1 depreciation will be £2,400. In year 2 the reduced balance of the car will be:

$$\begin{array}{ll} \text{Cost price} & £16,000 \\ \text{Less depreciation} & £\ 2,400 \\ \hline & £13,600 \end{array}$$

Thus depreciation in year 2 will be £2,040.

In year 3 the reduced balance of the car will be £11,560. Depreciation in year 3 will be £1,734.

2.18.3 RECORDING DEPRECIATION IN THE ACCOUNTS

To record depreciation in the accounts at the end of the financial year, the following entries are made:

(a) Credit the appropriate accumulated depreciation account with depreciation charged on the fixed asset.

(b) Debit the profit and loss account with the current year's depreciation, as an expense.

Note that if an asset is bought during the year it is usual to depreciate it for a full year. Do this unless you are told otherwise.

Example The firm buys a car for £6,000 in December 1998. The estimated life of the car is four years, at the end of which it should realise £1,200 on sale.

Annual depreciation on the car using the straight-line method is:

$$\frac{£6,000 - £1,200}{4} = £1,200$$

The firm's financial year ends on 30 November 1999.

ACCUMULATED DEPRECIATION (MOTOR CARS) ACCOUNT

Date	Details	Dr	Cr	Balance
1999 Nov 30	Profit and loss	£	£ 1,200	£ 1,200 Cr

Strictly, depreciation is a current liability but by convention it is shown on the balance sheet as a deduction of accumulated depreciation from the cost price of the asset. Continuing the example:

FINAL ACCOUNTS AND ADJUSTMENTS

PROFIT AND LOSS ACCOUNT FOR YEAR ENDED
30 NOVEMBER 1999

	£
INCOME	—
LESS EXPENDITURE	
Depreciation: motor cars	1,200

BALANCE SHEET AS AT 30 NOVEMBER 1999

FIXED ASSETS		
Motor cars at cost	6,000	
Less: accumulated depreciation	1,200	
		4,800
CURRENT ASSETS		XX
LESS CURRENT LIABILITIES		XX
		XX
CAPITAL EMPLOYED		XX

The accounts would be shown as follows at the end of year 2, which is 30 November 2000.

ACCUMULATED DEPRECIATION (MOTOR CARS) ACCOUNT

Date	Details	Dr	Cr	Balance
1999		£	£	£
Nov 30	Profit and loss		1,200	1,200 Cr
2000				
Nov 30	Profit and loss		1,200	2,400 Cr

PROFIT AND LOSS ACCOUNT FOR THE YEAR ENDED
30 NOVEMBER 2000

	£
INCOME	—
LESS EXPENDITURE	
Depreciation: motor cars	1,200

BALANCE SHEET AS AT 30 NOVEMBER 2000

FIXED ASSETS		XX
Motor cars at cost	6,000	
Less: accumulated depreciation	2,400	
		3,600
CURRENT ASSETS		XX
LESS CURRENT LIABILITIES		XX
		XX
CAPITAL EMPLOYED		XX

2.19 Sale of Assets

When an asset is sold a new account is opened called the asset disposal account. If the asset is sold for more than its book value too much depreciation has been provided for. This 'profit' must be shown as income in the profit and loss account for the year when the asset is sold. If the asset is sold for less than its book value, too little depreciation has been provided for. This 'loss' must be shown as an expense in the profit and loss account for the year in which the asset is sold.

The following entries will be made in the accounts when an asset is sold.

(a) Transfer the cost price of the asset from the asset account to the asset disposal account by making the following entries:

(i) Credit the asset account with the cost price of the asset.

(ii) Debit the asset disposal account with the cost price of the asset.

Continuing the example from **2.18.3**, assume that the car is sold in December 2000.

MOTOR CARS ACCOUNT

Date	Details	Dr	Cr	Balance
1998 Dec	Cash	£ 6,000	£	£ 6,000 Dr
2000 Dec	Asset disposal		6,000	—

ASSET DISPOSAL ACCOUNT (MOTOR CARS)

Date	Details	Dr	Cr	Balance
2000 Dec	Motor cars	£ 6,000	£	£ 6,000 Dr

(b) Transfer the accumulated depreciation from the depreciation account to the asset disposal account by making the following entries:

(i) Debit the depreciation account.

(ii) Credit the asset disposal account.

Continuing the example:

ACCUMULATED DEPRECIATION (MOTOR CARS) ACCOUNT

Date	Details	Dr	Cr	Balance
1999 Nov 30	Profit and loss depreciation	£	£ 1,200	£ 1,200 Cr
2000 Nov 30	Profit and loss depreciation		1,200	2,400 Cr
Dec	Asset disposal — transfer	2,400		—

FINAL ACCOUNTS AND ADJUSTMENTS

ASSET DISPOSAL ACCOUNT (MOTOR CARS)

Date	Details	Dr	Cr	Balance
2000 Dec	Motor cars cost price Accumulated depreciation	£ 6,000	£ 2,400	£ 6,000 Dr 3,600 Dr

(c) Record receipt of sale proceeds by making the following entries:

    (i) Debit the cash account.

    (ii) Credit the asset disposal account.

If the asset is sold on credit a personal account will be opened and the personal account of the buyer is debited with the sale price and *not* cash account.

Continuing the example, assume that the car is sold for £3,000.

CASH ACCOUNT

Date	Details	Dr	Cr	Balance
2000 Dec	Asset disposal (motor car)	£ 3,000	£	£ 3,000 Dr

ASSET DISPOSAL ACCOUNT (MOTOR CARS)

Date	Details	Dr	Cr	Balance
2000 Dec	Motor cars cost price Depreciation Cash	£ 6,000	£ 2,400 3,000	£ 6,000 Dr 3,600 Dr 600 Dr

(d) Transfer the balance on the asset disposal account to the profit and loss account as follows:

    (i) If the asset disposal account has a debit balance the firm has made a loss on the sale of the asset and the balance will be transferred to the profit and loss account as an expense. Continuing the example:

ASSET DISPOSAL ACCOUNT (MOTOR CARS)

Date	Details	Dr	Cr	Balance
2000 Dec	Motor cars Depreciation Cash	£ 6,000	£ 2,400 3,000	£ 6,000 Dr 3,600 Dr 600 Dr
2001 Nov 30	Profit and loss: transfer		600	—

FINAL ACCOUNTS AND ADJUSTMENTS

```
              PROFIT AND LOSS ACCOUNT FOR THE YEAR ENDED
                            30 NOVEMBER 2001
                                                          £           £
  INCOME                                                              XX
                                                                      —
  LESS EXPENDITURE
  Asset disposal: loss on sale of car                     600
```

(ii) If the asset disposal account has a credit balance the firm has made a profit on the sale of the asset and the balance on the asset disposal account is transferred to the profit and loss account as income.

Example In 2000 the firm bought a word processor for £1,000. Depreciation is charged on the word processor at the rate of £200 per annum. In 2001 the word processor was sold for £900 cash. The accounts would appear as follows:

OFFICE EQUIPMENT ACCOUNT

Date	Details	Dr	Cr	Balance
		£	£	£
2000	Cash cost price	1,000		1,000 Dr
2001	Asset disposal — transfer		1,000	—

ACCUMULATED DEPRECIATION (OFFICE EQUIPMENT) ACCOUNT

Date	Details	Dr	Cr	Balance
		£	£	£
2000	Profit and loss depreciation		200	200 Cr
2001	Asset disposal — transfer	200		—

ASSET DISPOSAL ACCOUNT (OFFICE EQUIPMENT)

Date	Details	Dr	Cr	Balance
2001		£	£	£
	Office equipment	1,000		1,000 Dr
	Depreciation (office equipment)		200	800 Dr
	Cash		900	100 Cr
	Profit and loss (profit on sale)	100		—

```
           PROFIT AND LOSS ACCOUNT FOR THE YEAR ENDED .... 2001

  INCOME                                                   £           £
  Costs                                                    XX
  Add: Closing work in progress                            XX
                                                           ——
                                                           XX
  Less: Opening work in progress                           XX          XX
                                                           ——
  Add: Asset disposal: profit on sale of word processor                100
```

FINAL ACCOUNTS AND ADJUSTMENTS

2.19.1 DISPOSING OF PART OF A GROUP OF ASSETS

Example Flynn, a solicitor, prepares final accounts on 31 December each year. The trial balance taken immediately before the preparation of the final accounts for the year ended 2000 shows a figure for motor cars, at cost, of £31,000. Accumulated depreciation on the cars at 31 December 1999 was £6,600. You are told that the trial balance figures include the cost of a car, £10,000, bought on 1 January 2000, and another car being sold by Flynn on the same day for £7,600 cash. The second car had been bought by Flynn for £9,000 on 1 January 1999. Depreciation is charged at 20% per annum of cost price. No provision had been made for the sale and this is done immediately before the final accounts are prepared on 31 December 2000. Flynn's accounts to record the above will be as follows.

MOTOR CARS ACCOUNT

Date	Details	Dr	Cr	Balance
2000		£	£	£
	Balance			31,000 Dr
Dec 31	Asset disposal		9,000	22,000 Dr

ASSET DISPOSAL ACCOUNT (MOTOR CARS)

Date	Details	Dr	Cr	Balance
2000		£	£	£
Dec 31	Motor cars	9,000		9,000 Dr
	Depreciation		1,800	7,200 Dr
	Cash		7,600	400 Cr
	Profit and loss account:			
	Transfer profit on sale	400		———

ACCUMULATED DEPRECIATION ACCOUNT (MOTOR CARS)

Date	Details	Dr	Cr	Balance
2000		£	£	£
Jan 1	Balance			6,600 Cr
	Asset disposal	1,800		4,800 Cr
Dec 31	Profit and loss		4,400	9,200 Cr

PROFIT AND LOSS ACCOUNT FOR THE YEAR ENDED 30 DECEMBER 2000

	£	£	£
INCOME		XX	
Profit on sale of car	400		
LESS EXPENDITURE			
Depreciation: motor cars	4,400		

BALANCE SHEET AS AT 31 DECEMBER 2000

FIXED ASSETS		
Motor cars at cost	22,000	
Less: Accumulated depreciation	9,200	
		12,800
CURRENT ASSETS	XX	
LESS CURRENT LIABILITIES		
	XX	
	XX	
CAPITAL EMPLOYED		
	XX	

Note: the current year's depreciation is calculated by taking the cost price of the car which has been sold (£9,000) from the balance on the motor cars account (£31,000), and finding 20% of the remainder (£22,000) = £4,400.

2.20 Exercises on Adjustments and Final Accounts

1   On 31 October 2001 the firm's light and heat account has a debit balance of £5,000. The firm estimates that a further £250 worth of gas has been used.

Show the state of the light and heat account on 1 November 2001 and the entries which you would make in the final accounts which are prepared on 31 October 2001.

2   The firm pays council tax of £1,000 on 1 April and 1 October for the following six months. The firm's final accounts are prepared on 31 December each year.

Show the rates account at 1 January 2001 and the entries you would make in the final accounts for the year ended 31 December 2000.

3   Final accounts are prepared on 30 June each year. On 30 June 2001 the stationery account shows a debit balance of £800. On checking the stationery it is discovered that there is £200 worth left.

Show the stationery account at 1 July 2001 and the entries in the final accounts for the year ended 30 June 2001.

4   At the end of its financial year, 31 December 1999, Grace & Co. had profit costs of £180,000 and its work in progress was valued at £18,000. At the end of its second year, 31 December 2000, the firm had delivered bills totalling £220,000 and its work in progress was valued at £25,000.

Show the costs account and also the final accounts for the year ended 31 December 2000.

5   On 1 July 2000 the balance on the cars account is £25,000 and accumulated depreciation is £7,000. Depreciation on cars is charged at 15% per annum. In December 2000 a car purchased in 1998 for £10,000 is sold for £8,000.

Prepare the ledger accounts to record the above events and show the final accounts as at 30 June 2001.

6   Smith, a sole practitioner, prepares final accounts on 31 December each year. Immediately prior to 31 December 1999 an inspection of Smith's accounts reveals the following:

(a) Debts due from Brown, Jones and Green of £124, £86 and £26, respectively, are irrecoverable and are to be written off.

(b) Black owes £235 (including £35 VAT). Black has been made bankrupt and there are no assets available. It is decided to write off the debt.

(c) The total amount of debts before any adjustments have been made for the above is £5,936.

(d) It is decided to provide for doubtful debts at 10% of total debtors, after the debts have been written off.

FINAL ACCOUNTS AND ADJUSTMENTS

During the year to December 2000 the following events take place:

(a) Green has been traced and has paid in full.

(b) It is decided to reduce the provision for doubtful debts to 5% of the debtors figure.

At the end of 2000 total debtors amount to £4,000.

You are required to show the bad debts account for both years, together with the necessary entries in the final accounts.

7 The trial balance of J. Milton, prepared on 31 December 2001, is as follows:

TRIAL BALANCE AS AT 31 DECEMBER 2001

Name of account	Dr	Cr
	£	£
Drawings	19,000	
Fixtures and fittings	5,200	
Cars	20,600	
Accumulated depreciation (cars)		4,120
Accumulated depreciation (fixtures and fittings)		1,300
Premises	132,000	
Capital		140,000
Telephone/postage	1,300	
Council tax	2,950	
Light and heat	1,550	
Salaries	25,270	
Cash at bank:		
Office account	14,190	
Client account	315,000	
Petty cash	123	
Debtors	4,422	
Due to creditors		4,763
Due to clients		315,000
Profit costs		76,422
	541,605	541,605

In addition:

(a) Depreciation at 10% and 5% is to be charged against the cost price of cars and fixtures and fittings respectively.

(b) At 31 December 2001 electricity and telephone bills outstanding amount to £551 and £505 respectively.

(c) Included in the amount for debtors is £122 which is to be written off. A provision for doubtful debts of 5% of remaining debtors is to be made.

(d) Work in progress at 31 December 2001 is valued at £8,569.

Prepare final accounts for the year ended 31 December 2001.

8 The following balances were taken from the accounts of C. Arnold, solicitor, on 31 December 2001.

	£
Capital	223,059
Work in progress at 1 January 2001	16,582
Petty cash	55
Bank overdraft on office account	4,552
Bank client account	450,000
Debtors	12,009
Creditors	9,235
Car: cost price	20,000
Accumulated depreciation: car	8,000
Drawings	20,459
Fixtures and fittings at cost	8,000
Accumulated depreciation: fixtures and fittings	1,200

	£
Costs	78,021
Rent and rates	2,626
Salaries	30,226
General expenses	12,500
Interest on overdraft	735
Insurance commission received	369
Freehold premises	200,500
Bad debts	2,400
Provision for doubtful debts b/d (last year's)	1,656
Due to clients	450,000

C. Arnold provides the following additional information about the practice:

(a) Work in progress was valued at £14,270 on 31 December 2001.

(b) Salaries outstanding on 31 December 2001 were £426.

(c) Council tax paid in advance on 31 December 2001 amounted to £500.

(d) This year's provision for doubtful debts is to be increased to £2,600.

(e) Depreciation is to be charged at 20% per annum on cost of cars and 5% per annum on cost of fixtures and fittings.

Prepare a profit and loss account and balance sheet for the year ended 31 December 2001.

2.21 Suggested Answers to Exercises on Adjustments and Final Accounts

1   LIGHT AND HEAT ACCOUNT

Date	Details	Dr	Cr	Balance
2001		£	£	£
Oct 31	Balance			5,000 Dr
	Provision: Gas c/d	250		5,250 Dr
	Profit and loss: transfer		5,250	
Nov 1	Provision: Gas b/d		250	250 Cr

FINAL ACCOUNTS AND ADJUSTMENTS

PROFIT AND LOSS ACCOUNT FOR THE YEAR ENDED 31 OCTOBER 2001

	£	£	£
INCOME			XX
LESS EXPENDITURE			
Light and heat	5,000		
Add provision	250	5,250	

BALANCE SHEET AS AT 31 OCTOBER 2001

FIXED ASSETS			XX
CURRENT ASSETS		XX	
LESS CURRENT LIABILITIES			
Provision for light and heat	250		
		XX	
			XX
CAPITAL EMPLOYED			
		XX	

2   COUNCIL TAX ACCOUNT

Date	Details	Dr	Cr	Balance
2000		£	£	£
Apr 1	Cash	1,000		1,000 Dr
Oct 1	Cash	1,000		2,000 Dr
Dec 31	Payment in advance c/d		500	1,500 Dr
	Profit and loss: transfer		1,500	—
2001				
Jan 1	Payment in advance b/d	500		500 Dr

PROFIT AND LOSS ACCOUNT FOR THE YEAR ENDED 31 DECEMBER 2000

	£	£	£
INCOME			XX
LESS EXPENDITURE			
Council tax	2,000		
Less paid in advance	500	1,500	

BALANCE SHEET AS AT 31 DECEMBER 2000

	£	£	£
FIXED ASSETS			XX
CURRENT ASSETS			
Council tax paid in advance	500		
		XX	
LESS CURRENT LIABILITIES			
		XX	
			XX
CAPITAL EMPLOYED			
		XX	

FINAL ACCOUNTS AND ADJUSTMENTS

3 STATIONERY ACCOUNT

Date	Details	Dr	Cr	Balance
2001		£	£	£
June 30	Balance			800 Dr
	Closing stock c/d		200	600 Dr
	Profit and loss: transfer		600	—
July 1	Opening stock b/d	200		200 Dr

PROFIT AND LOSS ACCOUNT FOR THE YEAR ENDED 30 JUNE 2001

	£	£	£
INCOME			XX
LESS EXPENDITURE			
Stationery	800		
Less closing stock	200	600	

BALANCE SHEET AS AT 30 JUNE 2001

	£	£	£
FIXED ASSETS			XX
CURRENT ASSETS			
Closing stock of stationery	200		
		XX	
LESS CURRENT LIABILITIES		XX	
			XX
CAPITAL EMPLOYED		XX	

4 PROFIT COSTS ACCOUNT

Date	Details	Dr	Cr	Balance
1999		£	£	£
Dec 31	Balance (bills delivered)			180,000 Cr
	Closing work in progress c/d		18,000	198,000 Cr
	Profit and loss: transfer	198,000		—
2000				
Jan 1	Opening work in progress b/d	18,000		18,000 Dr
Dec 31	Costs		220,000	202,000 Cr
	Closing work in progress c/d		25,000	227,000 Cr
	Profit and loss: transfer	227,000		—
2001				
Jan 1	Opening work in progress b/d	25,000		25,000 Dr

GRACE & CO
PROFIT AND LOSS ACCOUNT FOR THE YEAR ENDED 31 DECEMBER 2000

	£	£	£
INCOME			
Costs	220,000		
Add closing work in progress	25,000		
	245,000		
Less opening work in progress	18,000	227,000	
LESS EXPENDITURE		XX	

FINAL ACCOUNTS AND ADJUSTMENTS

GRACE & CO
BALANCE SHEET AS AT 31 DECEMBER 2000

FIXED ASSETS			XX
CURRENT ASSETS			
Closing work in progress	25,000		
	———		
		XX	
LESS CURRENT LIABILITIES			
		XX	
		———	
		XX	
CAPITAL EMPLOYED			
		XX	

5   MOTOR CARS ACCOUNT

Date	Details	Dr	Cr	Balance
2000		£	£	£
July 1	Balance			25,000 Dr
Dec	Asset disposal		10,000	15,000 Dr

ASSET DISPOSAL ACCOUNT

Date	Details	Dr	Cr	Balance
2000		£	£	£
Dec	Motor cars cost price	10,000		10,000 Dr
	Depreciation (2 years @ 1,500)		3,000	7,000 Dr
	Cash		8,000	1,000 Cr
2001				
June 30	Profit and loss: Profit on sale	1,000		—

ACCUMULATED DEPRECIATION ACCOUNT

Date	Details	Dr	Cr	Balance
2000		£	£	£
July 1	Balance			7,000 Cr
Dec	Asset disposal	3,000		4,000 Cr
2001				
June 30	Profit and loss: transfer		2,250	6,250 Cr

PROFIT AND LOSS ACCOUNT FOR THE YEAR ENDED
30 JUNE 2001

	£	£	£
INCOME			
Profit on sale of car		1,000	
LESS EXPENDITURE			
Depreciation: motor cars	2,250		

BALANCE SHEET AS AT 30 JUNE 2001

FIXED ASSETS			
Motor cars	15,000		
Less accumulated depreciation	6,250		
		8,750	
CURRENT ASSETS		XX	
LESS CURRENT LIABILITIES		XX	
			XX
CAPITAL EMPLOYED			XX

6 SMITH
BAD DEBTS ACCOUNT

Date	Details	Dr	Cr	Balance
1999		£	£	£
Dec 31	Brown	124		
	Jones	86		
	Green	26		236 Dr
	Black	200		436 Dr
	Provision c/d	550		986 Dr
	Profit and loss transfer		986	—
2000				
Jan 1	Provision b/d		550	550 Cr
	Cash bad debt recovered (Green)		26	576 Cr
Dec 31	Provision c/d	200		376 Cr
	Profit and loss transfer	376		—
2001				
Jan 1	Provision b/d		200	200 Cr

SMITH
PROFIT AND LOSS ACCOUNT FOR THE YEAR ENDED 31 DECEMBER 1999

	£	£	£
INCOME			XX
LESS EXPENDITURE			
Bad debts	436		
Provision	550	986	

SMITH
BALANCE SHEET AS AT 31 DECEMBER 1999

FIXED ASSETS			XX
CURRENT ASSETS			
Debtors	5,500		
Less provision for doubtful debts	550		
		4,950	
		XX	
LESS CURRENT LIABILITIES		XX	
			XX
CAPITAL EMPLOYED			XX

FINAL ACCOUNTS AND ADJUSTMENTS

SMITH
PROFIT AND LOSS ACCOUNT FOR THE YEAR ENDED 31 DECEMBER 2000

	£	£	£
INCOME			
Overestimate of provision for doubtful debts written off		376	

BALANCE SHEET AS AT 31 DECEMBER 2000

FIXED ASSETS			XX
CURRENT ASSETS			
Debtors	4,000		
Less provision for doubtful debts	200		
		3,800	
		XX	
LESS CURRENT LIABILITIES			
		XX	
			XX
CAPITAL EMPLOYED			
			XX

7   J MILTON
PROFIT AND LOSS ACCOUNT FOR THE YEAR ENDED 31 DECEMBER 2001

	£	£	£
INCOME			
Profit costs		76,422	
Add closing work in progress		8,569	84,991
LESS EXPENDITURE			
Telephone and postage	1,300		
Add provision	505	1,805	
Council tax		2,950	
Light and heat	1,550		
Add provision	551	2,101	
Salaries		25,270	
Depreciation:			
Motor cars	2,060		
Fixtures and fittings	260	2,320	
Bad debts and provision		337	34,783
(£122 + £215 provision)			
NET PROFIT			50,208

FINAL ACCOUNTS AND ADJUSTMENTS

J MILTON
BALANCE SHEET AS AT 31 DECEMBER 2001

	£	£	£
FIXED ASSETS			
Premises		132,000	
Fixtures and fittings at cost	5,200		
Less accumulated depreciation	1,560		
		3,640	
Motor cars at cost	20,600		
Less accumulated depreciation	6,180		
		14,420	
			150,060
CURRENT ASSETS			
Closing work in progress		8,569	
Debtors	4,300		
Less provision	215		
		4,085	
Cash at bank, office account		14,190	
Petty cash		123	
		26,967	
LESS CURRENT LIABILITIES			
Creditors	4,763		
Outstanding expenses	1,056		
		5,819	
NET CURRENT ASSETS			21,148
TOTAL			171,208
CAPITAL EMPLOYED			
Capital at start	140,000		
Add net profit	50,208		
		190,208	
Less drawings		19,000	
TOTAL			171,208
Client account			
Cash at bank, client account	315,000		
Due to clients	315,000		

FINAL ACCOUNTS AND ADJUSTMENTS

8   C. ARNOLD: PROFIT AND LOSS ACCOUNT FOR THE YEAR ENDED 31 DECEMBER 2001

	£	£	£
INCOME			
Profit costs		78,021	
Add: closing work in progress		14,270	
		92,291	
Less: opening work in progress		16,582	75,709
Additional income			
Insurance commission received			369
			76,078
LESS EXPENDITURE			
Rent and rates	2,626		
Less: paid in advance	500	2,126	
Salaries	30,226		
Plus: outstanding	426	30,652	
General expenses		12,500	
Interest		735	
Bad and doubtful debts		3,344* [see note below]	
Depreciation: cars	4,000		
Fixtures and fittings	400	4,400	53,757
NET PROFIT			22,321

Note:

Bad debts	2,400
Add this year's provision	2,600
	5,000
Less last year's provision	1,656
	3,344

C. ARNOLD: BALANCE SHEET AS AT 31 DECEMBER 2001

	£	£	£
FIXED ASSETS			
Freehold premises		200,500	
Fixtures and fittings at cost	8,000		
Less accumulated depreciation	1,600		
		6,400	
Motor cars at cost	20,000		
Less accumulated depreciation	12,000		
		8,000	
			214,900
CURRENT ASSETS			
Closing work in progress		14,270	
Debtors	12,009		
Less provision	2,600		
		9,409	

FINAL ACCOUNTS AND ADJUSTMENTS

	£	£	£
Petty cash		55	
Payment in advance			
Rates		500	
		24,234	
LESS CURRENT LIABILITIES			
Creditors	9,235		
Office bank account overdraft	4,552		
Outstanding expenses: salaries	426		
		14,213	
NET CURRENT ASSETS			10,021
TOTAL			224,921
CAPITAL EMPLOYED			
Capital at start	223,059		
Add net profit	22,321		
		245,380	
Less drawings		20,459	
TOTAL			224,921
CLIENT ACCOUNT			
Cash at bank, client account	450,000		
Less: due to clients	450,000		

THREE

PARTNERSHIP ACCOUNTS

3.1 The Accounts Kept by a Partnership

3.1.1 GENERAL

The accounts kept by a partnership are largely the same as those kept by a sole practitioner. The real and nominal accounts are the same and the clients' accounts are the same, as are the accounting procedures up to the preparation of final accounts.

3.1.1.1 Profit and loss account
There is an extension to the profit and loss account, known as the appropriation account, which will show how the profit is divided between the partners.

3.1.1.2 The balance sheet
The partners each have a separate capital account and a separate current account, which shows details of all the profit allocated to the partner, less drawings.

3.2 Final Accounts

3.2.1 PROFIT AND LOSS ACCOUNT — THE APPROPRIATION ACCOUNT

Up to the point of calculating the firm's net profit, the profit and loss account of a partnership is the same as that of a sole practitioner. In a partnership the profit and loss account is extended to show the allocation of the net profit amongst the partners in the profit-sharing ratio provided for in the partnership agreement after such items as salaries and interest on capital, also provided for in the partnership agreement, have been taken into account. The extension of the profit and loss account is called an appropriation account.

> **Example** The firm has three partners A, B and C. The profit and loss account records a net profit for the year of £120,000. The partnership agreement provides that A is to receive interest on capital of £2,000 and a salary of £8,000, C is to receive interest on capital of £1,000 and a salary of £2,000 and B is to receive a salary of £2,000. Profits are shared in the ratio A2 : B2 : C1. The appropriation account for A, B and C will appear as follows:
>
> A, B & C APPROPRIATION ACCOUNT FOR THE YEAR ENDING
>
> NET PROFIT   120,000

PARTNERSHIP ACCOUNTS

SALARIES:		
A	8,000	
B	2,000	
C	2,000	
		12,000
INTEREST ON CAPITAL:		
A	2,000	
C	1,000	3,000
PROFIT SHARE:		
A: 2/5ths	42,000	
B: 2/5ths	42,000	
C: 1/5th	21,000	105,000
		120,000

Note the following with regard to the appropriation account:

(a) Net profit is carried down from the profit and loss account. (Note if any interest on drawings is charged to the partners this would be added to the net profit.)

(b) Partners' entitlements to salary and interest on capital, for example, are deducted from the net profit (plus any interest on drawings).

(c) The resulting balance is shared amongst the partners in the profit-sharing ratio.

(d) The current account for each partner will show any salary, interest on capital and profit share that they are entitled to. This will form part of the balance sheet — see **3.3.5**.

To continue the above example, the current account for partner A would appear as follows:

PARTNERSHIP ACCOUNTS

CURRENT ACCOUNT: A

Date	Details	Dr	Cr	Balance
		£	£	£
	Appropriation: salary		8,000	8,000 Cr
	Appropriation: interest on capital		2,000	10,000 Cr
	Appropriation: profit share		42,000	52,000 Cr

Example where a net loss is made D and E are in partnership as solicitors. The partnership agreement provides that D is to receive a salary of £8,000 per annum and 6% per annum interest on capital, which stands at £50,000. E is to receive 6% per annum interest on capital, which stands at £25,000. D has made drawings of £14,000 and E has made drawings of £15,000. Profits and losses are shared equally. The profit and loss account shows a net loss of £2,000.

D & E APPROPRIATION ACCOUNT FOR THE YEAR ENDING

	£	£	£
NET LOSS b/d			2,000
SALARIES:			
D			8,000
INTEREST ON CAPITAL:			
D 6% on £50,000		3,000	
E 6% on £25,000		1,500	4,500
TOTAL LOSS			14,500
DIVISION OF NET LOSS:			
D:		7,250	
E:		7,250	

CURRENT ACCOUNT: D

Date	Details	Dr	Cr	Balance
		£	£	£
	Drawings	14,000		14,000 Dr
	Appropriation: salary		8,000	6,000 Dr
	Appropriation: interest on capital		3,000	3,000 Dr
	Appropriation: share of loss	7,250		10,250 Dr

CURRENT ACCOUNT: E

Date	Details	Dr	Cr	Balance
		£	£	£
	Drawings	15,000		15,000 Dr
	Appropriation: interest on capital		1,500	13,500 Dr
	Appropriation: share of loss	7,250		20,750 Dr

PARTNERSHIP ACCOUNTS

3.2.2 PARTNERS' EXPENSES

If bona fide expenses are paid by the partners these are business expenses and will be recorded by means of a debit entry in the appropriate nominal expense account. At the end of the year the balance on the nominal expense account will be transferred to the profit and loss account as a business expense.

> **Example** Edwina, a partner in a provincial firm, travels to London on firm's business. She travels first class and pays the return train fare of £50 out of her own money. Edwina submits a claim to recoup the £50.
>
> (a) If the cashier pays Edwina her £50, the entries in the accounts will be:
>
> (i) Debit travelling expenses account.
>
> (ii) Credit cash account.
>
> TRAVELLING EXPENSES ACCOUNT
>
> | Date | Details | Dr | Cr | Balance |
> |------|---------|----|----|---------|
> | | | £ | £ | £ |
> | | Cash (partner's travel) | 50 | | 50 Dr |
>
> This is a nominal expense account.
>
> CASH ACCOUNT
>
> | Date | Details | Dr | Cr | Balance |
> |------|---------|----|----|---------|
> | | | £ | £ | £ |
> | | Travelling expenses | | 50 | 50 Cr |
>
> (b) If Edwina is not to be paid in cash, the travelling expenses will be credited to her current account, in which case the entries in the accounts will be:
>
> (i) Debit the travelling expenses account.
>
> (ii) Credit the current account of Edwina.
>
> PROFIT AND LOSS ACCOUNT FOR THE YEAR ENDED .....
>
> INCOME £
> ———
>
> LESS EXPENDITURE
> Partners' travelling expenses 50
>
> CURRENT ACCOUNT: EDWINA
>
> | Date | Details | Dr | Cr | Balance |
> |------|---------|----|----|---------|
> | | | £ | £ | £ |
> | | Travelling expenses | | 50 | 50 Cr |

3.3 Drawings

A drawings account may be opened for each partner or alternatively drawings may be debited to the partners' current accounts when they are made.

Partners' drawings can be of two types:

(a) Cash drawings.

(b) Drawings in kind.

3.3.1 CASH DRAWINGS

If a drawings account is used the following entries will be made to record the partners' cash drawings.

(a) Debit drawings account.

(b) Credit cash account.

Example On 31 March partner A draws £2,000, on 30 April A draws £2,000, on 10 May the firm pays A's home gas bill, £150.

DRAWINGS ACCOUNT: A

Date	Details	Dr	Cr	Balance
		£	£	£
Mar 31	Cash	2,000		2,000 Dr
Apr 30	Cash	2,000		4,000 Dr
May 10	Cash: home gas bill	150		4,150 Dr

If the firm does not use a drawings account for the partners but debits drawings into the partners' current accounts, when the drawings are made, the above entries would have been recorded in A's current account.

3.3.2 DRAWINGS IN KIND

If a partner takes partnership property as personal property, the following entries will be made in the accounts when the asset is taken out of the practice.

(a) Transfer the cost price of the asset to the asset disposal account (see **2.13**).

(b) Transfer depreciation already charged on the asset from the depreciation account to the asset disposal account.

(c) Credit the asset disposal account with the value of the asset at the date of disposal to the partner.

PARTNERSHIP ACCOUNTS

(d) Debit the partner's current account with the value of the asset at the date of disposal to the partner.

(e) Transfer any profit or loss made on the disposal of the asset from the asset disposal account to the profit and loss account at the end of the financial year.

> **Example** On 5 January A takes over ownership of a firm's car valued at £12,500 as it is surplus to requirements.
>
> ### CURRENT ACCOUNT: A
>
> | Date | Details | Dr | Cr | Balance |
> |---|---|---|---|---|
> | | | £ | £ | £ |
> | Jan 5 | Asset disposal: car | 12,500 | | 12,500 Dr |

3.3.3 END OF THE FINANCIAL YEAR

At the end of the financial year the partner's drawings account will be closed and the balance on the account will be transferred to the partner's current account.

> **Example** Continuing the example from **3.3.1**, assume that the firm's financial year ends on 30 June and that the partners' drawings are debited to their drawings accounts during the year.
>
> ### DRAWINGS ACCOUNT: A
>
> | Date | Details | Dr | Cr | Balance |
> |---|---|---|---|---|
> | | | £ | £ | £ |
> | Mar 31 | Cash | 2,000 | | 2,000 Dr |
> | Apr 30 | Cash | 2,000 | | 4,000 Dr |
> | May 10 | Cash: home gas bill | 150 | | 4,150 Dr |
> | June 30 | Current account: transfer | | 4,150 | — |
>
> ### CURRENT ACCOUNT: A
>
> | Date | Details | Dr | Cr | Balance |
> |---|---|---|---|---|
> | | | £ | £ | £ |
> | Jan 5 | Asset disposal: car | 12,500 | | 12,500 Dr |
> | June 30 | Drawings | 4,150 | | 16,650 Dr |

3.3.4 CAPITAL ACCOUNTS

In a partnership the capital is introduced by more than one person and therefore a separate capital account is kept for each partner.

PARTNERSHIP ACCOUNTS

Note, however, that the net profit is not transferred from the profit and loss account to the partners' capital account at the end of the financial year as happens with a sole practitioner.

Drawings are not transferred to the partners' capital account at the end of the year as happens with a sole practitioner.

If partners wish to have their share of the profit capitalised, the balance on their current accounts will be transferred to their capital accounts at the end of the financial year.

Thus partners' capital accounts will only show capital which they introduced into the practice and any profit which they decide to capitalise.

Example A and B enter into partnership introducing £30,000 and £90,000 capital respectively.

CAPITAL ACCOUNT: A

Date	Details	Dr	Cr	Balance
	Balance	£	£	£ 30,000 Cr

CAPITAL ACCOUNT: B

Date	Details	Dr	Cr	Balance
	Balance	£	£	£ 90,000 Cr

3.3.5 CURRENT ACCOUNTS

A current account is opened for each partner.

A partner's current account is credited with any sums which the partner is entitled to receive from the practice, for example, the profit share, interest on capital and salary.

A partner's current account is debited with any sums which the partner has taken out of the practice or which are owed to the practice, for example, drawings (transferred at the end of the financial year from the partner's drawings account), interest charged on the partner's drawings or the partner's share of a loss made by the firm.

If a partner's current account has a credit balance, the firm owes money to the partner. If the current account has a debit balance, the partner owes money to the firm which is a current asset of the firm.

By convention, the balances on the partners' current accounts are always shown on the capital employed part (or liabilities part) of the balance sheet.

PARTNERSHIP ACCOUNTS

> **Example** In the example in **3.3.4**, assume that on 30 June 2001, the end of the financial year for A and B's first year of practice, A's share of the net profit is £35,000 and B's share is £40,000. Interest on capital is allowed to both partners at the rate of 5% per annum. A has made drawings of £20,000 and B has made drawings of £30,000. B is paid a salary of £5,000 per annum. B asks that any sums due to her at the end of the year be transferred to her capital account.
>
> ### CURRENT ACCOUNT: A
>
> | Date | Details | Dr | Cr | Balance |
> |---|---|---|---|---|
> | 2001 | | £ | £ | £ |
> | June 30 | Profit share | | 35,000 | 35,000 Cr |
> | | Interest on capital | | 1,500 | 36,500 Cr |
> | | Drawings | 20,000 | | 16,500 Cr |
>
> At the end of the year the firm owes A £16,500.
>
> ### CURRENT ACCOUNT: B
>
> | Date | Details | Dr | Cr | Balance |
> |---|---|---|---|---|
> | 2001 | | £ | £ | £ |
> | June 30 | Profit share | | 40,000 | 40,000 Cr |
> | | Salary | | 5,000 | 45,000 Cr |
> | | Interest on capital | | 4,500 | 49,500 Cr |
> | | Drawings | 30,000 | | 19,500 Cr |
> | | Capital account: transfer | 19,500 | | ——— |
>
> ### CAPITAL ACCOUNT: B
>
> | Date | Details | Dr | Cr | Balance |
> |---|---|---|---|---|
> | 2001 | | £ | £ | £ |
> | June 30 | Balance | | | 90,000 Cr |
> | | Current account transfer | | 19,500 | 109,500 Cr |

3.3.6 LOAN ACCOUNTS

If partners loan money to the firm over and above their capital contribution, a loan account will be opened in the partners' names and they will be treated as creditors of the firm.

Any loan will be shown on the balance sheet as a long-term liability.

If interest is payable on the loan, a nominal expense account will be opened to record the payment of interest; the interest payable account. At the end of the financial year the debit balance on the interest payable account will be transferred to the profit and loss account as a business expense.

The partner may take payment of the loan interest in cash or may have the loan interest credited to the current account.

The bookkeeping entries to record the payment of loan interest in cash will be:

(a) Debit interest payable account.

(b) Credit cash account.

The bookkeeping entries to record loan interest credited to the partner's current account will be:

(a) Debit interest payable account.

(b) Credit current account of partner making the loan.

Example Lawrence, Alice and Mark practise together in partnership. It is agreed that Lawrence will make a loan of £5,000 to the practice to be used towards the purchase of a word processor. Lawrence is to receive interest of £250 per annum for so long as the loan remains unpaid. Lawrence asks that the interest be dealt with in his current account.

When the loan is negotiated the entries in the accounts will be:

(a) Debit office cash account when the loan is paid into firm's bank account.

(b) Credit the loan account.

CASH ACCOUNT

Date	Details	Dr	Cr	Balance
	Loan: Lawrence	£ 5,000	£	£ 5,000 Dr

LOAN ACCOUNT: LAWRENCE

Date	Details	Dr	Cr	Balance
	Cash	£	£ 5,000	£ 5,000 Cr

When the first year's interest of £250 becomes due:

(a) Debit the loan interest payable account.

(b) Credit Lawrence's current account. (Had Lawrence asked for payment to be made to him, the cash account and not Lawrence's current account would have been credited.)

LOAN INTEREST PAYABLE ACCOUNT

Date	Details	Dr	Cr	Balance
	Current account: Lawrence	£ 250	£	£ 250 Dr

At the end of the financial year the balance will be transferred to the profit and loss account as a business expense and the loan interest payable account will be closed for that period.

CURRENT ACCOUNT: LAWRENCE

Date	Details	Dr	Cr	Balance
	Interest payable: loan	£	£ 250	£ 250 Cr

PARTNERSHIP ACCOUNTS

3.3.7 BALANCE SHEET

The balance sheet of a partnership is the same as that of a sole practitioner except:

(a) The capital accounts of the partners are shown separately. The capital accounts show capital at the start of the year. An exception to this is if the partner capitalises the current account balance, in which case the balance on the current account will be transferred to the partner's capital account before the final accounts are prepared.

(b) Net profit and drawings are *not* transferred to a partner's capital account and therefore are not shown as additions to and deductions from capital, respectively, as happens with a sole practitioner.

(c) The current accounts of the partners are shown on the liabilities part (capital employed) of the balance sheet. If there is a credit balance on the current accounts, this is added to the capital account balance. If there is a debit balance on the current accounts this is deducted from the capital account balance.

(d) It is usual to show movements on partners' current accounts on the balance sheet itself. At the end of the balance sheet is a schedule showing the movement on the current accounts.

3.3.8 EXAMPLE ON PARTNERS' FINAL ACCOUNTS

Ginger, Tom and Arnold are in partnership, sharing profits and losses in the ratio 2 : 2 : 1. Each partner is entitled to interest on capital at 10% per annum and to salaries of £10,000 to Ginger and £7,000 to Arnold.

An abridged trial balance prepared from the partnership books shows the following position at 30 September 2001.

	Dr £	Cr £
Total assets	320,000	
Total liabilities		150,000
Profit for the year from the profit and loss account		140,000
Drawings		
Ginger	30,000	
Tom	25,000	
Arnold	25,000	
Capital accounts		
Ginger		50,000
Tom		40,000
Arnold		20,000
	400,000	400,000

From the above, prepare the profit and loss appropriation account for the year ended 30 September 2001, together with a balance sheet as at that date.

PARTNERSHIP ACCOUNTS

3.3.9 ANSWER TO EXAMPLE ON PARTNERS' FINAL ACCOUNTS

PROFIT AND LOSS APPROPRIATION ACCOUNT FOR THE YEAR ENDED 30 SEPTEMBER 2001

	£	£
NET PROFIT		140,000
INTEREST ON CAPITAL:		
Ginger 10% on £50,000	5,000	
Tom 10% on £40,000	4,000	
Arnold 10% on £20,000	2,000	11,000
		129,000
SALARIES:		
Ginger	10,000	
Arnold	7,000	17,000
		112,000
SHARE OF PROFIT:		
Ginger: 2/5ths	44,800	
Tom: 2/5ths	44,800	
Arnold: 1/5th	22,400	112,000

GINGER, TOM AND ARNOLD BALANCE SHEET AS AT 30 SEPTEMBER 2001

Assets	320,000	
Less: liabilities	150,000	
Total		170,000
Capital employed		
Capital accounts:		
Ginger	50,000	
Tom	40,000	
Arnold	20,000	
	110,000	
Current accounts (see movements on current accounts):		
Ginger	29,800	
Tom	23,800	
Arnold	6,400	
	60,000	
Total		170,000

Movements on partners' current accounts

	Ginger	Tom	Arnold
Opening balance			
Salary	10,000	—	7,000
Interest on capital	5,000	4,000	2,000
Profit share	44,800	44,800	22,400
	59,800	48,800	31,400
Less: drawings	30,000	25,000	25,000
	29,800 Cr	23,800 Cr	6,400 Cr

PARTNERSHIP ACCOUNTS

3.4 Partnership Changes

The constitution of a partnership may change during the financial year as a result of a partner dying, retiring from the practice, a new partner joining the practice or because the partners decide to vary their profit sharing agreement.

When there is a partnership change during the year, the format of the balance sheet and the profit and loss account to the net profit stage will not change.

The format of the appropriation account will change in that there will be a split appropriation. This means that there will be one appropriation account for the period from the start of the financial year to the change and one for the period after the change to the end of the financial year. Each appropriation account will reflect the terms of the partnership agreement in force for the period to which the appropriation account relates. Unless you are told the net profit for the period before and after the change you will have to apportion the net profit for the year on a time basis.

The net profit, interest on drawings, interest on capital and salaries must be apportioned. For example, if there is a partnership change three months into the year, in the first appropriation account, net profit, etc., for the year will be divided by four to reflect the fact that the appropriation account relates to only one quarter of the year.

If a sole practitioner takes in a partner part way through the year, the profits for the time as a sole practitioner will belong wholly to the sole practitioner. There will be no salary, interest on capital, etc., in the first part of the appropriation account as these are relevant only where there is a partnership. It therefore follows that provision for salaries, etc., in the partnership agreement can apply only to the second appropriation period, that is, the period when the original sole practitioner has taken in a partner.

Example A and B are in partnership. A's capital is £60,000 and B's is £40,000. They share the profits in the ratio 3 : 2. Their financial year runs from 1 November to 31 October. C joins the partnership on 1 May 2001. C is to receive a salary of £12,000 per annum and A and B interest on capital of 10% per annum. A, B and C are to share the profits in the ratio of 2 : 2 : 1.
Net profit for the year ended 31 October 2001 is £140,000.

A, B & C: PROFIT AND LOSS ACCOUNT FOR THE YEAR ENDED
31 OCTOBER 2001

	£	£	£
NET PROFIT			140,000

APPROPRIATION ACCOUNT
1 NOVEMBER 2000 TO 30 APRIL 2001

	£	£	£
PROFIT SHARE:			
A: 3/5ths	42,000		
B: 2/5ths	28,000		70,000

---

	1 MAY 2001 to 31 OCTOBER 2001		
	£	£	£
INTEREST ON CAPITAL:			
A for half year	3,000		
B for half year	2,000	5,000	
SALARIES:			
C for half year		6,000	
PROFIT SHARE:			
A: 2/5ths	23,600		
B: 2/5ths	23,600		
C: 1/5th	11,800	59,000	70,000
			140,000

3.4.1 REVALUATION OF PARTNERSHIP ASSETS

As a consequence of a change in the partnership constitution the partners may decide to revalue some or all of the fixed assets. This ensures that the partners in the firm before the change takes place have the benefit of any increase in value and bear the burden of any reduction in value.

The revaluation of the fixed assets is recorded in a revaluation account, the corresponding double entries being made in the real account for the asset which is being revalued.

To record an increase in the value of an asset:

(a) Debit the asset account with the increase in value.

(b) Credit the revaluation account.

To record a reduction in the value of an asset:

(a) Credit the asset account with the reduction in value.

(b) Debit the revaluation account.

The revaluation account is closed by transferring the net increase or decrease in value to the existing partners' capital accounts in the old profit sharing ratio. If there is an increase in value the entries will be:

(a) Debit the revaluation account.

(b) Credit the capital accounts of the existing partners.

If the revaluation account shows a decrease in value the entries will be reversed.

If the partners receive interest on capital it is important to remember that the revaluation alters their capital account balances. Interest should therefore be calculated on the old balances for the period before the change, and on the new balances for the period after the change.

PARTNERSHIP ACCOUNTS

Example A and B are in partnership, sharing profits equally. They have capital account balances of £50,000 and £80,000 respectively. C is to be admitted into the partnership on 1 April. A and B revalue premises and motor cars which have a book value of £100,000 and £18,000 respectively. On revaluation, premises are valued at £125,000 and cars at £14,000.

REVALUATION ACCOUNT

Date	Details	Dr	Cr	Balance
		£	£	£
Mar 31	Premises		25,000	25,000 Cr
	Motor cars	4,000		21,000 Cr
	Capital: A	10,500		
	Capital: B	10,500		———
	(transfer profit on revaluation)			

PREMISES ACCOUNT

Date	Details	Dr	Cr	Balance
		£	£	£
	Balance b/d			100,000 Dr
Mar 31	Revaluation	25,000		125,000 Dr

MOTOR CARS ACCOUNT

Date	Details	Dr	Cr	Balance
		£	£	£
	Balance b/d			18,000 Dr
	Revaluation		4,000	14,000 Dr

CAPITAL ACCOUNT: A

Date	Details	Dr	Cr	Balance
		£	£	£
	Balance			50,000 Cr
	Revaluation		10,500	60,500 Cr

CAPITAL ACCOUNT: B

Date	Details	Dr	Cr	Balance
		£	£	£
	Balance			80,000 Cr
	Revaluation		10,500	90,500 Cr

3.5 Exercises on Partnership Final Accounts

1 The bookkeeper of the firm Bertram, Crawford and Norris, solicitors, draws up a trial balance in respect of the year ending 31 December 2001.

PARTNERSHIP ACCOUNTS

TRIAL BALANCE AT 31 DECEMBER 2001

	Dr £	Cr £
Profit Costs less work in progress at start of year		544,060
General and administrative expenses	372,900	
Due to clients		943,560
Bad debts	4,900	
Capital accounts		
Bertram		130,000
Crawford		100,000
Norris		80,000
Current Accounts		
Bertram		5,000
Crawford		4,000
Norris		6,000
Sundry creditors		8,100
Interest received		6,420
Freehold premises	320,000	
Library furniture & equipment at cost	42,000	
Accumulated depreciation on library Furniture & equipment		12,600
Motor cars	45,000	
Accumulated depreciation on motor cars		18,000
Due from clients	51,820	
Overdraft office account		3,000
Cash at bank client current account	493,560	
Cash at bank client deposit account	450,000	
Petty cash	560	
Drawings		
Bertram	30,000	
Crawford	25,000	
Norris	25,000	
	1,860,740	1,860,740

The partnership agreement provides that Crawford has a partnership salary of £5,000 per annum, interest on capital for the partners is 5% per annum and profits and losses are shared equally.

Work in progress as at 31 December 2001 is £50,000. Payments in advance are £1,800 and outstanding expenses are £2,100. Provision for doubtful debts for the year to 31 December 2001 is set at £1,200. Depreciation for the year on the library furniture and equipment is 10% of the cost price, and depreciation for the year on motor cars is 20% of the cost price.

Draw up the profit and loss and appropriation account for the partners together with the balance sheet. Show full details of the movement on current accounts.

2. Ash and Rowan are in partnership as solicitors, sharing profits and losses as to Ash two-thirds and Rowan one-third. Each partner is entitled to interest on capital in the firm at the rate of 5% per annum. Rowan is also entitled to a salary of £10,000 per annum. The following trial balance was prepared from the firm's accounts for the year ended 31 December 2001.

PARTNERSHIP ACCOUNTS

TRIAL BALANCE AT 31 DECEMBER 2001

	Dr £	Cr £
Capital accounts		
Ash		50,000
Rowan		25,000
Current accounts		
Ash		3,450
Rowan		1,620
Lease at cost price	15,000	
Motor cars	30,000	
Furniture, library and equipment	22,000	
Partners' drawings		
Ash	23,500	
Rowan	28,000	
Administration and general expenses	118,520	
Profit costs		190,425
Interest received		2,900
Due to clients		425,380
Provision for doubtful debts b/d		560
Creditors		18,375
Cash at bank: clients' account:		
Deposit account	350,000	
Current account	75,380	
Petty cash	270	
Cash at bank: office account	12,840	
Work in progress (1 January 2001)	34,200	
Due from clients	24,000	
Loan account: bank		10,000
Rent received		6,000
	733,710	733,710

Work in progress at 31 December 2001 is valued at £38,000. This year's provision for doubtful debts is £800.

Depreciation on motor cars for the year ending 31 December 2001 is £6,000. Depreciation on furniture, library and equipment is £4,800.

From the above information prepare a profit and loss and appropriation account for the year ended 31 December 2001 together with a balance sheet as at that date.

3   Beth and Amy are in partnership as solicitors sharing profits and losses in the ratio 3 : 2. Each partner is entitled, under the partnership agreement, to interest on capital at the rate of 10% per annum and Amy is entitled, in addition, to a partnership salary of £12,000 per annum.

On 1 January 2001, Jo is admitted into the partnership, contributing £10,000 as her share of the capital in the firm. The new partnership agreement provides that, as from 1 January 2001, profits and losses will be shared between Beth, Amy and Jo in the ratio 2 : 2 : 1 respectively. Furthermore, partnership salaries of £20,000, £15,000 and £10,000 per annum will be allowed

PARTNERSHIP ACCOUNTS

to Beth, Amy and Jo respectively. No interest is to be allowed on capital, and no interest is to be charged on partners' drawings.

An abridged trial balance, prepared from the partnership books, shows the following position as at 30 June 2001.

	£	£
NET PROFIT for the year, before charging interest on capital, and other appropriations		120,000
Partners' drawings:		
Beth	30,700	
Amy	28,400	
Jo	11,000	
Partners' capital accounts:		
Beth		70,000
Amy		50,000
Jo		10,000
Sundry assets	194,700	
Sundry liabilities		14,800
	264,800	264,800
Amounts due to clients		894,568
Cash at bank: clients	894,568	
	1,159,368	1,159,368

From the above information, prepare the profit and loss appropriation account for the year ended 30 June 2001, together with a balance sheet as at that date. The allocation of profits between the partners is to be determined on a time basis. (Calculations to be made in months.) Detailed movements on partners' current accounts should be shown.

4   Hale and Hearty are in partnership as solicitors. Hale and Hearty receive interest on capital of 5% per annum and Hearty receives a salary of £2,000 per annum. The remaining profits are shared equally. Their financial year ends on 31 December. On 31 December 2001 the trial balance is:

	Dr £	Cr £
Freehold premises	145,000	
Fixtures and fittings	15,000	
Accumulated depreciation on fixtures and fittings		3,000
Library	2,000	
Accumulated depreciation on library		500
Capital accounts:		
Hale		80,000
Hearty		75,000
Current accounts:		
Hale		2,500
Hearty		2,000
Drawings:		
Hale	24,000	
Hearty	24,500	

PARTNERSHIP ACCOUNTS

	£	£
Profit		
Costs		78,000
Insurance commission received		600
Salaries	20,000	
Insurance paid	1,500	
Council tax	1,620	
Light and heat	1,400	
Stationery	900	
Travelling	400	
Creditors		820
Debtors	3,000	
Office bank account	3,000	
Petty cash	100	
Client bank account	465,000	
Client ledger account		465,000
	707,420	707,420

At 31 December 2001 work in progress amounts to £5,000; there is a stock of stationery valued at £300. Depreciation is charged on fixtures and fittings and library at 10% on the cost price. There is an amount outstanding for electricity of £100.

Prepare final accounts for Hale and Hearty for the year ended 31 December 2001.

3.6 Suggested Answers to Exercises on Partnership Final Accounts

1 Bertram, Crawford and Norris

PROFIT AND LOSS ACCOUNT FOR THE YEAR
ENDING 31 DECEMBER 2001

INCOME	£	£	£
Profit costs		544,060	
Add: work in progress at end of year		50,000	
Value of work done			594,060
ADDITIONAL INCOME			
Add: interest received		6,420	600,480
LESS: EXPENDITURE			
General and admin expenses	372,900		
Bad debts	4,900		
Provision for doubtful debts	1,200		
depreciation on cars	9,000		
depreciation on furniture etc.	4,200		
Add: outstanding expenses	2,100		
	394,300		
Less: payments in advance	1,800		392,500
NET PROFIT			207,980

PARTNERSHIP ACCOUNTS

APPROPRIATION ACCOUNT
Profit available   207,980
SALARY
  Crawford   5,000
INTEREST ON CAPITAL
  Bertram   6,500
  Crawford   5,000
  Norris   4,000   15,500
PROFIT SHARE
  Bertram   62,494
  Crawford   62,493
  Norris   62,493   187,480

BERTRAM, CRAWFORD AND NORRIS BALANCE SHEET
AS AT 31 DECEMBER 2001

FIXED ASSETS
Freehold premises   320,000
Library etc. cost price   42,000
Less depreciation   168,000
                                                             25,200

Motor cars cost price   45,000
Less depreciation   27,000
                                                             18,000
                                                                              363,200
CURRENT ASSETS
Work in progress   50,000
Debtors (due from clients)   51,820
Less provision   1,200
                                                             50,620
Petty cash   560
Payments in advance   1,800
                                                                     102,980
Less CURRENT LIABILITIES
Sundry creditors   8,100
Overdraft office account   3,000
Outstanding expenses   2,100
                                                                      13,200

Net current assets   89,780

TOTAL   452,980

CAPITAL EMPLOYED
Capital accounts:
  Bertram   130,000
  Crawford   100,000
  Norris   80,000
                                                                      310,000

PARTNERSHIP ACCOUNTS

Current accounts (see schedule movement on current accounts)
Bertram 43,994
Crawford 51,493
Norris 47,493

142,980

TOTAL 452,980

CLIENT ACCOUNT
Due to clients 943,560
Cash at bank client
 current account 493,560
Cash at bank client
 deposit account 450,000

943,560

MOVEMENTS ON PARTNERS' CURRENT ACCOUNTS

	Bertram	Crawford	Norris
Opening Balance	5,000	4,000	6,000
Salary	—	5,000	—
Interest on capital	6,500	5,000	4,000
Profit share	62,494	62,493	62,493
	73,994	76,493	72,493
Less: Drawings	30,000	25,000	25,000
	43,994	51,493	47,493

2 Ash and Rowan

PROFIT AND LOSS APPROPRIATION ACCOUNT FOR THE YEAR ENDED 31 DECEMBER 2001

INCOME	£	£	£
Profit costs		190,425	
Add: closing work in progress		38,000	
		228,425	
Less: opening work in progress		34,200	
Value of work done		194,225	
ADDITIONAL INCOME			
Interest received	2,900		
Rent received	6,000		
		8,900	
			203,125

LESS: EXPENDITURE
Administrative and general expenses   118,520
Provision for doubtful debts
  This year's provision   800
  Less: last year's   560   240

Depreciation:
  Cars   6,000
  Furniture etc.   4,800   10,800   129,560

NET PROFIT   73,565
APPROPRIATION   73,565
SALARIES:
  Rowan   10,000
INTEREST ON CAPITAL:
  Ash   2,500
  Rowan   1,250   3,750

PROFIT SHARE:
  Ash: 2/3rds   39,877
  Rowan: 1/3rd   19,938

(round up or down to nearest pound to balance)

Note that last year's provision for doubtful debts brought down will reduce the expense this year.

Schedule to Balance Sheet

MOVEMENT ON PARTNERS' CURRENT ACCOUNTS

	Ash £	Rowan £
Balance	3,450 Cr	1,620 Cr
Salary	—	10,000
Interest on capital	2,500	1,250
Profit share	39,877	19,938
	45,827	32,808
Less: drawings	23,500	28,000
	22,327 Cr	4,808 Cr

ASH AND ROWAN BALANCE SHEET
AS AT 31 DECEMBER 2001

FIXED ASSETS
Leasehold premises   15,000
Furniture, library and equipment
  at cost   22,000
  Less: depreciation   4,800

                                                                             17,200

PARTNERSHIP ACCOUNTS

Motor cars		30,000	
Less: depreciation		6,000	
		24,000	
			56,200
CURRENT ASSETS			
Closing work in progress		38,000	
Debtors	24,000		
Less: provision	800		
		23,200	
Cash at bank office account		12,840	
Petty cash		270	
		74,310	
Less: CURRENT LIABILITIES			
Creditors		18,375	
NET CURRENT ASSETS			55,935
			112,135
Less: LONG TERM LIABILITIES			
Bank loan			10,000
TOTAL			102,135
CAPITAL EMPLOYED			
Capital accounts:			
Ash	50,000		
Rowan	25,000		
		75,000	
Current accounts:			
(see schedule to the Balance sheet)			
Ash	22,327		
Rowan	4,808		
		27,135	
TOTAL			102,135
CLIENT ACCOUNT			
Bank balance:			
Deposit account	350,000		
Current account	75,380		
		425,380	
Less: Due to clients		425,380	

3 Beth, Amy and Jo

PROFIT AND LOSS APPROPRIATION ACCOUNT FOR PERIOD 1 JULY 2000 TO 31 DECEMBER 2001

	£	£
NET PROFIT (for 6 months)		60,000
SALARY (for 6 months):		
Amy	6,000	
INTEREST ON CAPITAL (for 6 months):		
Beth	3,500	
Amy	2,500	
		12,000
PROFIT SHARE:		
Beth: 3/5ths	28,800	
Amy: 2/5ths	19,200	48,000

PROFIT AND LOSS APPROPRIATION ACCOUNT FOR PERIOD 1 JANUARY 2001 TO 30 JUNE 2001

	£	£
NET PROFIT (for 6 months)		60,000
SALARIES (for 6 months):		
Beth	10,000	
Amy	7,500	
Jo	5,000	
		22,500
PROFIT SHARE:		
Beth: 2/5ths	15,000	
Amy: 2/5ths	15,000	
Jo: 1/5th	7,500	37,500

Schedule to Balance Sheet

MOVEMENT ON PARTNERS' CURRENT ACCOUNTS

	Beth £	Amy £	Jo £
Salary	10,000	13,500	5,000
Interest on capital	3,500	2,500	—
Profit share	43,800	34,200	7,500
	57,300	50,200	12,500
Less balance	30,700	28,400	11,000
	26,600 Cr	21,800 Cr	1,500 Cr

PARTNERSHIP ACCOUNTS

BETH, AMY AND JO
BALANCE SHEET AS AT 30 JUNE 2001

ASSETS		194,700	
Less: liabilities		14,800	
TOTAL			179,900
CAPITAL EMPLOYED			
Capital accounts:			
Beth	70,000		
Amy	50,000		
Jo	10,000		
			130,000
Current accounts:			
Beth	26,600 Cr		
Amy	21,800 Cr		
Jo	1,500 Cr		
			49,900
TOTAL			179,900
CLIENT ACCOUNT			
Client bank balance		894,568	
Less: due to clients		894,568	

4 Hale and Hearty

PROFIT AND LOSS ACCOUNT FOR THE YEAR ENDED
31 DECEMBER 2001

	£	£	£
INCOME			
Profit costs		78,000	
Add closing work in progress		5,000	
Value of work done			83,000
Add insurance commission received		600	
			83,600
LESS EXPENDITURE			
Salaries		20,000	
Insurance paid		1,500	
Council tax		1,620	
Light and heat	1,400		
Plus outstanding expense	100	1,500	
Stationery	900		
Less closing stock	300	600	
Travel expenses		400	
Depreciation:			
Fixtures and fittings	1,500		
Library	200	1,700	27,320
NET PROFIT			56,280

APPROPRIATION ACCOUNT

Salary:
Hearty		2,000	2,000

Interest on capital:
Hale		4,000	
Hearty		3,750	7,750

Profit share:
Hale: ½		23,265	
Hearty: ½		23,265	46,530
			56,280

HALE AND HEARTY BALANCE SHEET
AS AT 31 DECEMBER 2001

FIXED ASSETS

Premises		145,000	
Fixtures and fittings	15,000		
Less accumulated depreciation	4,500		
		10,500	
Library	2,000		
Less accumulated depreciation	700		
		1,300	
			156,800

CURRENT ASSETS

Closing work in progress	5,000		
Debtors	3,000		
Office bank account	3,000		
Petty cash	100		
Stock of stationery	300		
		11,400	

Less CURRENT LIABILITIES

Creditors	820		
Outstanding expenses	100		
		920	

NET CURRENT ASSETS			10,480
TOTAL			167,280

CAPITAL EMPLOYED

Capital accounts:
Hale	80,000		
Hearty	75,000		
			155,000

Current accounts: see movement on current accounts
Hale	5,765		
Hearty	6,515		
			12,280
TOTAL			167,280

PARTNERSHIP ACCOUNTS

CLIENT ACCOUNT
Client bank balance	465,000
Less amount due to clients	465,000

MOVEMENT ON PARTNERS' CURRENT ACCOUNTS

	Hale	Hearty
Opening balance	2,500	2,000
Salary		2,000
Interest on capital	4,000	3,750
Profit share	23,265	23,265
	29,765	31,015
Less drawings	24,000	24,500
	5,765	6,515

3.7 Test on Partnership Final Accounts

Allow 2 to 3 hours to complete this test.

1 The bookkeeper of the firm Gold and Silver solicitors, extracts the following information from the books of account in respect of the year ended 31 December 2001.

	£
Due to clients	440,460
Profit costs	160,500
Interest received	7,450
General and administrative expenses	94,840
Rent received	4,000
Provision for doubtful debts (last year's)	600
Partners' capital accounts	
Gold	30,000
Silver	20,000
Partners' current accounts	
Gold	2,500 Dr
Silver	800 Cr
Leasehold property at cost	34,000
Library, furniture and equipment at cost	16,500
Accumulated depreciation on library, furniture and equipment to 31 December 2000	3,300
Due from clients	21,790
Work in progress at 1 January 2001	12,100
Cash at the bank: client account	440,460
office account	7,360
Petty cash balance	140
Partners' drawings:	
Gold	24,960
Silver	18,890
Creditors	6,430

PARTNERSHIP ACCOUNTS

The following information is relevant:

(a) Profits and losses are shared between Gold and Silver so that Gold receives three-fifths and Silver two-fifths.

(b) Silver is to receive a partnership salary of £8,000 per year.

(c) Interest is to be allowed on partners' capital, as follows:

        Gold   £3,000

        Silver   £2,000

(d) Work in progress at 31 December 2001 is valued at £14,150.

(e) At 31 December 2001, prepaid general expenses amount to £350, whilst there are administration expenses outstanding and not yet accounted for amounting to £900.

(f) The provision for doubtful debts is to be increased to £760.

(g) Depreciation of £1,650 is to be charged against library, furniture and equipment.

From the above information prepare a Profit and Loss Appropriation account for the year ended 31 December 2001, together with the Balance Sheet as at that date.

2 From the Trial Balance of Rip, Van and Winkle set out below draw up a profit and loss account and appropriation account for the year ended 31 December 2001, together with a balance sheet as at that date.

	Dr £	Cr £
Current accounts		
Rip		2,771
Van		3,055
Winkle	760	
Capital accounts		
Rip		160,000
Van		120,000
Winkle		80,000
Drawings		
Rip	25,000	
Van	25,000	
Winkle	25,000	
Creditors		5,923
Premises — cost price	300,000	
Office equipment — cost price	25,000	
Office furniture — cost price	30,000	
Motor cars — cost price	45,000	
Accumulated depreciation on office equipment		5,000
Accumulated depreciation on office furniture		6,000
Accumulated depreciation on motor cars		9,000

PARTNERSHIP ACCOUNTS

General expenses	415,000	
Cash at bank — office account	7,543	
Petty cash	96	
Profit costs		539,700
Interest received		7,150
Work in progress as at 1 January 2001	35,000	
Cash at Bank Client account		
current account	176,000	
deposit account	490,000	
Amount due to clients		666,000
Due from clients	5,200	
	1,604,599	1,604,599

Note the following:

Expenses due and not yet paid during the year amount to £895, those expenses prepaid amount to £625. A bad debt has to be written off in the sum of £600, and provision for bad and doubtful debts amounts to £530. Work in progress as at 31 December 2001 amounts to £38,800. Depreciation on office equipment and on office furniture is 10% per annum on the cost price, and depreciation on cars is 20% per annum on the cost price. Rip has a partnership salary of £5,000, and the partners allow interest on capital at 5% per annum. The profits are then shared equally between the partners.

3.8 Suggested Answers to Test on Partnership Final Accounts

1 Gold and Silver

PROFIT AND LOSS APPROPRIATION ACCOUNT FOR THE YEAR
ENDED 31 DECEMBER 2001

INCOME	£	£	£
Profit costs	160,500		
Add: closing work in progress	14,150		
		174,650	
Less: opening work in progress		12,100	
Value of work done			162,550
ADD			
Interest received		7,450	
Rent received		4,000	
			11,450
Total income			174,000
LESS EXPENDITURE			
General and administrative expenses	94,840		
Add: outstanding expenses	900		
	95,740		
Less: paid in advance	350		
		95,390	
Bad debts		160	
Depreciation: library, furniture and equipment		1,650	
Total expenses			97,200

NET PROFIT		76,800
APPROPRIATION		
Profit		76,800
SALARY		
Silver		8,000
INTEREST ON CAPITAL		
Gold	3,000	
Silver	2,000	
		5,000
SHARE OF PROFIT		
Gold: 3/5ths	38,280	
Silver: 2/5ths	25,520	
		63,800

Workings

BAD DEBTS ACCOUNT

Date	Details	Dr	Cr	Balance
2001		£	£	£
Jan 1	Provision b/d (last year's)		600	600 Cr
Dec 31	Provision c/d (this year's)	760		160 Dr
	Transfer to Profit and Loss		160	—

Schedule to the Balance Sheet

MOVEMENT ON PARTNERS' CURRENT ACCOUNTS

	Gold	Silver
	£	£
Balance	2,500 (Dr)	800 Cr
Interest on capital	3,000	2,000
Salary	—	8,000
Profit share	38,280	25,520
	38,780	36,320
Less: drawings	24,960	18,890
	13,820 Cr	17,430 Cr

GOLD AND SILVER BALANCE SHEET AS AT 31 DECEMBER 2001

	£	£	£
FIXED ASSETS			
Leasehold property at cost		34,000	
Library, furniture and equipment at cost	16,500		
Less: accumulated depreciation	4,950		
		11,550	
			45,550

PARTNERSHIP ACCOUNTS

CURRENT ASSETS			
Closing work in progress		14,150	
Debtors (due from clients)	21,790		
Less: provision for this year	760		
		21,030	
Cash at bank: office account	7,360		
Petty cash	140		
Payments in advance re general expenses	350		
		43,030	
Less CURRENT LIABILITIES			
Creditors	6,430		
Outstanding expenses	900		
		7,330	
NET CURRENT ASSETS			35,700
TOTAL			81,250
CAPITAL EMPLOYED			
Capital accounts:			
Gold	30,000		
Silver	20,000		
			50,000
Current accounts:			
Gold	13,820		
Silver	17,430		
			31,250
TOTAL			81,250
CLIENT ACCOUNT			
Client bank balance	440,460		
Amount due to clients	440,460		

2 Rip, Van and Winkle

PROFIT AND LOSS ACCOUNT FOR THE YEAR ENDED 31 DECEMBER 2001

INCOME	£	£	£
Profit costs	539,700		
Add: Work in progress at the end of the year 31 December 2001	38,800		
	578,500		
Less: Work in progress at the start of the year 1 January 2001	35,000		
Value of work done	543,500		

PARTNERSHIP ACCOUNTS

ADD ADDITIONAL INCOME			
Interest received	7,150		
	———		
			550,650
Less: EXPENDITURE			
Admin and General Expenses	415,000		
Outstanding expenses	895		
Bad debt written off	600		
Provision for doubtful debts	530		
	———		
	417,025		
Less: prepaid	625		
	———		
	416,400		
Add: depreciation			
On office equipment	2,500		
On office furniture	3,000		
On motor cars	9,000		
	———	14,500	
		———	430,900
			———
NET PROFIT			119,750
APPROPRIATION ACCOUNT			
Profit available for distribution			119,750
SALARY			
Rip			5,000
INTEREST ON CAPITAL			
Rip	8,000		
Van	6,000		
Winkle	4,000		
	———		18,000
Profit share			
Rip	32,250		
Van	32,250		
Winkle	32,250		
	———		96,750
			———

RIP, VAN AND WINKLE
BALANCE SHEET AS AT 31 DECEMBER 2001

FIXED ASSETS			
Premises cost price		300,000	
Office equipment cost price	25,000		
Less: Total depreciation	7,500		
	———	17,500	
Office furniture cost price	30,000		
Less: Total depreciation	9,000		
	———	21,000	
Motor cars cost price	45,000		
Less: Total depreciation	18,000		
	———	27,000	
		———	365,500

PARTNERSHIP ACCOUNTS

CURRENT ASSETS			
Work in Progress		38,800	
Debtors (5,200 − 600)	4,600		
Less: Provision	530		
		4,070	
Cash at Bank office		7,543	
Petty cash		96	
Prepaid		625	
			51,134
Less: CURRENT LIABILITIES			
Creditors		5,923	
Outstanding expenses		895	
			6,818
NET CURRENT ASSETS			44,316
TOTAL			409,816
CAPITAL EMPLOYED			
CAPITAL ACCOUNTS			
Rip		160,000	
Van		120,000	
Winkle		80,000	
			360,000
CURRENT ACCOUNTS			
See schedule movement on current accounts			
Rip		23,021	
Van		16,305	
Winkle		10,490	
			49,816
TOTAL			409,816

Schedule Movement on Current Accounts

	Rip	Van	Winkle
Opening Balance	2,771	3,055	− 760 (Dr)
Salary	5,000	—	—
Interest on Capital	8,000	6,000	4,000
Profit share	32,250	32,250	32,250
	48,021	41,305	35,490
Less drawings	25,000	25,000	25,000
	23,021	16,305	10,490

FOUR

BASIC ACCOUNTING CONCEPTS AND MANUFACTURING AND TRADING ACCOUNTS

4.1 Financial Accounting Concepts

Having seen how final accounts are drawn up and some of the adjustments made, at this stage we will look at accounting concepts. The accounting profession has formed standard accounting practices which were set out in Statements of Standard Accounting Practice (SSAPs). These were issued by the Accounting Standards Committee, replaced in 1990 by the Accounting Standards Board, which now issues accounting standards called Financial Reporting Standards. The methods of accounting described are intended to give a true and fair view of the profit or loss of a business enterprise and its value in the balance sheet. SSAP2, issued in 1971, dealt with disclosure of accounting policies, the relationship between accounting concepts, accounting methods and accounting policies.

Fundamental accounting concepts are the assumptions on which accounts of businesses are drawn up. They include the following:

4.1.1 THE BUSINESS ENTITY CONCEPT

This means that for accounting purposes a business is treated as a separate entity from its owner or owners, even though in law this may not be the case, e.g., a sole trader or a partnership. Thus when an owner puts money into the business this is recorded as the business having received the money and that the business owes that money to the proprietor (see capital accounts at **1.3.2.1**).

4.1.2 THE MONEY MEASUREMENT CONCEPT

Accounts give information about a business, but only in money terms. They do not, for example, give information about the motivation of the workforce or how competent the managing director is.

4.1.3 THE COST CONCEPT

This means that assets would be valued at cost price rather than by estimating their current value.

BASIC ACCOUNTING CONCEPTS AND MANUFACTURING AND TRADING ACCOUNTS

4.1.4 THE GOING-CONCERN CONCEPT

This is the assumption that the business will continue to operate in the future. Thus the profit and loss account and the balance sheet will be drawn up on the assumption that the business will continue at the same level and not be sold. For example, if a business ceases to operate, its assets may be worth considerably less on a closing down sale than if the business continues.

4.1.5 THE ACCRUALS CONCEPT

This is the assumption that income and expenses should be matched and actually recorded in the period in which they are earned or incurred, rather than the period in which they are actually received or paid, e.g., adjustments for work in progress, payments in advance, outstanding expenses, etc., that we have seen previously (see **Chapter 2**). Thus if work has been carried out within a particular accounting period, then the amount earned in respect of that work should be shown as income. Or if a payment is made in advance it should not be treated as an expense of the period in which it has been paid, but should be shown as an expense in the next period.

4.1.6 THE CONSISTENCY CONCEPT

This means that there should be consistency in the accounting methods used for similar items, in the same accounting period and in later periods. If a firm changes the basis on which it values stock or work in progress then the profit figure may be different from the figure that would be obtained had stock or work in progress been valued in the same way. Thus if businesses wish to change the basis on which they value stock, or value assets, then they must mention the effect on the profit of the change in accounting method.

4.1.7 THE CONCEPT OF PRUDENCE

This is the principle that profit should not be overstated. Thus income should not be anticipated and should be recorded in the profit and loss account only when received in cash, or as assets (e.g., debtors) which can be converted readily into cash. However, provision should be made for all possible known or expected future losses.

4.1.8 THE CONCEPT OF MATERIALITY

This means that there is no need to make detailed accounting records of items which are regarded as not material. For example, small items purchased, e.g., biros used in the office, will be treated as part of the expenses in the period in which they are purchased, and there will be no need to record on the balance sheet at the end of the year that the firm has six biros. Firms will decide individually whether an item is material, e.g., for a large firm items costing less than £500 may be treated as not material, if the firm is smaller then it may treat items costing less than £50 as not material. All such items will be treated as expenses and any remaining items will not be shown on the balance sheet, i.e., there is no need to make adjustments for small amounts.

4.2 Accounting Bases and Policies

Accounting bases are methods which have been developed for applying the accounting concepts to accounting transactions and items. These will vary according to the type of business and business transaction. They can be used, for example, to decide the accounting periods in which income and expenses should be recognised in the profit and loss account, and to decide the amounts at which items are considered material for inclusion in the balance sheet.

Accounting policies are particular accounting bases which are considered by individual businesses to be most appropriate to their particular circumstances, and best suited to show their financial position fairly. Accounting policies used by a business should be disclosed by

BASIC ACCOUNTING CONCEPTS AND MANUFACTURING AND TRADING ACCOUNTS

way of a note to the accounts, e.g., how depreciation is treated, or how work in progress or stock is valued.

4.3 Manufacturing and Trading Accounts

4.3.1 INTRODUCTION AND EXAMPLE

We have previously looked at the accounts of solicitors, who derive their income from services, or work done (see **Chapters 1–3**). With a trader, goods will be purchased for resale, there will be an account to record the value of all purchases, and a separate account to record the value of all sales.

Example Gary starts business with £20,000 cash, being the capital he has introduced.

Debit the cash book £20,000

Credit the capital account £20,000

CASH BOOK

Date	Details	Dr £	Cr £	Balance £
	Capital	20,000		20,000 Dr

CAPITAL ACCOUNT

Date	Details	Dr £	Cr £	Balance £
	Cash		20,000	20,000 Cr

He then buys goods for £10,000 cash.

Debit the purchases account (an expense account) £10,000

Credit the cash book £10,000 recording the payment out

PURCHASES

Date	Details	Dr £	Cr £	Balance £
	Cash	10,000		10,000 Dr

CASH BOOK

Date	Details	Dr £	Cr £	Balance £
				20,000 Dr
	Purchases		10,000	10,000 Dr

Gary then buys further goods from Suppliers Ltd for £5,000 on credit.

Debit the purchases account £5,000

Credit Suppliers Ltd's account (the creditor) £5,000

BASIC ACCOUNTING CONCEPTS AND MANUFACTURING AND TRADING ACCOUNTS

PURCHASES

Date	Details	Dr £	Cr £	Balance £
	Balance			10,000 Dr
	Suppliers Ltd	5,000		15,000 Dr

SUPPLIERS LTD

Date	Details	Dr £	Cr £	Balance £
	Purchases		5,000	5,000 Cr

Gary then sells all his goods for £40,000 cash.

Debit the cash book £40,000.

Credit the sales account (income account) £40,000.

CASH BOOK

Date	Details	Dr £	Cr £	Balance £
	Balance			10,000 Dr
	Sales	40,000		50,000 Dr

SALES

Date	Details	Dr £	Cr £	Balance £
	Cash		40,000	40,000 Cr

4.3.2 TRADING ACCOUNT

When Gary draws up his final accounts, a trading account will be drawn up, showing the sales less purchases, to give the gross profit. This will be followed by the profit and loss account, showing income, the gross profit and other income not derived from trading, e.g., interest receivable, less expenses, administrative expenses, financial expenses, etc.

TRADING ACCOUNT

Sales	£40,000
Less purchases	£15,000
Gross profit	£25,000

This is a simple form of trading account. Additional items to be taken into account might include sales returns: e.g., where goods have been returned to the business, the sales returns account would be debited and then the cash book or the customer's personal ledger card would be credited. The debit balance on the sales returns account will be deducted from the sales figure, to give net sales. For example:

BASIC ACCOUNTING CONCEPTS AND MANUFACTURING AND TRADING ACCOUNTS

Sales	£700,000
Less sales returns	£10,000
	£690,000

The purchases figure will have to be adjusted, to take account of any stock held by the trader at the start of the year, and any stock left at the end of the year, to give the actual cost of the goods sold.

Example A trader starts the year with £60,000 worth of goods (opening stock). During the year a further £300,000 worth of goods is purchased, and at the end of the year there is £40,000 worth of goods remaining.

The cost of goods sold is therefore:

	£	£
Opening stock	60,000	
Plus purchases	300,000	
		360,000
Less closing stock		40,000
Cost of goods sold		320,000

The adjustment for stock will be shown on the purchases account.

PURCHASES ACCOUNT

Date	Details	Dr £	Cr £	Balance £
	Opening stock brought down from previous period	60,000		60,000 Dr
	Purchases during the year	300,000		360,000 Dr
	Closing stock		40,000	320,000 Dr
	Transfer to profit and loss		320,000	
	Opening stock b/d	40,000		40,000 Dr

The trading and profit and loss account would therefore appear as set out below:

TRADING AND PROFIT AND LOSS ACCOUNT FOR THE YEAR ENDING
31 DECEMBER 200–

	£	£
Sales	700,000	
Less returns	10,000	
		690,000

BASIC ACCOUNTING CONCEPTS AND MANUFACTURING AND TRADING ACCOUNTS

	£	£
Less		
Cost of goods sold		
Opening stock	60,000	
Plus purchases	300,000	
	360,000	
Less closing stock	40,000	
Cost of goods sold		320,000
GROSS PROFIT		370,000
Less general expenses		100,000
NET PROFIT		270,000

4.3.3 MANUFACTURING ACCOUNT

If the trader is manufacturing goods for sale, i.e., processing raw materials, then the trading account will be preceded by a manufacturing account, showing the cost of manufacturing the goods sold. This will show all the costs and expenses directly and indirectly incurred in producing the goods. Total costs will be divided between:

(a) *Direct costs*   The prime cost, which is the total of costs directly associated with the finished products, consisting of:

   (i) direct materials — the cost of the raw materials;

   (ii) direct labour — wages paid to the employees directly involved in producing the goods;

   (iii) direct expenses — e.g., the cost of sub-contracting any process needed to produce the goods;

(b) *Indirect costs*   Works overheads or factory overheads — these are the indirect expenses of production including:

   (i) indirect materials, e.g., consumable stores (oil to lubricate) and supplies of materials for repairs and maintenance;

   (ii) indirect labour, e.g., supervisors, inspectors, cleaners;

   (iii) indirect expenses, e.g., heat, light, power, rent, depreciation of factory buildings, plant and machinery.

4.3.3.1 Stock and work in progress

Adjustments will have to be made for the closing stock of raw materials, and partly finished goods (work in progress), as well as finished goods. We saw that the stock of finished goods will appear in the trading account (see **4.3.2**); the stock of raw materials and partly finished goods will appear in the manufacturing account.

BASIC ACCOUNTING CONCEPTS AND MANUFACTURING AND TRADING ACCOUNTS

4.3.4 EXAMPLE OF A MANUFACTURING ACCOUNT

Example   Jenny Wren & Co.   Clothing Manufacturers

MANUFACTURING AND TRADING ACCOUNT FOR THE YEAR TO 1 APRIL 2001

	£ '000	£ '000
Opening stock of raw materials (cloth)	10,000	
Plus work in progress (partly finished clothes)	20,000	
		£
		30,000
Plus purchase of cloth during the year		100,000
		130,000
Less		
Closing stock of raw material (cloth)	15,000	
Closing work in progress (partly finished clothes)	30,000	
		45,000
Cost of materials		85,000
Add direct wages		60,000
Prime cost of production		145,000
Add works overheads inc. heat, light, power, depreciation etc.		20,000
Carried to trading account (trading account section)		165,000

TRADING ACCOUNT

Net sales		350,000
Less cost of sales		
Opening stock of finished clothes	25,000	
Manufacturing account b/d	165,000	
	190,000	
Less closing stock of finished clothes	22,000	
Production cost of clothes sold		168,000
Gross profit		182,000

This will be followed by a profit and loss account, showing the gross profit plus any other income, less expenses, e.g., administrative, financial, selling expenses, with the usual adjustments for any payments in advance and outstanding expenses.

The resulting net profit (or loss) will be transferred to the credit (debit if loss) of a sole manufacturer's capital account, or, if there is a partnership, it will be appropriated between the partners and then credited to their current accounts (see **Chapter 3** on partnership accounts). Company accounts are dealt with in **Chapter 5**.

The balance sheet will be drawn up in the way previously shown (see **Chapter 2**).

BASIC ACCOUNTING CONCEPTS AND MANUFACTURING AND TRADING ACCOUNTS

4.4 Practice Exercise

From the trial balance of Bucket drawn up on 31 July 2001 show the manufacturing, trading and profit and loss account and the balance sheet.

TRIAL BALANCE

	Dr £	Cr £
Capital		270,000
Drawings	210,000	
Work in progress at start of year	104,000	
Stock of raw material at start of year	65,000	
Stock of finished goods at start of year	89,000	
Purchases of raw materials	521,000	
Sales		2,140,000
Factory wages	400,000	
Office salaries	300,000	
Factory general expenses	56,000	
Office general expenses	32,000	
Factory light/heat	20,000	
Factory rent	120,000	
Office light/heat	10,000	
Office rent	80,000	
Insurance (factory)	10,000	
Insurance (office)	9,000	
Advertising	40,000	
Bad debts	28,000	
Plant and machinery	150,000	
Motor cars	81,000	
Bank account	49,000	
Petty cash	7,000	
Creditors		81,000
Debtors	110,000	
	2,491,000	2,491,000

At 31 July 2001 closing stock of raw materials was £90,000, work in progress was £120,000 and stock of finished goods was £112,000. For the purposes of this example please ignore depreciation.

4.5 Suggested Answer to Practice Exercise

Bucket Manufacturing, Trading and Profit and Loss account for the year ending 31 July 2001.

MANUFACTURING ACCOUNT

	£	£
Opening stock raw materials	65,000	
Add opening work in progress	104,000	
		169,000
Plus purchases	521,000	
		690,000

Less closing stock raw materials	90,000	
Closing stock work in progress	120,000	
		210,000
Cost of materials		480,000
Add direct factory wages		400,000
Prime cost		880,000
Add factory light/heat	20,000	
factory rent	120,000	
factory insurance	10,000	
factory general expenses	56,000	
		206,000
Factory cost of production carried down		1,086,000

TRADING ACCOUNT

	£	£
Sales		2,140,000
Less cost of sales		
Opening stock of finished goods	89,000	
Plus cost of production carried down	1,086,000	
	1,175,000	
Less closing stock of finished goods	112,000	
Production costs of goods sold		1,063,000
Gross profit		1,077,000

PROFIT AND LOSS ACCOUNT

	£	£
Gross profit brought down		1,077,000
Less		
office salaries	300,000	
office general expenses	32,000	
office light and heat	10,000	
office rent	80,000	
office insurance	9,000	
advertising	40,000	
bad debts	28,000	
		499,000
Net profit		578,000

BUCKET — BALANCE SHEET AS AT 31 JULY 2001

FIXED ASSETS		
Plant and machinery	150,000	
Motor cars	81,000	
		231,000

CURRENT ASSETS			
Stock raw materials	90,000		
Work in progress	120,000		
Stock of finished goods	112,000		
Debtors	110,000		
Bank account	49,000		
Petty cash	7,000		
		488,000	
Less CURRENT LIABILITIES			
Creditors		81,000	
NET CURRENT ASSETS			407,000
			638,000
Less long-term liabilities			—
TOTAL			638,000
CAPITAL EMPLOYED			
Capital		270,000	
Add net profit	578,000		
Less drawings	210,000		
		368,000	
TOTAL			638,000

FIVE

COMPANY ACCOUNTS AND CONSOLIDATED GROUP ACCOUNTS

5.1 Accounts of Limited Companies

Companies may be incorporated under the provisions of the Companies Acts 1985 and 1989. Companies so incorporated may be:

(a) A company limited by shares, a member's liability being limited to any part of the issued price of the member's shares not yet paid to the company.

(b) A company limited by guarantee, a member's liability being limited to the sum that the member undertook to contribute to the company in the event of its being wound up.

(c) An unlimited company with no limit on a member's liability.

We will look at companies limited by shares.

5.1.1 SHARE CAPITAL

The capital of a limited company is divided into shares which will have a nominal value, e.g., £1 each, or £5 or £10. When the company issues shares for cash, the entries are the same as the entries made when a sole proprietor or a partner introduces capital. The capital account will be known as the share capital account.

Example A company issues 60,000 £1 ordinary shares for £60,000 cash.

CASH BOOK

Date	Details	Dr	Cr	Balance
		£	£	£
	Share capital	60,000		60,000 Dr

SHARE CAPITAL ACCOUNT
£1 Ordinary Shares

Date	Details	Dr	Cr	Balance
		£	£	£
	Cash		60,000	60,000 Cr

COMPANY ACCOUNTS AND CONSOLIDATED GROUP ACCOUNTS

A company may issue the shares at par, i.e., sell the shares at their nominal value. Thus if the company above issued 60,000 shares at a nominal value of £1 for £1 each, then the entries would be as above.

The balance sheet would show:

FIXED ASSETS		XX
CURRENT ASSETS		
Cash	60,000	
CAPITAL EMPLOYED		
Share capital £1 ordinary shares	60,000	

5.1.2 ISSUING SHARES AT A PREMIUM

A company may, however, set a price which is higher than the nominal value, when it will issue the shares at a premium. For example, the company issues 60,000 £1 shares at £1.20 each, giving total cash of £72,000. The cash book will be debited with the total amount received, broken down into the nominal value of £60,000 and the premium of £12,000. The share capital account will be credited with the £60,000 and the share premium account will be credited with the £12,000.

CASH BOOK

Date	Details	Dr	Cr	Balance
		£	£	£
	Share capital	60,000		60,000Dr
	Share premium	12,000		72,000Dr

SHARE CAPITAL ACCOUNT

Date	Details	Dr	Cr	Balance
		£	£	£
	Cash		60,000	60,000 Cr

SHARE PREMIUM ACCOUNT

Date	Details	Dr	Cr	Balance
		£	£	£
	Cash		12,000	12,000 Cr

The balance sheet would show:

FIXED ASSETS		XX
CURRENT ASSETS		
Cash		72,000
CAPITAL EMPLOYED		
Share capital £1 ordinary shares	60,000	
Share premium	12,000	
		72,000

Note that a company may not issue all the shares which it is authorised to sell. The shares sold are called the issued capital.

Different types of shares may be offered, e.g., ordinary, preference or deferred shares. There may also be voting and non-voting shares.

5.1.3 PREFERENCE SHARES

These will get an agreed percentage rate of dividend before the ordinary shareholders, i.e., they have priority. There may be different classes of preference shares, e.g.:

5.1.3.1 Non-cumulative preference shares

These receive the dividend before the ordinary shareholders up to an agreed percentage. However, if the amount paid in a year is less than the maximum agreed percentage, the shareholder cannot claim the shortage in the next year or years.

5.1.3.2 Cumulative preference shares

In this case, if a full dividend is not received in a year, the arrears of dividend can be carried forward and paid together with the dividend due in the next year before the ordinary shareholders are entitled to receive any dividend.

5.1.3.3 Participating preference shares

In this case the shareholders, e.g., also have the right to participate in any remaining profits after the ordinary shareholders have received their dividend.

5.1.3.4 Redeemable preference shares

In such a case the shares will be repaid by the company at some time in the future.

This may sound complicated, but the accounting entries for the issue of all types of preference shares will be the same. A separate share capital account for each type of shares will be opened.

COMPANY ACCOUNTS AND CONSOLIDATED GROUP ACCOUNTS

Example A company issues 50,000 ordinary shares at £1 each, and 10,000 7% preference shares at £1.

CASH BOOK

Date	Details	Dr	Cr	Balance
		£	£	£
	Ordinary shares	50,000		50,000 Dr
	7% preference shares	10,000		60,000 Dr

ORDINARY SHARE CAPITAL ACCOUNT

Date	Details	Dr	Cr	Balance
		£	£	£
	Cash		50,000	50,000 Cr

7% PREFERENCE SHARE CAPITAL ACCOUNT

Date	Details	Dr	Cr	Balance
		£	£	£
	Cash		10,000	10,000 Cr

Note: the cash received from the share issue will be used in the business, e.g., to purchase assets.

5.1.4 DEBENTURES

A debenture is a bond which acknowledges a loan to a company and which bears a fixed rate of interest. As this is really a type of loan to the company, the debenture holder is not a member of the company like a shareholder and the interest will be paid whether the company makes a profit or not. A debenture may be redeemable, i.e., repayable at or before a specified date, or irredeemable and thus only repayable when the company is liquidated.

When debentures are issued, then the entries will be similar to those shown on the issue of share capital.

Example A company issues debentures of £60,000 at fixed interest of 10%.

CASH BOOK

Date	Details	Dr	Cr	Balance
		£	£	£
	10% debentures	60,000		60,000 Dr

10% DEBENTURE STOCK

Date	Details	Dr	Cr	Balance
		£	£	£
	Cash		60,000	60,000 Cr

COMPANY ACCOUNTS AND CONSOLIDATED GROUP ACCOUNTS

5.1.5 ISSUING DEBENTURES AT A DISCOUNT

Example A company issues 12% (interest) debentures at a discount of 10%. The debentures have a nominal value of £40,000. With the discount of 10%, i.e., £4,000, the cash received will be £36,000. The 12% debenture account will be credited with £40,000, broken down into the cash received and the amount of the discount. The cash book will be debited with the cash received, and a debenture discount account will be debited with the discount.

12% DEBENTURE ACCOUNT

Date	Details	Dr	Cr	Balance
		£	£	£
	Cash		36,000	36,000 Cr
	Discount		4,000	40,000 Cr

CASH BOOK

Date	Details	Dr	Cr	Balance
		£	£	£
	12% debenture	36,000		36,000 Dr

DEBENTURE DISCOUNT ACCOUNT

Date	Details	Dr	Cr	Balance
		£	£	£
	12% debenture	4,000		4,000 Dr

When the company redeems the debentures, it will repay them at the full price, i.e., £40,000. This is shown by the credit balance on the debenture account, i.e., the company owes £40,000. The debit balance on the debenture discount account shows the loss in issuing the debenture. If, e.g., the ordinary share capital of the company was £100,000 the balance sheet would show:

LONG-TERM LIABILITY
12% Debenture   40,000
CAPITAL EMPLOYED
Ordinary share capital   100,000

The debit balance on the debenture discount account will be shown as a deduction in the capital employed section until it has been written off.

LONG-TERM LIABILITY
12% debenture   40,000
CAPITAL EMPLOYED
Ordinary share capital   100,000
Reserves say (see **5.2.6**)   80,000
Less debenture discount   4,000
                                     _____
                                                   76,000
                                                  _____
                                                  176,000

COMPANY ACCOUNTS AND CONSOLIDATED GROUP ACCOUNTS

5.2 Limited Companies' Profit and Loss Accounts

A company may draw up its own final accounts for internal use in any way it considers most suitable. However, when the accounts are sent to the Registrar of Companies or to a shareholder, the Companies Acts lay down the information that must be shown, and also how it should be shown, in line with European Community requirements.

There is a choice of layout, four forms for profit and loss account, and two forms for the balance sheet.

The (vertical form) Format 1 Profit and Loss account is set out below:

PROFIT AND LOSS ACCOUNT

1. Turnover
2. Cost of sales
3. Gross profit or loss
4. Distribution costs
5. Administrative expenses
6. Other operating income
7. Income from shares in group undertakings
8. Income from participating interests
9. Income from other fixed asset investments
10. Other interest receivable and similar income
11. Amounts written off investments
12. Interest payable and similar charges
13. Tax on profit or loss on ordinary activities
14. Profit or loss on ordinary activities after taxation
15. Extraordinary income
16. Extraordinary charges
17. Extraordinary profit or loss
18. Tax on extraordinary profit or loss
19. Other taxes not shown under the above items
20. Profit or loss for the financial year

A company's profit and loss account is similar to that of a sole trader or a partnership. However, there will be some differences.

Salaries paid to directors will be shown as an expense of the company (like wages of employees). Contrast this with a salary paid to a partner, which is shown as an allocation of profit in the appropriation account. This particular account shows how the net profit will be used. After the net profit has been calculated, tax will have to be considered, and provided for. Once this has been done then dividends should be provided for, and then any surplus may be retained or transferred to reserves.

5.2.1 APPROPRIATION OF PROFIT — TAXATION

It must be remembered that corporation tax is not an expense of the company but regarded as an appropriation of profit.

Since 6 April 1999 corporation tax is paid by quarterly equal instalments by large companies, to be phased in over four years. The instalments will be paid on the basis of anticipated current year liabilities for tax. The quarterly instalments will start in month 7 of the accounting year, so that two instalments will be within the accounting year, i.e., month 7 and month 10. Medium and small companies will not have to pay their corporation tax by instalments.

At the same time, self assessment for companies was introduced; this affects accounting periods ending on or after 1 July 1999.

To provide for taxation, the appropriation account above will be debited (remember this forms part of the double-entry system), and a taxation account will be credited. The rate of corporation tax at present is 20% for small companies and 30% for large companies. From 1 April 2000 there is a new starter rate of corporation tax at 10% for companies with profits up to £10,000. There is a sliding scale between £10,000 and £50,000 when the small companies' rate comes into force.

Large companies are those whose taxable profits are at least £1.5 million per annum. Medium size companies are those with taxable profits of between £0.3 million and £1.5 million per annum. Small companies are those with taxable profits of up to £0.3 million per annum. For convenience, in the following examples, rates have been taken that are easy to calculate.

Example The net profit of a company is £200,000. Assuming the rate of corporation tax to be 20% the tax would be £40,000.

Profit and loss account
Net profit   200,000
Less corporation tax (debit)   40,000

                                     160,000

TAXATION ACCOUNT

Date	Details	Dr	Cr	Balance
		£	£	£
	Profit and loss account		40,000	40,000 Cr

These entries do not involve any payment or transfer of cash. The net profit is merely appropriated, and the credit balance on the taxation account shows that £40,000 is due to the Inland Revenue. Until the tax is paid this will be shown as a current liability on the balance sheet. When the tax is actually paid, the cash book will be credited, and the taxation account debited. Continuing the above example:

CASH BOOK

Date	Details	Dr	Cr	Balance
		£	£	£
	Balance say			150,000 Dr
	Taxation — Inland Revenue		40,000	110,000 Dr

TAXATION ACCOUNT

Date	Details	Dr	Cr	Balance
		£	£	£
	Balance			40,000 Cr
	Cash	40,000		Nil

5.2.2 DEFERRED TAXATION

This is to take account of the fact that the figure for profits shown on the company's profit and loss account may not be the same as the figure for profits on which tax is payable. The reasons for this include:

(a) The difference between the figures used for depreciation by the company each year and the figures for capital allowances allowed by the Inland Revenue.

(b) That the Inland Revenue may not allow all the figures that have been shown as expenses on the profit and loss account.

Where there is a difference between the figures used for depreciation and the capital allowances, this will lead to timing differences, as the capital allowances allowed by the Inland Revenue may fall into different periods from the depreciation figures used by the company, even though in the end the amount overall may be the same.

So that a true picture can be given to, e.g., shareholders, deferred taxation is used to adjust the tax shown on the appropriation account. The tax will be adjusted to show the tax on the profit based on depreciation used by the company, rather than based on the capital allowances allowed by the Inland Revenue.

Where the taxation payable for the year is lower than it would be based on the company's own figures then: *debit the profit and loss appropriation account and credit the deferred taxation account.*

The credit balance will be shown as a separate item on the balance sheet under provisions for liabilities and charges.

Where the taxation payable is higher than it would be based on the company's calculation of profit then the entries would be: *credit the profit and loss appropriation account and debit the deferred taxation account.*

Example Year 1

Profit based on the company's calculations:	£200,000
Tax payable based on taxable profit of £160,000 at 20% 32,000	
Deferred taxation 8,000	40,000
Balance retained profit	160,000

TAXATION ACCOUNT

		Dr	Cr	Balance
		£	£ 32,000	£ 32,000 Cr

DEFERRED TAXATION ACCOUNT

		Dr	Cr	Balance
		£	£ 8,000	£ 8,000 Cr

The balance sheet would show:
Creditors due within one year
taxation   32,000
Provisions for liabilities and charges
Deferred taxation   8,000

Year 2
Profit based on company's
calculations   £200,000
Less tax based on taxable profit of
£240,000 at 20%   − 48,000
Add deferred tax adjustment   + 8,000
                                                                                  40,000
Balance retained profit   160,000

TAXATION ACCOUNT

		Dr	Cr	Balance
		£	£ 48,000	£ 48,000 Cr

DEFERRED TAXATION ACCOUNT

		Dr	Cr	Balance
		£	£	£
	Brought down			8,000 Cr
	Year 2	8,000		nil

The balance sheet would show
Creditors amounts due within one
year taxation   £48,000
Provisions for liabilities and charges
Deferred taxation   —

COMPANY ACCOUNTS AND CONSOLIDATED GROUP ACCOUNTS

5.2.3 DIVIDENDS

The directors of a company will propose that part of the net profit be distributed to the shareholders, usually expressed as a percentage of the nominal value of the shares.

5.2.3.1 Appropriation of dividend

Example A company declares a dividend of 10% in respect of ordinary shares with a nominal value of £100,000, being £10,000. Net profit after tax is £96,000. The directors will not allocate all the profit remaining after taxation, as:

(a) Profit will need to be retained to run the business, or for expansion.

(b) Net profit will not necessarily be represented by cash at the bank.

Profit and loss account	
Net profit	120,000
Less corporation tax (debit)	24,000
	96,000
Less dividend	10,000
	86,000

DIVIDEND ACCOUNT

Date	Details	Dr	Cr	Balance
		£	£	£
	Profit and loss account		10,000	10,000 Cr

The amount shown on the dividend account shows the amount due for the dividend. This will be shown as a current liability on the balance sheet. The size of the dividend will be agreed at the annual general meeting of the company, when the accounts are agreed. The dividend can then be paid. Continuing the above example:

5.2.3.2 Payment of dividend

CASH BOOK

Date	Details	Dr	Cr	Balance
		£	£	£
	Balance say			25,000 Dr
	Dividend		10,000	15,000 Dr

DIVIDEND ACCOUNT

Date	Details	Dr	Cr	Balance
		£	£	£
	Balance			10,000 Cr
	Cash	10,000		Nil

COMPANY ACCOUNTS AND CONSOLIDATED GROUP ACCOUNTS

5.2.3.3 Payment of interim dividend

If the company has paid an interim dividend before the end of the year, the entries to record the payment of the interim dividend will be the same as the payment of the dividend above. The interim dividend will be shown in the appropriation section of the profit and loss account, in the same way that the end of year dividend was shown.

> **Example** During the year a company pays an interim dividend of £10,000. At the end of the year the net profit after taxation is £80,000. A final dividend of £15,000 is recommended by the directors.
>
> 1. Payment of the interim dividend during the year.
>
> CASH BOOK
>
> | Date | Details | Dr | Cr | Balance |
> |------|---------|----|----|---------|
> | | | £ | £ | £ |
> | | Balance say | | | 48,000 Dr |
> | | Interim dividend | | 10,000 | 38,000 Dr |
>
> DIVIDEND ACCOUNT
>
> | Date | Details | Dr | Cr | Balance |
> |------|---------|----|----|---------|
> | | | £ | £ | £ |
> | | Cash — interim dividend | 10,000 | | 10,000 Dr |
>
> 2. Final dividend at end of year
>
> Profit and loss account
> Net profit after taxation   80,000
> Less dividend
>   interim   10,000
>   final   15,000
>   ──────
>   25,000
>   ──────
>   55,000
>
> DIVIDEND ACCOUNT
>
> | Date | Details | Dr | Cr | Balance |
> |------|---------|----|----|---------|
> | | | £ | £ | £ |
> | | Balance (interim dividend) | | | 10,000 Dr |
> | | Profit and loss account | | | |
> | | Interim dividend | | 10,000 | Nil |
> | | Final dividend | | 15,000 | 15,000 Cr |

The £15,000 credit balance on the dividend account will be shown on the balance sheet as a current liability, being the amount due to the shareholders. When the final dividend is paid the entries will be as shown previously.

COMPANY ACCOUNTS AND CONSOLIDATED GROUP ACCOUNTS

5.2.4 APPROPRIATION — RETAINED PROFIT AND RESERVES

After providing for taxation and dividends, the balance of the net profit is retained on the appropriation account, or it may be transferred to a reserve account. Either way it will be shown as a reserve on the balance sheet, in the capital employed section (like the net profit due to a sole proprietor).

Net profit is not necessarily represented by cash — it is represented by an increase in recorded net assets. Thus 'retention of profit' or 'reserves' are merely retaining in the business the assets which are attributable to profit.

The balance of net profit will be transferred to a reserve account if it is to be retained for a specific purpose, e.g., replacement of fixed assets, or redemption (repayment) of debentures. The entries to record a transfer to a reserve account are: *debit the appropriation account and credit the reserve account.*

Example Net profit after taxation is £40,000. A dividend of £10,000 is declared. Of the remaining £30,000, £16,000 is transferred to a reserve account.

Net profit after taxation	£40,000
Less dividend	£10,000
	£30,000
Transferred to reserve	£16,000
	£14,000

Note: both the balance of £14,000 and the reserve of £16,000 will be shown on the balance sheet as part of the capital employed.

Capital employed		
Share capital		100,000 (say)
Reserves		
Special reserve	16,000	
Profit and loss	14,000	
		30,000
		130,000

As mentioned in **2.3.4**, this is the same principle as in the balance sheet of a sole proprietor, where the net profit would be shown added to their capital.

The share capital and reserves shown above are known as the shareholders' equity, or the ordinary shareholders' funds. These will be represented by the assets of the company, shown in the employment of capital section of the balance sheet.

In the event of the company being wound up the shareholders would be entitled to the return of their capital, plus a share in the surplus assets of the company, represented by the reserves.

5.2.5 PROVISIONS, RESERVES AND LIABILITIES

A provision, as we have seen in **2.11.4**, may be debited to the profit and loss account, or it may be debited to the appropriation account of a company. A provision may be created in respect of a known liability which exists at the date of the balance sheet where the amount cannot be determined with substantial accuracy. The provision may, for example, be for (estimated) doubtful debts, or depreciation, which would be debited to the profit and loss section. Provision may also be made for estimated taxation, or a dividend, which would be debited to the appropriation section.

Provisions are in contrast to liabilities, which are amounts owed and which can be determined with substantial accuracy, e.g., rent due. Provisions may also be contrasted with reserves, which can only be debited to the appropriation section, and which do not relate to any liability or loss which is known to exist at the time of the balance sheet.

Definitions of these are contained in the Companies Act 1985, sch. 9, para. 32.

5.2.6 CAPITAL AND REVENUE RESERVES

5.2.6.1 Revenue reserves

These are reserves transferred from the profit and loss appropriation account (i.e., retained profit) which can be general, or for some particular purpose, e.g., a foreign exchange reserve account, to meet any possible losses through devaluation of a foreign currency. General revenue reserve accounts may be used in future years, should profit be insufficient for dividends, when the reserve may be used for the payment of dividends, provided that cash is available. (If this was done then the revenue reserve account would be debited and the profit and loss appropriation account would be credited.)

General reserve accounts may also be used to increase the capital required with inflation as the amount of working capital required by the company will increase. When we looked at final accounts in **Chapter 2**, we saw on the balance sheet a figure for net current assets, or working capital — this means the portion of capital invested in the business which is left to run the business after providing the fixed assets.

5.2.6.2 Capital reserves

These are not available for distribution by way of dividend under the Companies Acts.

Capital reserves which cannot be used for the declaration of dividends payable in cash are:

(a) capital redemption reserves;

(b) a share premium account;

(c) a revaluation reserve.

Capital redemption reserves include a preference shares redemption reserve, which can be used to redeem redeemable preference shares, or, e.g., a debenture redemption reserve, which can be used to redeem debentures on the date specified. A company may transfer a certain amount of net profit each year to a redemption reserve account.

A share premium account is needed when the company issues shares at a premium — the additional amount over the nominal value of the shares is shown in the share premium account.

A revaluation reserve is used when a company revalues its assets. If the value of the assets is increased, then there must be a corresponding increase in the capital employed section of the balance sheet. The asset account is to be debited and the revaluation reserve account is to be credited. This cannot be used to pay a dividend as it merely represents the increase in value of the assets.

COMPANY ACCOUNTS AND CONSOLIDATED GROUP ACCOUNTS

5.2.7 CAPITALISATION OF RESERVES: BONUS ISSUE OF SHARES

Although reserves may not be available for distribution by way of dividend, they may be capitalised by issuing bonus or free shares to shareholders.

Example A company has an issued share capital of £40,000,000 and general reserves of £15,000,000. It makes a bonus issue of one share for every four shares held. The bonus issue will therefore be £10,000,000.

Before the bonus issue the balance sheet would show:

	£000
Capital employed	
Share capital	40,000
General reserves	15,000
	55,000

After the bonus issue the balance sheet will show:

	£000
Capital employed	
Share capital	50,000
General reserves	5,000
	55,000

The entries on the accounts would be:

SHARE CAPITAL ACCOUNT

Date	Details	Dr	Cr	Balance
		£000	£000	£000
	Balance			40,000 Cr
	General reserve		10,000	50,000 Cr

GENERAL RESERVE ACCOUNT

Date	Details	Dr	Cr	Balance
		£000	£000	£000
	Balance			15,000 Cr
	Share capital	10,000		5,000 Cr

Although each shareholder will own more shares, these will be worth less individually, as the shares are still represented by the same amount of assets. Any dividend payable in respect of the shares may be at a lower percentage, as the same net profit will have to be apportioned between the shares.

5.2.8 SINKING FUNDS

As mentioned in **5.2.4**, retained net profit is not equivalent to cash, it merely represents an increase in assets. If cash is required then it will be necessary, at the same time as profit is transferred to a reserve, to transfer the required amount of cash, or easily realisable assets, to a sinking fund (or reserve fund) which can then be used when needed.

Example A company transfers £200,000 to debenture redemption reserve from net profit after taxation and dividends of £500,000. It also transfers £200,000 from the cash at the bank to a deposit account, to be used as a reserve fund for debenture redemption.

Profit and loss appropriation account
Net profit after tax and dividend   £500,000
Transfer to debenture redemption reserve   £200,000
                                             _____
                                             £300,000

DEBENTURE REDEMPTION RESERVE ACCOUNT

Date	Details	Dr	Cr	Balance
		£	£	£
	Profit and loss		200,000	200,000 Cr

CASH BOOK

Date	Details	Dr	Cr	Balance
		£	£	£
	Balance say			350,000 Dr
	Debenture redemption reserve (sinking) fund		200,000	150,000 Dr

DEBENTURE REDEMPTION RESERVE (SINKING) FUND ACCOUNT

Date	Details	Dr	Cr	Balance
		£	£	£
	Cash	200,000		200,000 Dr

The balance sheet would show:

FIXED ASSETS
Debenture redemption
reserve (sinking fund)   200,000
NET CURRENT ASSETS
CAPITAL EMPLOYED
Share capital   XX
Debenture redemption reserve   200,000

COMPANY ACCOUNTS AND CONSOLIDATED GROUP ACCOUNTS

5.3 Reports and Records Required under the Companies Acts

The Companies Acts 1985 and 1989 set out the requirements: every company must maintain adequate accounting records, and prepare financial statements in respect of each accounting year.

At the annual general meeting of shareholders the following should be presented:

(a) A profit and loss account.

(b) A balance sheet.

(c) A directors' report.

(d) An auditors' report.

The auditors must confirm the requirement that the balance sheet shall give a true and fair view of the state of affairs of the company as at the end of its financial year, and every profit and loss account shall give a true and fair view of the profit or loss of the company for the financial year. Accounting standards and practices should be observed.

The accounting concepts previously mentioned in **4.1** must be used:

(a) The going concern concept.

(b) Accounting principles must be applied consistently from one year to the next.

(c) The concept of prudence.

(d) The accruals or matching concept.

Historical cost and alternative accounting rules are prescribed, e.g., current cost accounting. This is outside the scope of this book. The publicity and filing requirements of companies will vary according to their size. Although small and medium size companies must present a full set of accounts to their shareholders they can file modified reports with the Registrar of Companies.

Except for small and medium size companies there is a requirement under the Companies Act 1989 that a statement should be given explaining whether the accounts have been prepared in accordance with applicable accounting standards and giving details of, and the reasons for, any material departures.

5.3.1 SMALL AND MEDIUM SIZE COMPANIES

A company is defined in the Companies Acts as small or medium sized for a financial year if, both for that year and the preceding year, it satisfies any two or more of the following conditions:

COMPANY ACCOUNTS AND CONSOLIDATED GROUP ACCOUNTS

Condition	Small company	Medium size company
Turnover not exceeding	£2.8 million	£11.2 million
Balance sheet total not exceeding	£1.4 million	£5.6 million
Employees less than	50	250
Modifications applicable:		
Directors' report	Not required	Required
Profit and loss account	Not required	Modified
Balance sheet	Only main headings and amounts required but aggregate debtors/creditors due after more than one year must be disclosed	Required
Particulars of salaries of directors and higher paid employees	Not required	Required

There are also modifications to the notes to the accounts.

5.3.2 THE FORM OF THE BALANCE SHEET

There are two formats, the vertical form and the horizontal form. The vertical format is set out below:

Balance sheet: Format 1 — the vertical

A CALLED UP SHARE CAPITAL NOT PAID*
B FIXED ASSETS
I Intangible assets
   1 Development costs
   2 Concessions, patents, licences, trademarks
   and similar rights and assets
   3 Goodwill
   4 Payments on account
II Tangible assets
   1 Land and buildings
   2 Plant and machinery
   3 Fixtures, fittings, tools and equipment
   4 Payments on account and assets in course of construction
III Investments
   1 Shares in group undertakings
   2 Loans to group undertakings
   3 Participating interests
   4 Loans to undertakings in which the company has a participating interest
   5 Other investments other than loans
   6 Other loans
   7 Own shares

COMPANY ACCOUNTS AND CONSOLIDATED GROUP ACCOUNTS

C CURRENT ASSETS
I Stocks
  1 Raw materials and consumables
  2 Work in progress
  3 Finished goods and goods for resale
  4 Payments on account
II Debtors
  1 Trade debtors
  2 Amounts owed by group undertakings
  3 Amounts owed by undertakings in which the company has a participating interest
  4 Other debtors
  5 Called up share capital not paid*
  6 Prepayments and accrued income**
III Investments
  1 Shares in group undertakings
  2 Own shares
  3 Other investments
IV Cash at bank and in hand

D PREPAYMENTS AND ACCRUED INCOME**

E CREDITORS: AMOUNTS FALLING DUE WITHIN ONE YEAR
  1 Debenture loans
  2 Bank loans and overdrafts
  3 Payments received on account
  4 Trade creditors
  5 Bills of exchange payable
  6 Amounts owed to group undertakings
  7 Amounts owed to undertakings in which the company has a participating interest
  8 Other creditors including taxation and social security
  9 Accruals and deferred income***

F NET CURRENT ASSETS (LIABILITIES)

G TOTAL ASSETS LESS CURRENT LIABILITIES

H CREDITORS: AMOUNTS FALLING DUE AFTER MORE THAN ONE YEAR
  1 Debenture loans
  2 Bank loans and overdrafts
  3 Payments received on account
  4 Trade creditors
  5 Bills of exchange payable
  6 Amounts owed to group undertakings
  7 Amounts owed to related undertakings in which the company has a participating interest
  8 Other creditors including taxation and social security
  9 Accruals and deferred income***

I PROVISIONS FOR LIABILITIES AND CHARGES
  1 Pensions and similar obligations
  2 Taxation, including deferred taxation
  3 Other provisions

J ACCRUALS AND DEFERRED INCOME***

K CAPITAL AND RESERVES
I Called up share capital
II Share premium account
III Revaluation reserve
IV Other reserves
  1 Capital redemption reserve
  2 Reserve for own shares
  3 Reserves provided for by the articles of association
  4 Other reserves
V PROFIT AND LOSS ACCOUNT

* ** *** These items may be shown in either of the two positions indicated.

COMPANY ACCOUNTS AND CONSOLIDATED GROUP ACCOUNTS

Items preceded by letters or Roman numerals must be disclosed on the face of the balance sheet, e.g., B fixed assets, K I called up share capital, but those with ordinary Arabic numbers, e.g., 1, 2, 3, may be combined where they are not material or the combination aids assessment of the company's affairs. Where they are combined the details of each item should be shown in the notes to the accounts.

5.3.2.1 Public companies and the Stock Exchange

Shares of most public companies are dealt with on the Stock Exchange. Private companies cannot issue their shares to the public, their shares cannot be bought and sold on the Stock Exchange. Sale and purchase of shares on the Stock Exchange will have no effect on the accounting entries made in the company's books. However, the price of the shares on the Stock Exchange will affect, e.g., the price at which any new shares are to be issued.

5.3.3 EXAMPLE BALANCE SHEET

What follows is an example of a balance sheet using the format required by the Companies Acts.

BALANCE SHEET AS AT —

	£ '000	£ '000	£ '000
FIXED ASSETS			
Intangible assets			
Goodwill		10,000	
Tangible assets			
Premises	200,000		
Machinery	80,000		
Motor cars	40,000		
		320,000	
			330,000
CURRENT ASSETS			
Stock	30,000		
Debtors	26,000		
Cash at bank	20,000		
		76,000	
LESS CREDITORS			
Amounts falling due within one year			
Proposed dividend	10,000		
Creditors	18,000		
Corporation tax due	9,000		
		37,000	
			39,000
TOTAL ASSETS LESS CURRENT LIABILITIES			369,000
CREDITORS			
Amounts falling due after more than one year			90,000
TOTAL			279,000

COMPANY ACCOUNTS AND CONSOLIDATED GROUP ACCOUNTS

CAPITAL AND RESERVES	
Authorised and issued fully paid ordinary £1 shares	240,000
Share premium account	13,000
General reserve	15,000
Profit and loss account	11,000
TOTAL	279,000

5.4 Practice Exercises

1 From the following trial balance of Randall Limited drawn up on 31 March 200—, draw up the profit and loss account and the balance sheet for the year ending 31 March 200—.

Trial Balance	Dr £	Cr £
Ordinary share capital		120,000
10% preference share capital		25,000
Debentures		20,000
Buildings	150,000	
Equipment	45,000	
Motor cars	20,000	
Accumulated depreciation: equipment		5,000
Accumulated depreciation: motor cars		10,000
Stock at start of year	19,000	
Sales		375,000
Purchases	149,000	
Wages	40,000	
Directors' remuneration	70,000	
Motor expenses	6,000	
Rates insurance	3,000	
General expenses	19,000	
Debenture interest payable	2,000	
Debtors	29,000	
Creditors		18,000
Cash at bank	26,000	
Interim ordinary dividend paid	10,000	
General reserve		15,000
	588,000	588,000

Additional information required to complete the accounts:

- stock at the end of the year is £21,000;
- depreciation on equipment is £2,000, and on motor cars is £5,000;
- taxation is estimated at £20,000;
- the preference share dividend is £2,500; and
- the final dividend for the ordinary shareholders is £2,000.

2 The trial balance of Campion Limited as at 31 August 2001 was as follows:

	Dr £ '000	Cr £ '000
Share capital ordinary £1 shares		350,000
Reserves		32,000
Profit and loss account 31 August 1999		10,560

COMPANY ACCOUNTS AND CONSOLIDATED GROUP ACCOUNTS

Freehold premises at cost	320,000	
Machinery at cost	70,000	
Accumulated depreciation on machinery		14,000
Purchases	310,000	
Sales		483,000
General expenses	40,000	
Wages	40,000	
Directors' fees	50,000	
Light and heat	1,500	
Bad debts	2,000	
Debtors	30,060	
Creditors		25,000
Stock as at 31 August 1999	41,000	
Cash at bank	10,000	
	914,560	914,560

Additional information is as follows:

stock as at 31 August 2001 is	38,000
expenses due amount to	2,400
tax due is	9,090
prepayments amount to	4,200
a dividend is proposed	17,500
a provision for doubtful debts is suggested for this year	1,000
depreciation for this year on machinery at cost is 10%.	

Draw up a trading and profit and loss account for the year ending 31 August 2001 and a balance sheet as at 31 August 2001.

3 From the trial balance of Down and Out Limited shown below, draw up a profit and loss account and a balance sheet, in the format required under the Companies Acts.

TRIAL BALANCE AS AT 31 DECEMBER 2001

	Dr £ '000	Cr £ '000
Ordinary share capital £1 shares fully paid		160,000
12% debentures repayable in 2005		40,000
Goodwill at cost	20,000	
Buildings	150,000	
Fixtures and fittings	40,000	
Motor cars	25,000	
Accumulated depreciation: fixtures and fittings		8,000
Accumulated depreciation: motor cars		10,000
Stock as at 1 January 2001	23,000	
Sales		179,000
Purchases	70,000	
Salaries/wages	33,000	
Directors' fees	39,000	
Motor expenses	2,500	
Council tax	2,300	
General expenses	11,400	
Debenture interest	6,000	
Debtors	26,500	
Creditors		19,900

COMPANY ACCOUNTS AND CONSOLIDATED GROUP ACCOUNTS

Cash at bank	13,200	
General reserve		15,000
Share premium account		16,000
Interim ordinary dividend paid	3,000	
Profit and loss account 2000		17,000
	464,900	464,900

The following should be taken into account:

	£ '000
stock at the end of the year	26,000
depreciation on cars for the year	5,000
depreciation on fixtures was	4,000
proposed final dividend is	2,000
provision for corporation tax due is	2,640

4 From the trial balance of Rosa Limited following, draw up a trading and profit and loss account and a balance sheet.

TRIAL BALANCE AS AT 31 DECEMBER 2001

	Dr £	Cr £
Premises	290,000	
Fixtures at cost	50,000	
Accumulated depreciation on fixtures		5,000
Stock at the start of the year	21,000	
Debtors	18,000	
Cash at bank	17,000	
Creditors		19,000
Share capital		320,000
Reserves		6,500
Purchases	110,000	
Sales		290,000
Salaries	35,000	
Council tax	3,000	
Office expenses	6,000	
Sundry expenses	500	
Directors' fees	90,000	
	640,500	640,500

Note the following:

	£
stock at the end of the year was	23,000
outstanding expenses were	1,000
depreciation on fixtures and fittings was	5,000
taxation is estimated at	8,500
the proposed dividend totals	16,000
transfer to reserves	10,000

5.5 Suggested Answers to Practice Exercises

1 RANDALL LIMITED TRADING AND PROFIT AND LOSS ACCOUNT FOR THE YEAR ENDING 31 MARCH 200—

	£	£	£
Sales			375,000
Less cost of goods sold			
Opening stock	19,000		
Add purchases	149,000		
	168,000		
Less closing stock	21,000		
			147,000
Gross profit			228,000
Less expenses			
Wages	40,000		
Motor expenses	6,000		
Directors' remuneration	70,000		
Rates and insurance	3,000		
General expenses	19,000		
Debenture interest payable	2,000		
Depreciation on equipment	2,000		
Depreciation on cars	5,000		
			147,000
Profit before taxation			81,000
Taxation			20,000
Profit after taxation			61,000
Less appropriation			
Preference share dividend		2,500	
Ordinary share dividend			
Interim paid	10,000		
Final dividend	2,000		
		12,000	
			14,500
Reserves (retained profit)			46,500

RANDALL LIMITED BALANCE SHEET AS AT 31 MARCH 200—

	£	£	£
FIXED ASSETS			
Buildings		150,000	
Equipment	45,000		
Less depreciation	7,000		
		38,000	
Motor cars	20,000		
Less depreciation	15,000		
		5,000	
			193,000

COMPANY ACCOUNTS AND CONSOLIDATED GROUP ACCOUNTS

CURRENT ASSETS			
Stock	21,000		
Debtors	29,000		
Cash at bank	26,000		
		76,000	
Less			
CURRENT LIABILITIES			
Creditors	18,000		
Preference share dividend	2,500		
Final dividend	2,000		
Taxation	20,000		
		42,500	
NET CURRENT ASSETS			33,500
TOTAL ASSETS LESS CURRENT LIABILITIES			226,500
Less			
Debentures			20,000
			206,500
CAPITAL AND RESERVES			
Ordinary share capital		120,000	
Preference shares		25,000	
		145,000	
Reserves	15,000		
This year	46,500		
		61,500	
			206,500

2 CAMPION LIMITED
TRADING AND PROFIT AND LOSS ACCOUNT FOR THE YEAR
ENDING 31 AUGUST 2001

	£ '000	£ '000	£ '000
Sales			483,000
Less cost of goods sold			
opening stock	41,000		
add purchases	310,000		
	351,000		
Less closing stock	38,000		
			313,000
Gross profit			170,000

Less expenses			
General expenses	40,000		
Wages	40,000		
Directors' fees	50,000		
Light and heat	1,500		
Bad debts	2,000		
Provision for doubtful debts	1,000		
Depreciation: machinery	7,000		
Add outstanding expenses	2,400		
		143,900	
Less prepaid		4,200	
			139,700
Net profit			30,300
Less provision for taxation			9,090
Profit after taxation			21,210
Add retained profit from last year			10,560
			31,770
Less proposed dividend			17,500
Retained profit carried forward to next year			14,270

CAMPION LIMITED
BALANCE SHEET AS AT 31 AUGUST 2001

	£ '000	£ '000	£ '000
FIXED ASSETS			
Premises at cost		320,000	
Machinery at cost	70,000		
Less accumulated depreciation	21,000		
		49,000	
			369,000
CURRENT ASSETS			
Stock		38,000	
Debtors	30,060		
Less provision	1,000		
		29,060	
Cash at bank		10,000	
Prepayment		4,200	
		81,260	
LESS CURRENT LIABILITIES			
Creditors	25,000		
Oustanding expenses	2,400		
Proposed dividend	17,500		
Corporation tax due	9,090		
		53,990	
NET CURRENT ASSETS			27,270
			396,270
LESS LONG-TERM LIABILITIES			—
TOTAL			396,270

COMPANY ACCOUNTS AND CONSOLIDATED GROUP ACCOUNTS

CAPITAL EMPLOYED	
Share capital ordinary £1 shares fully paid	350,000
Reserves	32,000
From profit and loss account	14,270
TOTAL	396,270

3 DOWN AND OUT LIMITED TRADING AND PROFIT AND LOSS ACCOUNT FOR THE YEAR ENDING 31 DECEMBER 2001

	£'000	£'000	£'000
Sales			179,000
Less cost of goods sold			
opening stock	23,000		
plus purchases	70,000		
	93,000		
Less closing stock	26,000		
			67,000
Gross profit			112,000
Less expenses			
Salaries	33,000		
Directors' fees	39,000		
Motor expenses	2,500		
Council tax	2,300		
General expenses	11,400		
Debenture interest	6,000		
Depreciation on fixtures	4,000		
Depreciation on cars	5,000		
			103,200
Profit for the year			8,800
Less provision for corporation tax			2,640
Profit after tax			6,160
Add retained profit from last year			17,000
			23,160
Less dividends			
Interim dividend paid	3,000		
Final dividend proposed	2,000		
			5,000
Retained profit carried forward to next year			18,160

DOWN AND OUT LIMITED
BALANCE SHEET AS AT 31 DECEMBER 2001

	£'000	£'000	£'000
FIXED ASSETS			
Intangible assets			
Goodwill			20,000
Tangible assets			
Premises		150,000	
Fixtures costs	40,000		
Less depreciation	12,000		
		28,000	
Cars cost	25,000		
Less depreciation	15,000		
		10,000	
			188,000
			208,000
CURRENT ASSETS:			
Stock		26,000	
Debtors		26,500	
Cash at bank		13,200	
		65,700	
Creditors: amounts falling due within one year			
Creditors	19,900		
Proposed dividend	2,000		
Taxation due	2,640		
		24,540	
NET CURRENT ASSETS			41,160
Total assets less current liabilities			249,160
Less longterm liabilities			
Debentures			40,000
TOTAL			209,160
CAPITAL AND RESERVES			
Share capital £1 ordinary shares		160,000	
Share premium		16,000	
General reserve		15,000	
Profit and loss account		18,160	
TOTAL			209,160

COMPANY ACCOUNTS AND CONSOLIDATED GROUP ACCOUNTS

4

ROSA LIMITED
TRADING AND PROFIT AND LOSS ACCOUNT FOR THE YEAR ENDING
31 DECEMBER 2001

	£	£	£
Sales			290,000
Less cost of goods sold			
opening stock	21,000		
add purchases	110,000		
	131,000		
Less closing stock	23,000		
			108,000
Gross profit			182,000
Less expenses			
Salaries	35,000		
Council tax	3,000		
Office expenses	6,000		
Sundry expenses	500		
Depreciation on fixtures and fittings	5,000		
Directors' fees	90,000		
Outstanding expenses	1,000		
			140,500
Net profit			41,500
Less taxation			8,500
Profit after taxation			33,000
Less appropriations			
Proposed dividend	16,000		
To general reserve	10,000		
			26,000
			7,000

ROSA LIMITED
BALANCE SHEET AS AT 31 DECEMBER 2001

	£	£	£
FIXED ASSETS			
Premises		290,000	
Fixtures cost	50,000		
Less depreciation	10,000		
		40,000	
			330,000
CURRENT ASSETS			
Stock at end of year	23,000		
Debtors	18,000		
Cash at bank	17,000		
		58,000	

LESS CURRENT LIABILITIES		
Creditors	19,000	
Oustanding expenses	1,000	
Proposed dividend	16,000	
Tax due	8,500	
	44,500	
NET CURRENT ASSETS		13,500
		343,500
LESS LONG-TERM LIABILITIES		—
TOTAL		343,500
CAPITAL EMPLOYED		
Share capital authorised and issued		
Ordinary £1 shares		320,000
Reserves £6,500 plus £10,000		16,500
Profit and loss account		7,000
TOTAL		343,500

5.6 Group Companies and Consolidated Accounts

Separate companies operating independently will have separate accounting records and financial statements. Where one company controls another then this is regarded as a group, with a controlling, or parent, company which is called the parent undertaking, and the subsidiary company, called the subsidiary undertaking. Although the companies are still separate legal entities with separate financial records, the idea is that the shareholders of the parent company should be given some information about the subsidiary company. This information is provided by consolidated accounts for the group, being a consolidated profit and loss account and a consolidated balance sheet. These are created by aggregating the separate profit and loss accounts and balance sheets of the parent and subsidiary undertaking and are produced *in addition* to the separate final accounts for each company.

An undertaking is a parent undertaking in relation to another undertaking, a subsidiary, if:

(a) it holds a majority of the voting rights in the undertaking; or

(b) it is a member of the undertaking and has the right to appoint or remove a majority of its board of directors; or

(c) it has the right to exercise a dominant influence over the undertaking;

   (i) by virtue of provisions contained in the undertaking's memorandum or articles; or

   (ii) by virtue of a control contract; or

(d) it is a member of the undertaking and controls alone, pursuant to an agreement with other shareholders or members, a majority of the voting rights in the undertaking.

An undertaking is also a parent undertaking in relation to another undertaking, a subsidiary undertaking, if it has a participating interest in the undertaking, and:

COMPANY ACCOUNTS AND CONSOLIDATED GROUP ACCOUNTS

(a) it actually exercises a dominant influence over it; or

(b) it and the subsidiary undertaking are managed on a unified basis.

The above is really based on a company's ability to exercise control over another company. A group will thus exist whenever legal entities which are independent of each other are under central management, regardless of the share ownership. This legislation implements the EC Seventh Directive. It should be noted that certain partnerships and joint ventures can also come within the consolidation requirement.

5.6.1 THE CONSOLIDATED BALANCE SHEET

The balance sheets of each company will be merged. The issued capital shown will be that of the parent company only, represented by the assets of the two companies. Merging does not mean that the two balance sheets are added together: the inter company shares should be cancelled out first, and then the assets of the two companies will be added together. Inter company shares mean those shares in the subsidiary undertaking owned by the parent undertaking shown in its balance sheet, and the subsidiary company's capital and reserves which represent those shares shown in the subsidiary undertaking's balance sheet.

Example Company P Ltd owns the whole share capital of company S Ltd and the two separate balance sheets show:

	P Ltd £ '000	(parent company)
Fixed assets	25,000	
Shares in B Ltd (at cost)	15,000	inter company shares (investment in subsidiary)
Net current assets	10,000	
	50,000	
Share capital	50,000	
	50,000	

	S Ltd £ '000	(subsidiary company)
Fixed assets	10,000	
Net current assets	5,000	
	15,000	
Share capital	15,000	(representing the above)
	15,000	

The inter company shares are to be cancelled out, i.e., the shares held in S Ltd by P Ltd are to be taken out from P Ltd's balance sheet and the share capital representing this must be taken out from S Ltd's balance sheet.

COMPANY ACCOUNTS AND CONSOLIDATED GROUP ACCOUNTS

	P Ltd £'000	(parent company)
Fixed assets	25,000	
Net current assets	10,000	
	35,000	
Share capital	50,000	
	50,000	

	S Ltd £'000	(subsidiary company)
Fixed assets	10,000	
Net current assets	5,000	
	15,000	

Next, the assets of S Ltd must be added into P Ltd's balance sheet to make the consolidated account for P Ltd and S Ltd.

P LTD AND S LTD CONSOLIDATED GROUP BALANCE SHEET

		£'000	£'000
Fixed assets:	P Ltd		25,000
	S Ltd		10,000
			35,000
Net current assets:	P Ltd	10,000	
	S Ltd	5,000	
			15,000
Total			50,000
Share capital			50,000

If the subsidiary undertaking has reserves, then the share capital and the reserves (shareholder's funds) in the subsidiary undertaking must be excluded.

COMPANY ACCOUNTS AND CONSOLIDATED GROUP ACCOUNTS

Example P Ltd has purchased all the shares in S Ltd. The two balance sheets are as follows:

	P Ltd £'000	(parent company)
Fixed assets	40,000	
Shares in S Ltd (at cost)	30,000	investment in subsidiary
Net current assets	10,000	
	80,000	
Share capital	60,000	
Reserves	20,000	
	80,000	

	S Ltd £'000	(subsidiary company)
Fixed assets	25,000	
Net current assets	5,000	
	30,000	
Share capital	20,000	
Reserves	10,000	(representing the above)
	30,000	

The inter company shares and reserves (in S) must be cancelled out and then the assets of both companies added together.

P LTD AND S LTD CONSOLIDATED BALANCE SHEET

		£'000	£'000
Fixed assets:	P Ltd	40,000	
	S Ltd	25,000	
			65,000
Net current assets:	P Ltd	10,000	
	S Ltd	5,000	
			15,000
			80,000
Share capital		60,000	
Reserves		20,000	
			80,000

In the above two examples, P Ltd, the acquiring company, paid the book value of the assets owned by S Ltd. However, the acquiring company may pay more, or less, than the book value of the assets of the subsidiary undertaking.

5.6.1.1 Acquiring shares for more than the book value of the assets

Example P Ltd purchases the shares and reserves of S Ltd for £100,000,000. The balance sheet value of these are £90,000,000. The excess paid of £10,000,000 is known as goodwill, which will be included in the consolidated balance sheet.

The balance sheets before consolidation will look like this:

	P Ltd £'000	(parent company)
Fixed assets	200,000	
Shares in S Ltd (at cost)	100,000*	less £90,000,000 (book value of investment in S Ltd)
Net current assets	30,000	
	330,000	
Share capital	250,000	
Reserves	80,000	
	330,000	

	S Ltd £'000	(subsidiary company)
Fixed assets	80,000	
Net current assets	10,000	
	90,000	
Share capital	75,000	
Reserves	15,000	
	90,000*	(representing the above inter company shares)

The book value of the investment in S Ltd and the share capital and reserves of S Ltd totalling £90,000,000 must be cancelled out from the shares in S Ltd shown on P Ltd's balance sheet. This will leave £10,000,000 on P Ltd's balance sheet in respect of the shares in S Ltd, which will be called goodwill, being the additional payment in respect of the shares.

The assets of the two companies are then to be added together as before.

P LTD AND S LTD CONSOLIDATED BALANCE SHEET

		£'000	£'000
Goodwill re S Ltd shares			10,000
Fixed assets:	P Ltd	200,000	
	S Ltd	80,000	
			280,000

COMPANY ACCOUNTS AND CONSOLIDATED GROUP ACCOUNTS

Net current assets:	P Ltd	30,000	
	S Ltd	10,000	
		40,000	
			330,000
Share capital			250,000
Reserves			80,000
			330,000

5.6.1.2 Acquiring shares for less than the book value of the assets

Example Company P Ltd acquires all the share capital and reserves of S Ltd for £100,000,000 when the balance sheet value of these is £120,000,000. P Ltd has therefore made a 'profit' in respect of the purchase. This is due to the shareholders of P Ltd, but it cannot be distributed to them. A capital reserve account will be opened in respect of the profit of £20,000,000.

The balance sheets before consolidation will look like this:

	P Ltd	(parent company)
	£	£
	'000	'000
Fixed assets	200,000	
Shares in S Ltd		
(at cost)	100,000	(less value of S Ltd £120,000,000)*
Net current assets	150,000	
		450,000
Share capital	400,000	
Reserves	50,000	
		450,000
	S Ltd	(subsidiary company)
Fixed assets	85,000	
Net current assets	35,000	
		120,000
Share capital	110,000	
Reserves	10,000	
		120,000* (representing the above)

When the total value of S Ltd, i.e., £120,000,000, is removed from P Ltd's balance sheet, this would result in a minus figure of £20,000,000 in the assets. This is a credit balance which should be shown as a capital reserve in the share capital and reserves section.

	P Ltd	(parent company)
	£	£
	'000	'000
Fixed assets	200,000	

(Shares in S Ltd — £20,000,000 now a credit — move to the share capital and reserves section)

Net current assets   150,000

The consolidated balance sheet will appear as follows:

COMPANY ACCOUNTS AND CONSOLIDATED GROUP ACCOUNTS

P LTD AND S LTD CONSOLIDATED BALANCE SHEET

		£'000	£'000
Fixed assets:	P Ltd	200,000	
	S Ltd	85,000	
			285,000
Net current assets:	P Ltd	150,000	
	S Ltd	35,000	
			185,000
			470,000
Share capital		400,000	
Capital reserve (re shares in S Ltd)		20,000	
Other reserves		50,000	
			470,000

5.6.2 THE CONSOLIDATED PROFIT AND LOSS ACCOUNT

These can be fairly complicated. The sales, cost of sales and expenses will be merged and the net profits, taxation, and transfers to reserves will be merged, but the dividend payable to the parent undertaking (inter company dividend) will be excluded. In order to keep things simple, the following example will just show the net profit onwards.

Example The profit and loss accounts of P Ltd and S Ltd are as follows:

P Ltd (parent)

	£'000	£'000
Net profit		50,000
Add dividend from S Ltd		10,000
		60,000
Taxation, say		15,000
Profit after tax		45,000
Dividend (to P Ltd's shareholders)		15,000
Retained profit (reserves)		30,000

S Ltd (subsidiary)

	£'000	£'000
Net profit		40,000
Taxation		12,000
Profit after tax		28,000
Dividend to P Ltd		10,000
Retained profit (reserves)		18,000

COMPANY ACCOUNTS AND CONSOLIDATED GROUP ACCOUNTS

P LTD AND S LTD CONSOLIDATED PROFIT AND LOSS ACCOUNT

		£'000	£'000
Net profit:	P Ltd	50,000	
	S Ltd	40,000	
			90,000
Taxation:	P Ltd	15,000	
	S Ltd	12,000	
			27,000
			63,000
Dividend			15,000
Reserves:	P Ltd	30,000	
	S Ltd	18,000	
			48,000

5.6.2.1 Effect on the consolidated balance sheet

The share capital of P Ltd will be shown, together with the increased reserves of P Ltd and the increase in reserves of S Ltd. This will be represented by the increased assets of P Ltd and S Ltd.

Example Consolidated balance sheet before the profit and loss accounts

		£'000	£'000
Fixed assets:	P Ltd	100,000	
	S Ltd	60,000	
			160,000
Net current assets:	P Ltd	65,000	
	S Ltd	25,000	
			90,000
			250,000
Share capital		200,000	
Reserves		50,000	
			250,000

COMPANY ACCOUNTS AND CONSOLIDATED GROUP ACCOUNTS

CONSOLIDATED BALANCE SHEET AFTER THE PROFIT AND LOSS ACCOUNTS

		£'000	£'000
Fixed assets:	P Ltd	100,000	
	S Ltd	60,000	
			160,000
Net current assets:	P Ltd	95,000	
	S Ltd	43,000	
			138,000
TOTAL			298,000
Share capital			200,000
Reserves:	P Ltd	80,000	
	S Ltd	18,000	
			98,000
TOTAL			298,000

5.6.3 WHERE A COMPANY HOLDS A MAJORITY INTEREST IN THE SUBSIDIARY

In these circumstances consolidated final accounts will still be required.

5.6.3.1 The balance sheet

This will show the whole of the subsidiary's assets and liabilities. The minority shareholders' interest will be shown as liabilities.

Example Company P Ltd has acquired 80% of the issued share capital of S Ltd: the balance sheets show:

P Ltd (parent company)

	£'000	£'000
Fixed assets	200,000	
80% of shares (reserves) in S Ltd at cost	80,000	
Net current assets	70,000	
		350,000
Share capital	300,000	
Reserves	50,000	
		350,000

149

COMPANY ACCOUNTS AND CONSOLIDATED GROUP ACCOUNTS

S Ltd (subsidiary company)

	£'000	£'000
Fixed assets	60,000	
Net current assets	40,000	
		100,000
Share capital	80,000	
Reserves	20,000	
		100,000

To consolidate the accounts the inter company shares figure must be excluded, i.e., £80,000,000. This is attributable to the share capital and reserves of S Ltd, i.e., it is made up of:

	£'000
80% of £80,000,000 share capital of S Ltd	64,000
80% of reserves of £20,000,000 of S Ltd	16,000
	80,000

Thus the amount of share capital and reserves attributable to the minority shareholders will be:

	£'000
Share capital	80,000
Less 80%	64,000
20%	16,000
Reserves	20,000
Less 80%	16,000
20%	4,000

The consolidated balance sheet will show:

		£'000	£'000
Fixed assets:	P Ltd	200,000	
	S Ltd	60,000	
			260,000
Net current assets:	P Ltd	70,000	
	S Ltd	40,000	
			110,000
Total assets less current liabilities			370,000
Less			
Interest of minority shareholders			
in S Ltd capital		16,000	
reserves		4,000	20,000
			350,000
Share capital		300,000	
Reserves		50,000	
			350,000

COMPANY ACCOUNTS AND CONSOLIDATED GROUP ACCOUNTS

5.6.3.2 **The profit and loss account where a company holds a majority of shares**

That part of the subsidiary's net profit after tax which belongs to the minority shareholders in respect of dividend and reserves will be deducted first, before appropriations are made for dividend and reserves.

Example Company P Ltd holds 80% of the share capital of S Ltd. The profit and loss accounts for P Ltd and S Ltd are as follows:

P Ltd (parent company)

	£'000	£'000
Net profit		90,000
Dividend from S Ltd		8,000
		98,000
Taxation, say		27,000
		71,000
Dividend		20,000
Reserves		51,000

S Ltd (subsidiary company)

	£'000	£'000
Net profit		40,000
Taxation		12,000
		28,000
Dividend: P Ltd	8,000	
Others	2,000	
		10,000
Reserves: P Ltd	14,400	
Others	3,600	
		18,000

Consolidated profit and loss account for P Ltd and S Ltd

	£'000	£'000
Net profit: P Ltd	90,000	
S Ltd	40,000	
		130,000
Taxation: P Ltd	27,000	
S Ltd	12,000	
		39,000
		91,000
Less minority interest		
Dividend	2,000	
Reserve	3,600	
		5,600
		85,400
Dividend		20,000
Reserves: P Ltd	51,000	
S Ltd	14,400	
		65,400

COMPANY ACCOUNTS AND CONSOLIDATED GROUP ACCOUNTS

5.7 Practice Exercises

1 Ball Limited owns all the shares in Chain Limited. The summarised profit and loss accounts and balance sheets for Ball and Chain drawn up on 30 September 200— are shown below. The balance sheets take into account retained profit (reserves) shown on the profit and loss account. Draw up the consolidated profit and loss account and the consolidated balance sheet for Ball Limited and Chain Limited.

BALL LIMITED
PROFIT AND LOSS ACCOUNT FOR THE YEAR ENDING 30 SEPTEMBER 200—

	£ '000	£ '000
Net profit	100,000	
Add dividend from Chain Limited	12,000	
	112,000	
Less taxation, say	30,000	
Profit after tax	82,000	
Dividend to Ball Limited's shareholders	20,000	
Reserves	62,000	

CHAIN LIMITED
PROFIT AND LOSS ACCOUNT FOR THE YEAR ENDING 30 SEPTEMBER 200—

	£ '000	£ '000
Net profit	44,000	
Less taxation	13,200	
Profit after tax	30,800	
Dividend to Ball Limited	12,000	
Reserves	18,800	

BALL LIMITED
BALANCE SHEET AS AT 30 SEPTEMBER 200—

	£ '000	£ '000
Fixed assets		300,000
Shares in Chain Limited at cost		89,000
Net current assets		192,000
TOTAL		581,000
Share capital		500,000
Reserves	19,000	
	62,000	
		81,000
TOTAL		581,000

CHAIN LIMITED
BALANCE SHEET AS AT 30 SEPTEMBER 200—

	£ '000	£ '000
Fixed assets		65,000
Net current assets		42,800
TOTAL		107,800
Share capital		80,000
Reserves	9,000	
This year's	18,800	
		27,800
TOTAL		107,800

2 Ash Limited has 80% of the share capital of Willow Limited. The summary balance sheets of the two companies are as follows:

ASH LIMITED BALANCE SHEET AS AT 30 NOVEMBER 200—

	£ '000	£ '000
Fixed assets		320,000
Shares in Willow Limited at cost		160,000
Net current assets		120,000
		600,000
Share capital		500,000
Reserves		100,000
		600,000

WILLOW LIMITED BALANCE SHEET AS AT 30 NOVEMBER 200—

	£ '000	£ '000
Fixed assets		150,000
Net current assets		50,000
		200,000
Share capital		180,000
Reserves		20,000
		200,000

Draw up the consolidated balance sheet for the two companies.

COMPANY ACCOUNTS AND CONSOLIDATED GROUP ACCOUNTS

5.8 Suggested Answers to Practice Exercises

1 Ball Limited

CONSOLIDATED PROFIT AND LOSS ACCOUNT FOR BALL LIMITED AND CHAIN LIMITED FOR THE YEAR ENDING 30 SEPTEMBER 200—

	£ '000	£ '000
Net profit: Ball Limited	100,000	
Chain Limited	44,000	
		144,000
Less taxation: Ball Limited	30,000	
Chain Limited	13,200	
		43,200
		100,800
Dividend to Ball Limited shareholders		20,000
Reserves: Ball Limited	62,000	
Chain Limited	18,800	
		80,800

CONSOLIDATED BALANCE SHEET FOR BALL LIMITED AND CHAIN LIMITED AS AT 30 SEPTEMBER 200—

	£ '000	£ '000
Fixed assets: Ball Limited	300,000	
Chain Limited	65,000	
		365,000
Net current assets: Ball Limited	192,000	
Chain Limited	42,800	
		234,800
		599,800
Share capital		500,000
Reserves: Ball Limited	19,000	
plus this year's	62,000	
	81,000	
Chain: increase in reserve	18,800	
		99,800
TOTAL		599,800

2 **Ash Limited**

CONSOLIDATED BALANCE SHEET FOR ASH LIMITED AND WILLOW LIMITED AS AT 30 NOVEMBER 200—

		£ '000	£ '000
Fixed assets:	Ash Limited	320,000	
	Willow Limited	150,000	
			470,000
Net current assets:	Ash Limited	120,000	
	Willow Limited	50,000	
			170,000
Total assets less current liabilities			640,000
Less interest of minority shareholders			
(being 20% of share capital		36,000	
20% of reserves)		4,000	
			40,000
TOTAL			600,000
Share capital		500,000	
Reserves		100,000	
TOTAL			600,000

SIX

INTERPRETATION OF ACCOUNTS AND ACCOUNTING RATIOS

6.1 Introduction

Accounts may be used by many different people, e.g., by the management of a business, by employees, by investors in the business, by shareholders, by long-term lenders or trade creditors or by the Government for taxation and statistics. Each of these may be looking for different things in the accounts. A creditor, for example, would want to make sure that the debt could be repaid, whereas a shareholder in the business may be looking for increasing profit, so that dividends will be higher, or may be looking for capital appreciation.

The interpretation of accounts can help to assess how a business is performing at present and can also enable inferences to be made about its future performance. The current level of profit may be compared with other similar businesses to see if it is satisfactory, and whether it can be improved. By looking at the accounts of a business over a number of years trends may be seen. A business may have sufficient assets to cover liabilities, but if these are tied up in fixed assets, or stock which is not selling, or work in progress, or debtors who are unlikely to pay, it may not be able to pay its current liabilities.

You may wonder whether you need to know about interpretation of accounts at all. Why not leave it to the accountants? One good reason is that, as a sole practitioner or as a partner, the accounts will explain the profit due to you. It is not a good idea to leave the understanding of accounts to your accountants or to one or two of the other partners. You will not be able to make informed decisions about the business where necessary, for example, whether to retain staff, or take on more staff, or change the type of work done by the firm. Understanding accounts will also be necessary where you are dealing with commercial work; even where accountants are involved, you should have at least some idea of the advice given. You may be asked to give advice on proposed investments suggested by a stockbroker for a client or, for example, a trust in which you are a trustee. Note that there may be financial services implications here. There are few areas of work today where an understanding of accounts will not be needed.

6.2 Check Factors Outside the Accounts

To interpret accounts, ratio analysis may be used, as ratios can be used to compare performances from year to year and to compare different companies. Take care, however, as

INTERPRETATION OF ACCOUNTS AND ACCOUNTING RATIOS

reading the accounts and looking at ratios on their own will not provide sufficient information about a company; other information should be sought as well. A company may have been doing very well, but may have just lost its managing director, or industrial action may be threatened by its workforce. The business may possibly have been involved in an area which has now expanded to saturation point, and the market may no longer be there. A business should be compared with others of a similar type, i.e., dealing with the same services or products and of a similar size. If profits are disappointing there may be a recession generally. Are the markets for the business still there? Is there increased competition, e.g., from abroad?

6.3 General Areas to Look At

When accounts are looked at, absolute changes may be found, e.g., is this year's profit more than last year's, have the expenses of the business gone up? Relative changes should also be found, e.g., what are the expenses of the business as a percentage of the turnover or sales? What is the profit as a percentage of the sales? How much profit has been generated from the capital employed (i.e., total assets less current liabilities)? The business may have invested heavily in fixed assets, but profit may have gone up by only a modest amount.

6.3.1 ACCOUNTS FOR PAST YEARS

In interpreting accounts, the accounts for the last few years should be looked at as these should establish general trends. It should be noted that the figures shown on the accounts may not always be accurate. The business may be overstating the value of its assets. Examples may include stock or work in progress. If stock is valued at cost price, rather than its sale price, this may sound reasonable, but the stock may not have been sold for some time, and it may be necessary to sell the stock at a lower price than that shown on the balance sheet. How work in progress is valued should be checked — is this based on an accurate time recording system, or does it involve some guesswork? Other assets shown may be falling in value, e.g., office furniture, office equipment, and it is important that sufficient provision for depreciation has been made. If the business has freehold premises shown at cost price then the present value should be checked.

The figure for debtors (an asset) may be high, but if this is in respect of one or two debtors who are in trouble themselves, the debts may not be paid. Check that sufficient provision has been made for bad debts and doubtful debts.

There may also be changes in circumstances. A company may have just employed a new managing director who has a reputation as a troubleshooter, able to improve companies with poor performance. Thus in future years profit may go up dramatically.

It is also worth reading the information supplied by a company and the notes attached to the accounts.

There are two main areas that will be looked at in any analysis:

(a) The solvency or liquidity of the business.

(b) The profitability of the business.

6.4 Trends

Figures over the years may be compared, e.g., the profit over the last five years may show a general trend up, even though there may be the odd year when profit has fallen. Has the turnover increased? Have expenses increased?

INTERPRETATION OF ACCOUNTS AND ACCOUNTING RATIOS

6.5 Ratios

These will be calculated from a set of accounts for a year, but can then be compared with other years.

6.5.1 LIQUIDITY RATIOS

Liquidity means the ability of a business to pay its short-term debts. This is not the same as solvency, which means the ability of the business to pay all its liabilities. A firm may have sufficient assets to pay all its liabilities, but will still not be able to pay off short-term liabilities because it has insufficient cash or easily realisable assets.

6.5.1.1 The current assets ratio

$$\frac{\text{Current assets}}{\text{Current liabilities}}$$

This compares current assets with current liabilities. There should normally be enough current assets to cover current liabilities. The comparison is between assets which should be converted into cash in approximately 12 months; with liabilities which will be due for payment within the same 12 months. What is a satisfactory figure will vary with the type of business or with the reputation of the business. For example:

$$\frac{\text{Current assets}}{\text{Current liabilities}} \quad \frac{40{,}000}{20{,}000} = 2:1 \quad \text{('000)}$$

This would be a satisfactory ratio.

For example:

$$\frac{\text{Current assets}}{\text{Current liabilities}} \quad \frac{30{,}000}{20{,}000} = 1.5:1$$

Again this may be an acceptable ratio.

A very high figure may not mean that the business is safe and it is essential to look behind the figures. The company may have overvalued its current assets, e.g., the stock (or work in progress). Generally, if the ratio is less than 1 : 1, there may be a problem.

Where, however, the company has a bank overdraft and the bank is prepared to allow the overdraft to continue long term, this may then be treated as a long-term liability instead of a short-term liability and thus can be left out of the ratio. This will clearly improve the ratio.

6.5.1.2 The acid test

This ratio uses only cash or assets which can be converted quickly into cash, thus stock or work in progress will be excluded from the figure for current assets.

$$\frac{\text{Current assets less stock (or work in progress)}}{\text{Current liabilities}}$$

If this is 1 : 1 or better then the company will have sufficient liquid assets to meet its current liabilities: this is provided that the creditors are paid and debtors pay at approximately the

INTERPRETATION OF ACCOUNTS AND ACCOUNTING RATIOS

same time. Sometimes an even stricter test is used, that of measuring cash as against current liabilities. If debtors have been included in the ratio then, to check how fast debts will be paid, another ratio can be used; see **6.5.2**.

6.5.2 THE AVERAGE COLLECTION PERIOD — TRADE DEBTORS TO SALES RATIO

To find the length of time in days that debtors will pay debts, the following formula is used:

$$\frac{\text{Trade debtors}}{\text{Sales}} \times 365 \quad \text{or for solicitors' use} \quad \frac{\text{Debtors}}{\text{Profit costs}} \times 365$$

> **Example** Sales are £200,000 for the year and trade debtors are £10,000.
>
> $$\frac{£10,000}{£200,000} \times 365 = 18.25 \text{ days}$$
>
> If, e.g., sales are £200,000 for the year and trade debtors are £40,000:
>
> $$\frac{£40,000}{£200,000} \times 365 = 73 \text{ days}$$

The ratio may not accurately reflect the length of time allowed to debtors. If, for example, sales had been strong just before the balance sheet was drawn up, this may give a high debtors figure, which would distort the ratio, making it appear that the length of credit given was much longer, as in the second example.

If the length of time allowed for debtors to pay is too long, then steps should be taken to tighten up debt collection. It is usual for a business to allow a specified length of time for debtors to pay the amount due before action is taken by the business. This time should be compared with the actual time which the debtors are taking. Whether the time has increased from previous years will need to be checked, as will the times for other similar businesses. It may also be advisable to check the individual debts to see how long each one has been outstanding. Some of them may be irrecoverable.

To check how quickly the business pays its creditors, a similar ratio is used; see **6.5.3**.

6.5.3 THE AVERAGE PAYMENT PERIOD — TRADE CREDITORS TO PURCHASES RATIO

$$\frac{\text{Trade creditors}}{\text{Purchases}} \times 365$$

If purchases for the year are £90,000 and trade creditors are £20,000:

$$\frac{£20,000}{£90,000} \times 365 = 81.1 \text{ days}$$

Again this should be compared with previous years, with similar businesses, and the length of time that creditors allow for payment. Note that a business may deliberately delay payment of creditors for as long as reasonably possible. Large companies in particular may do this as they have stronger bargaining power than their smaller creditors. If the period has dramatically increased, it may be that the business is having difficulty in paying its bills. However, a

INTERPRETATION OF ACCOUNTS AND ACCOUNTING RATIOS

large figure for creditors may just be due to an increase in purchases just before the date of the balance sheet, and this may have been in anticipation of increased sales, or to buy in before prices are increased.

6.5.4 SHORTAGE OF WORKING CAPITAL

Working capital or net current assets is that portion of capital left to run the business after providing for fixed assets. A business needs to pay out money to run the business, e.g., paying salaries and other expenses, or buying goods or services, before receiving payment itself for the goods or services it provides. How much will be needed will vary. It may be that credit is given on purchases: if this is a longer period than the time in which the business collects its own debts, then not as much working capital will be required. The amount of working capital will need to increase if there is inflation, as expenses will increase. If the business wishes to expand then again more working capital will be required. Reserve funds based on retained profit (see **5.2.6**) can be used to finance the increased requirement. If this is not possible then the business will have to raise funds by issuing more shares, or borrowing.

If a business runs short of working capital then it will have insufficient funds to meet its short-term liabilities, and may not be able to take advantage of, e.g., discounts for prompt payment. It may also have to offer discounts itself to customers for prompt payment.

Indications of a shortage of working capital may be found from using the following ratios:

6.5.4.1 The working capital ratio

$$\frac{\text{Net current assets (working capital)}}{\text{Sales (or use profit costs for solicitors)}}$$

> **Example** A company has net current assets of £20,000 and sales are £200,000. The working capital ratio is:
>
> $$\frac{20,000}{200,000} = 0.1 : 1$$
>
> If net current assets were still £20,000 and sales were £400,000 then the ratio would be 0.05 : 1, clearly a lower ratio.

6.5.4.2 The ratio between debtors and creditors

$$\frac{\text{Debtors}}{\text{Creditors}}$$

If this ratio falls then again it may be a sign of overtrading. There may also be a shortage of cash. If the company is unable to find more capital to finance working capital, through borrowing or from the shareholders, then it may have to sell fixed assets, and lease instead, although there may be disadvantages in doing this.

Alternatively the business may be able to reduce the requirement for working capital, by ensuring that stock or work in progress is kept to a minimum and that debtors pay quickly, thereby releasing cash to use in the business.

If the company has over-expanded, i.e., sales have increased too fast, it may be necessary to halt the expansion.

INTERPRETATION OF ACCOUNTS AND ACCOUNTING RATIOS

6.5.5 PROFITABILITY RATIOS

6.5.5.1 Return on capital employed

This is the most important ratio in relation to profitability, for those who invest in the business it shows the rate of return on the capital used in the business. If net assets of the business are £2,000,000 and the profit is £20,000 then the return is only 1%, which is too low; as an investment the money would be better used elsewhere.

The ratio is:

$$\frac{\text{Operating profit (before interest and tax)}}{\text{Capital employed (total assets less current liabilities)}} \times 100\%$$

$$\frac{£20,000}{£2,000,000} \times 100\% = 1\%$$

The figure taken for profit is before tax and interest. If the figure was taken after interest on debentures, loans and overdrafts, the return on assets would be understated. Any interest received should also be excluded from the calculation, to ensure that the profit shown is that made by operations.

A problem with this particular ratio is that the capital employed is measured at the date of the balance sheet. This may be misleading if, for example, the company has recently increased its capital to fund expansion, by purchasing fixed assets, which have not yet created any increased profit. The figure for capital employed could be taken from the balance sheet at the end of the year, or at the start of the year, or an average of the figure at the start of the year and the figure at the end of the year.

Even if the return is satisfactory, it should be looked at with caution. The true value of the assets on the balance sheet should be checked. They may have been undervalued, e.g., premises may have been shown at cost price.

The ratio may also be adjusted in respect of a bank overdraft. If this is effectively long-term lending, it should be included in the figure for capital employed, i.e., added back.

$$\frac{\text{Operating profit (before taxation and interest)}}{\text{Total assets less current liabilities + overdraft}} \times 100\%$$

6.5.5.2 The gross profit percentage

$$\frac{\text{Gross profit}}{\text{Sales}} \times 100\%$$

This shows the profitability of the sales. Even if sales have increased, this does not necessarily mean that the gross profit has increased.

Example Year 1 $\quad \dfrac{30,000}{125,000} \times 100\% = 24\%$

Example Year 2 $\quad \dfrac{40,000}{200,000} \times 100\% = 20\%$

INTERPRETATION OF ACCOUNTS AND ACCOUNTING RATIOS

Although the sales and the gross profit have increased in year 2, it should be noted that the gross profit percentage is lower. If the gross profit percentage has fallen this may be because:

(a) the cost of goods sold has increased, but that selling prices have not been increased by an equivalent amount;

(b) sale prices have been reduced in order to sell more goods;

(c) if different types of goods have been sold, profit margins on some goods may be greater than on other goods.

6.5.5.3 Net profit percentage

$$\frac{\text{Operating or trading profit before interest and tax}}{\text{Sales}} \times 100\%$$

or for solicitors' use $\quad \dfrac{\text{Net profit}}{\text{Profit costs}} \times 100\%$

Both this ratio and the ratio in **6.5.5.2** will vary, depending on the type of business being carried out. As with all ratios they should be compared with similar businesses. Some businesses operate with a very low profit margin, relying on a large turnover.

If the gross profit ratio has remained the same, but the net profit ratio has fallen, then the expenses must have increased.

Each type of expense can be compared with the sales figure, for the current year and previous years, to find whether the increase is general or limited to a particular area.

> **Example** $\quad \dfrac{\text{Marketing costs}}{\text{Sales}} \times 100\%$
>
> $\dfrac{\text{Administrative expenses}}{\text{Sales}} \times 100\%$

6.5.6 EFFICIENCY RATIO — RATE OF STOCK TURNOVER

The faster stock is turned over, or sold, the more profit will be made, provided the gross profit percentage stays the same. There are two ratios which may be used to find stock turnover:

(a) either divide stocks by sales:

$$\frac{\text{Stocks (based on the selling price)}}{\text{Sales}}$$

> **Example** If stock was £80,000 and sales were £700,000 the ratio would be:
>
> $\dfrac{80,000}{700,000} = 0.114$ or every 41.7 days

INTERPRETATION OF ACCOUNTS AND ACCOUNTING RATIOS

(b) or probably the better ratio, divide cost of goods sold by average stock:

$$\frac{\text{Cost of goods sold (sales at cost price)}}{\text{Average stock (at cost)}}$$

As you will not have the detailed accounts of the business to find average stock, use the average of the opening and closing stock:

Example If opening stock was £50,000 and closing stock was £80,000 then the average would be:

$$\frac{50,000 + 80,000}{2} = 65,000$$

If the cost of goods sold was £450,000 then the stock turnover would be:

$$\frac{450,000}{65,000} = 6.92 \text{ times per year, i.e., stock is turned over 6.92 times per year, or every 52.75 days}$$

The rate of stock turnover will vary, depending on the type of stock being carried. Although a fast rate of stock turnover should lead to increased profit, the business must be careful to have enough stock at any given time to meet demand.

If the rate of stock turnover has fallen then the business should check whether it is carrying too much stock, or whether sales have decreased generally.

After analysing the profitability of the business, it may be that profitability is satisfactory, or it may be considered that there is room for improvement. The business may attempt to reduce expenses, or increase prices or sales, to improve profitability. Increasing prices may not be the best solution, as customers may decide to go somewhere cheaper. If sales are to be increased the business will have to work more efficiently, or expect its workforce to work harder. It may be that the business decides to reduce its workforce but expects them to retain the same level of sales. Increased sales will be possible only if the market for those goods is there.

6.5.7 CAPITAL GEARING RATIOS

Gearing relates to the capital structure of the company, the relationship between the capital provided by shareholders and the capital provided by borrowing. A high-geared company is one which has a high proportion of borrowing. A company with low gearing has most of its funds provided by the ordinary shareholder. The ratios used may be calculated in different ways.

6.5.7.1 A commonly used ratio

$$\frac{\text{Preference shares + long-term loans}}{\text{All shareholders funds + long-term loans}} \times 100\%$$

> **Example 1** A company has share capital and long-term borrowings as follows:
>
> | | £— |
> |---|---|
> | Ordinary share capital | 100 |
> | Reserves | 50 |
> | 7% preference shares | 10 |
> | 12% debentures | 30 |
> | | 190 |
>
> $$\frac{10 + 30}{190} \times 100 = 21.05\%$$

> **Example 2** A company has share capital and long-term borrowings as follows:
>
> | | £— |
> |---|---|
> | Ordinary share capital | 80 |
> | Reserves | 20 |
> | Preference shares | 10 |
> | Debentures | 40 |
> | | 150 |
>
> $$\frac{10 + 40}{150} \times 100 = 33.33\%$$

The second company is a higher geared company than the first company.

If a company is highly geared, then any change in the profits will affect the shareholders more than in a low-geared company, as the interest on the borrowing will have to be paid before any dividend is available to the ordinary shareholders. The company will be susceptible to changes in interest rates, e.g., if these increase substantially. The borrowing will also have to be repaid at some stage. If the company requires additional capital to expand the business it may be better to do this through increasing the share capital.

6.5.7.2 An alternative ratio

Another ratio is the ratio of borrowings to shareholders' funds.

> **Example** If borrowing is £200,000 and shareholders' funds are £500,000 then the ratio will be:
>
> | | £ |
> |---|---|
> | Borrowing: | 200,000 |
> | Shareholders' funds | 500,000 |
> | Gearing | 2 : 5 |

INTERPRETATION OF ACCOUNTS AND ACCOUNTING RATIOS

6.5.8 INVESTMENT RATIOS

An investor will be concerned with the profitability of a business, and whether the investment will give a good return.

6.5.8.1 The return on capital employed ratio

This ratio, shown previously, can be used.

$$\frac{\text{Net profit (before interest and tax)}}{\text{Capital employed}} \times 100\%$$

6.5.8.2 Return on ordinary shareholders' interest

The return on capital employed shows only the return before tax and interest. An ordinary shareholder will want to know what the return is after payment of interest and tax, and after payment of any preference shares dividends.

$$\frac{\text{Net profit after interest, tax and preference share dividend}}{\text{Ordinary shareholders' interest (ordinary share capital plus any reserves attributable to them)}} \times 100\%$$

6.5.8.3 Earnings per share

This will show the return per single share, in money.

$$\frac{\text{Net profit after interest, tax and preference share dividend}}{\text{Number of ordinary shares}}$$

This is an important ratio and FRS14 requires limited companies to show the earnings per share in the published accounts.

However, this figure will not be the amount that the shareholder receives per share — the amount received will be the dividend declared by the directors. As we have seen in **5.2.6**, part of the profit will often be transferred to reserves and, although these belong to the shareholders, they may not be available for distribution.

6.5.8.4 Dividend yield

This is the annual return by way of dividend based on an investment of £100 in the shares at the current price. If, e.g., the shares cost £2.00 each, then 50 shares could be purchased for £100. If the dividend was 10p per share, then the total would be £5.00, giving a dividend yield of 5%.

6.5.8.5 Dividend cover

$$\frac{\text{Earnings per share}}{\text{Dividend per share}}$$

This shows the proportion of earnings distributed against the proportion retained by way of reserves.

INTERPRETATION OF ACCOUNTS AND ACCOUNTING RATIOS

> **Example** If net profit after tax and any preference share dividend was £8,000,000 and the number of ordinary shares was 4,000,000, then the earnings per share would be £2.00. If the dividend was £2,000,000, then the dividend per share would be 50p.
>
> $$\frac{2.00}{.50} = 4 \text{ times}$$

An alternative way of showing this would be:

$$\frac{\text{Net profit after tax and preference share dividend}}{\text{Dividend to ordinary shareholders}}$$

Continuing the above example:

> $$\frac{8,000,000}{2,000,000} = 4 \text{ times}$$

This shows that the dividend is covered four times by the profit earned, after tax and the preference share dividend. The higher this is, the more the company is reinvesting its profits in the business.

The amount retained will not only increase the underlying value of the shares but ensure that dividends can be paid if in any future year there is insufficient net profit available.

6.5.8.6 Price earnings ratio (PE ratio)

Once the earnings per share has been calculated, the actual earnings based on the present market price of the share (where applicable), rather than the value at which the share was issued, can be calculated.

$$\frac{\text{Market price per share}}{\text{Earnings per share}}$$

E.g. $\dfrac{£2.00}{.20} = 10$

This means that the investor has to pay £2.00 to get the benefit of earnings of 20p per annum — 10 times the year's earnings have been paid, or 10 years' purchase of earnings.

When the market is convinced that the future earnings of a company are going to increase, the market price of the shares may go up. The price earnings ratio will therefore be higher. If the market is convinced that future earnings are not going to be as good, then the price of the shares may go down, and the PE ratio will be lower. However, PE ratios will vary depending on the type of business being carried out.

If a takeover bid is rumoured in respect of the company then the value of the shares may well go up, which will lead to a high PE ratio.

INTERPRETATION OF ACCOUNTS AND ACCOUNTING RATIOS

If a PE ratio for a company is higher than other companies in a similar business, it may be that the company is highly regarded, or possibly that the shares are overvalued. A lower PE ratio may mean that the company is not highly regarded, or possibly that the shares are undervalued.

6.6 Example

DILLEY TANTE LIMITED
PROFIT AND LOSS ACCOUNTS FOR THE YEAR ENDING

	31 Dec 2000	31 Dec 2001
	£ '000	£ '000
Sales	800,000	1,200,000
Less cost of sales	500,000	700,000
Gross profit	300,000	500,000
Less expenses	132,000	240,000
Loan interest	8,000	40,000
Profit before tax	160,000	220,000
Taxation say	40,000	55,000
Profit after tax	120,000	165,000
Dividends	30,000	40,000
Retained profit	90,000	125,000

DILLEY TANTE LIMITED
BALANCE SHEET AS AT 31 DECEMBER

	2000	2001
	£ '000	£ '000
Fixed assets		
Tangible assets	810,000	960,000
Current assets		
Stock	80,000	175,000
Debtors	50,000	110,000
Cash	10,000	5,000
	140,000	290,000
Creditors:		
Amounts falling due within one year	80,000	80,000
Net current assets	60,000	210,000
Total assets less current liabilities	870,000	1,170,000
Creditors:		
Amounts falling due after more than one year		
Loans and other borrowings	50,000	225,000
	820,000	945,000

INTERPRETATION OF ACCOUNTS AND ACCOUNTING RATIOS

	2000	2001
Capital and reserves		
Called up share capital		
Ordinary £1 shares	600,000	600,000
Profit and loss account		
Retained profit	220,000	345,000
	820,000	945,000

Ratios
Liquidity

Current ratio '000 '000

$$\frac{\text{Current assets}}{\text{Current liabilities}} \qquad \frac{140,000}{80,000} = 1.75 \text{ to } 1 \qquad \frac{290,000}{80,000} = 3.625 \text{ to } 1$$

The liquidity ratio or the acid test

$$\frac{\text{Current assets less stock}}{\text{Current liabilities}} \qquad \frac{60,000}{80,000} = 0.75 \text{ to } 1 \qquad \frac{115,000}{80,000} = 1.438 \text{ to } 1$$

The average collection period – debtors to sales ratio

$$\frac{\text{Debtors}}{\text{Sales}} \times 365 \qquad \frac{50,000}{800,000} \times 365 = 22.8 \text{ days} \qquad \frac{110,000}{1,200,000} \times 365 = 33.46 \text{ days}$$

The average payment period – creditors to purchases ratio

$$\frac{\text{Creditors}}{\text{Purchases}} \times 365 \qquad \frac{80,000}{500,000} \times 365 \qquad \frac{80,000}{700,000} \times 365$$

Note: no purchases figure shown
Cost of sales taken as an approximation = 58.4 days   = 41.7 days

The working capital ratio

$$\frac{\text{Net current assets (working capital)}}{\text{Sales}} \qquad \frac{60,000}{800,000} = 0.075 \text{ to } 1 \qquad \frac{210,000}{1,200,000} = 0.175 \text{ to } 1$$

The ratio between debtors and creditors

$$\frac{\text{Debtors}}{\text{Creditors}} \qquad \frac{50,000}{80,000} = 0.625 \text{ to } 1 \qquad \frac{110,000}{80,000} = 1.375 \text{ to } 1$$

INTERPRETATION OF ACCOUNTS AND ACCOUNTING RATIOS

Return on capital employed

$$\frac{\text{Operating profit (before tax and interest)}}{\text{Capital employed (total assets less current liabilities)}} \times 100\%$$

$$\frac{168{,}000}{870{,}000} \times 100\% \qquad \frac{260{,}000}{1{,}170{,}000} \times 100\%$$
$$= 19.31\% \qquad = 22.22\%$$

The gross profit percentage

$$\frac{\text{Gross profit}}{\text{Sales}} \qquad \frac{300{,}000}{800{,}000} \times 100\% \qquad \frac{500{,}000}{1{,}200{,}000} \times 100\%$$
$$= 37.5\% \qquad = 41.67\%$$

The net profit percentage

$$\frac{\text{Operating or trading profit before interest and tax}}{\text{Sales}} \times 100\%$$

$$\frac{168{,}000}{800{,}000} \times 100\% \qquad \frac{260{,}000}{1{,}200{,}000} \times 100\%$$
$$= 21\% \qquad = 21.67\%$$

Rate of stock turnover

$$\frac{\text{Stocks}}{\text{Sales}} \qquad \frac{80{,}000}{800{,}000} \qquad \frac{175{,}000}{1{,}200{,}000}$$
$$0.1 \quad 36.5 \text{ days} \qquad 0.146 \quad 53.29 \text{ days}$$

Capital gearing

$$\frac{\text{Preference shares + long-term liabilities}}{\text{Capital employed}} \times 100\%$$

$$\frac{50{,}000}{870{,}000} \times 100\% \qquad \frac{225{,}000}{1{,}170{,}000} \times 100\%$$
$$= 0.057 \text{ to } 1 \qquad = 0.192 \text{ to } 1$$

or $\qquad\qquad\qquad\qquad\qquad 5.7\% \qquad\qquad\qquad 19.2\%$

Return on ordinary shareholders' interest

$$\frac{\text{Net profit after interest, tax and preference share dividend}}{\text{Ordinary shareholders' interest}} \times 100\%$$

$$\frac{120{,}000}{820{,}000} \times 100\% \qquad \frac{165{,}000}{945{,}000} \times 100\%$$
$$= 14.63\% \qquad = 17.46\%$$

Earnings per share

$$\frac{\text{Net profit after interest, tax and preference share dividend}}{\text{Number of ordinary shares}}$$

$$\frac{120{,}000}{600{,}000} \qquad \frac{165{,}000}{600{,}000}$$
$$= 20\text{p} \qquad = 27.5\text{p}$$

Dividend cover

$$\frac{\text{Net profit after tax, etc.}}{\text{Dividend to ordinary shareholders}} \qquad \frac{120{,}000}{30{,}000} \qquad \frac{165{,}000}{40{,}000}$$
$$= 4 \text{ times} \qquad = 4.125 \text{ times}$$

INTERPRETATION OF ACCOUNTS AND ACCOUNTING RATIOS

Comment

Liquidity: the current ratio was acceptable in 2000 at 1.75 to 1. In 2001 it increased to 3.625 to 1 as current assets, particularly stock and debtors, have increased dramatically, but creditors have remained the same. Clearly sales have increased, but the rate of stock turnover has reduced from 36.5 days to 53.29 days. This should be checked; also debtors should be checked to make sure that these will pay. Funding has come from increased long-term borrowing, now £225,000,000 instead of £50,000,000. Presumably the company has decided to increase turnover. The liquidity or acid test again shows an improvement from a rather weak 0.75 to 1 to an acceptable 1.438 to 1.

Given the high debtors figure, the average collection period has increased from 22.8 days to 33.46 days. This should be looked at with care and possibly steps taken to ensure that debtors pay within a set time.

The average payment period shown is an approximation; seemingly this has improved from 58.4 days to 41.7 days.

The working capital ratio has again improved, showing more working capital as mentioned above. The ratio of debtors to creditors has increased.

Return on capital employed has improved from 19.31% to 22.22%. There is also an improvement in the gross profit percentage. However, the net profit percentage has not improved much, i.e., from 21% to 21.67%. Expenses have increased, in particular the loan interest on the increased borrowing.

As mentioned previously, the rate of stock turnover has slowed and this should be looked at.

Given the increased long-term borrowing the gearing is now higher at 19.2% instead of the very low 5.7%. However, this is still not a high-geared company.

The return on ordinary shareholders' interest has improved as have earnings per share. Dividend cover remains approximately the same.

Clearly a decision was made to increase borrowing to invest in the company. Perhaps a further year is needed to consolidate.

6.7 Exercise

Below are shown the accounts of Perry and Mason for the year ending 30 November 2001.

PERRY AND MASON
PROFIT AND LOSS ACCOUNT FOR THE YEAR ENDING 30 NOVEMBER 2001

Income	£	£	£
Profit costs	300,000		
Add work in progress at 30 Nov 2001	50,000		
	350,000		
Less work in progress at 1 December 2000	40,000		
Work done			310,000
Interest received			4,000
			314,000

INTERPRETATION OF ACCOUNTS AND ACCOUNTING RATIOS

Less expenses				
General and administrative expenses including staff wages		210,000		
Add outstanding expenses		920		
		210,920		
Less payments in advance		1,040		
		209,880		
Travelling expenses		1,000		
Depreciation: library, furniture and equipment		7,000		
			217,880	
Net profit				96,120
Appropriation account				
Interest on capital at 5%	Perry	8,500		
	Mason	6,000		
			14,500	
Profit share	Perry	40,810		
	Mason	40,810		
			81,620	
				96,120

PERRY AND MASON
BALANCE SHEET AS AT 30 NOVEMBER 2001

FIXED ASSETS			
Freehold premises		240,000	
Library furniture and equipment	35,000		
Less depreciation	14,000		
		21,000	
			261,000
CURRENT ASSETS			
Work in progress	50,000		
Debtors	60,000		
Petty cash	360		
Payments in advance	1,040		
		111,400	
LESS CURRENT LIABILITIES			
Creditors	10,000		
Outstanding expenses	920		
Bank overdraft	35,000		
		45,920	
NET CURRENT ASSETS			65,480
			326,480
LESS LONG-TERM LIABILITIES			—
			326,480

INTERPRETATION OF ACCOUNTS AND ACCOUNTING RATIOS

```
CAPITAL EMPLOYED
Capital accounts:
    Perry                                    170,000
    Mason                                    120,000
                                             -------
                                                                    290,000

Current accounts: see movement on current accounts:
    Perry                                     22,310
    Mason                                     14,170
                                             -------
                                                                     36,480
                                                                    -------
                                                                    326,480
                                                                    -------

Client account
Cash at the bank client account
    Current account                          190,510
    Deposit account                          266,380
                                             -------
                                                       456,890
Amount due to clients                                  456,890

Movement on current accounts
                                              Perry     Mason
Interest on capital                           8,500     6,000
Profit share                                 40,810    40,810
                                             ------    ------
                                             49,310    46,810
Less drawings                                27,000    32,640
                                             ------    ------
                                             22,310    14,170
                                             ------    ------
```

From these calculate:

(a) the current ratio;

(b) the acid test;

(c) the net profit percentage;

(d) the average collection period;

(e) the return on capital employed.

Comment on these ratios and on the accounts themselves. How relevant is the return on capital employed ratio? What suggestions would you have for the partners, who are concerned at the overdraft and would like to draw out more cash if possible. What further information would you ask for?

6.8 Suggested Answer to Exercise

The current ratio

$$\frac{\text{Current assets}}{\text{Current liabilities}} \qquad \frac{111,400}{45,920} = 2.43 \text{ to } 1$$

INTERPRETATION OF ACCOUNTS AND ACCOUNTING RATIOS

The acid test

$$\frac{\text{Current assets less work in progress}}{\text{Current liabilities}} \qquad \frac{61{,}400}{45{,}920} = 1.34 \text{ to } 1$$

The net profit percentage

$$\frac{\text{Net profit}}{\text{Profit costs}} \qquad \frac{96{,}120}{300{,}000} \times 100 = 32.04\%$$

The average collection period

$$\frac{\text{Debtors}}{\text{Profit costs}} \qquad \frac{60{,}000}{300{,}000} \times 365 = 73 \text{ days}$$

The return on capital employed

$$\frac{\text{Net profit}}{\text{Capital employed}} \times 100 \qquad \frac{96{,}120}{326{,}480} \times 100 = 29.44\%$$

The current ratio measures the short-term financial position of the firm. Here clearly there are sufficient current assets to cover current liabilities, a ratio of 2.43 to 1 is good. The acid test is also satisfactory at 1.34 to 1. However, the figures for work in progress and debtors are high; there is no cash at the bank. The value of work in progress should be checked, and bills should be sent out. Debtors should also be checked. There may be some debtors that have been outstanding for a long time, some of these may be irrecoverable, and provision for doubtful debts should be checked. Debtors should be chased, and much tighter control exerted over the length of time that they are taking to pay — see the average collection period of 73 days. However, if a large number of bills were sent out just before the balance sheet was drawn up this would distort the period calculated.

The net profit percentage at 32.04% may be reasonable, but previous years should be checked, and comparison made, if possible, with similar firms.

The return on capital employed is not very useful in a partnership, as account must be taken of the partners' work — notional salaries could be taken to give a more accurate ratio. The partners have provided for interest on capital as part of the appropriation of profit.

Note that the profit is not cash, and the partners must solve the cash flow problem. Provided that the work in progress figure is realistic, and that the bulk of the debtors are able to pay, this should be possible — see above. It is also possible that the bank is happy to continue financing the firm by way of an overdraft, when the overdraft could be treated as long-term lending. However, given the work in progress and debtors, this would not seem to be necessary, and the firm will save interest charges, etc. if they manage to convert these assets into cash.

As mentioned above, previous years' accounts would be helpful to establish any trends. Is the firm checking bad debts, provision, etc.? What are other similar firms doing? The value of the premises should be checked — is this the correct value, or has it increased or decreased? Should the partners consider sale/leaseback or do they regard this as investment for the future? Any new partner coming in would have to fund this, if, e.g., one of the existing partners left. How old are the partners? Possibly check expenses; can these be reduced?

SEVEN

BASIC SOLICITORS' ACCOUNTS

7.1 Introduction

You should have a thorough understanding of the Solicitors' Accounts Rules 1998. These rules should have been implemented by 1 May 2000.

7.1.1 DUTY TO KEEP ACCOUNTS

A solicitor has a duty to keep accounts to record transactions involving clients' money. The accounts and all bank statements must be preserved for a minimum period of six years from the date of the last entry in the case of accounts, or from the date of issue by the bank in the case of bank statements (r. 32(9) of the Solicitors' Accounts Rules 1998). Where a computerised system is used the solicitor must ensure that a hard copy can be produced reasonably quickly and that it remains capable of reproduction for at least six years.

In addition, all paid cheques and copies of authorities for withdrawal of money from a client account must be retained for at least two years. To avoid the practical problems associated with storage, there is provision in the rules for the solicitor to obtain written confirmation from the bank that it will retain cheques for the required two-year period.

Under Rule 35, solicitors who hold client money or controlled trust money during an accounting period must have their client accounts inspected by an accountant 'qualified' within the meaning of the rules, and must submit an accountant's report to the Law Society for that accounting period within six months of the end of the accounting period.

The Law Society has the power to appoint an accountant to investigate a solicitor's practice.

7.2 The Solicitors' Accounts Rules 1998 (SAR)

7.2.1 BASIC PRINCIPLES RULE 1

This rule gives the principles which underpin the SAR.

Solicitors must:

(a) comply with the requirements of practice rule 1 re the solicitor's integrity, the duty to act in the client's best interests, and the good repute of the solicitor and the profession;

(b) keep other people's money separate from money belonging to the solicitor or the practice;

BASIC SOLICITORS' ACCOUNTS

(c) keep other people's money safely in a bank or building society account identifiable as a client account (except where the rules specifically provide otherwise);

(d) use each client's money for the client's matters only;

(e) use controlled trust money for the purposes of that trust only;

(f) establish and maintain proper accounting systems, and proper internal controls over those systems, to ensure compliance with the rules;

(g) keep proper accounting records to show accurately the position with regard to the money held for each client and each controlled trust;

(h) account for interest on other people's money in accordance with the rules;

(i) cooperate with the Law Society in checking compliance with the rules; and

(j) deliver annual accountant's reports as required by the rules.

7.2.2 KEEPING CLIENTS' AND OFFICE MONEY SEPARATE

Solicitors must keep money belonging to clients (clients' money) separate from their own money (office money). This necessitates having at least two separate accounts at the bank or building society, the client bank account and the office bank account. The rules define a client account as a current or deposit account at a bank or a deposit account at a building society in the name of the solicitor, the solicitor's firm or recognised body, in the title of which the word 'client' appears.

It follows that the solicitor must also have two cash accounts in the ledger system: the office cash account and the client cash account. For convenience these two are shown side by side, as follows:

CASH ACCOUNT

Date	Details	Office account			Client account		
		Dr £	Cr £	Balance £	Dr £	Cr £	Balance £

Each client ledger card will also show that there are two accounts:

SMITH: RE CONVEYANCING

Date	Details	Office account			Client account		
		Dr £	Cr £	Balance £	Dr £	Cr £	Balance £

Although the money for all clients will, as a general rule, be kept in one bank account, the solicitor must record separately in respect of each client the money which is being held for that client. This means that the solicitor must not use money belonging to one client for the purposes of another client, nor may the solicitor transfer the money of one client from that client's ledger account to the ledger account of another client except as provided for in the rules (see **7.6.3**).

BASIC SOLICITORS' ACCOUNTS

7.2.3 THE DEFINITION OF CLIENTS' MONEY

Whenever a solicitor receives or pays money on behalf of a client, the solicitor must decide whether it is clients' or office money. The rules define clients' money as money held or received by a solicitor for a client, or as agent, bailee, stakeholder or as the donee of a power of attorney, or as a liquidator, trustee in bankruptcy or Court of Protection receiver.

7.2.4 PAYMENTS INTO CLIENT ACCOUNT

Where a solicitor holds clients' money, the solicitor must pay it into a client account without delay. This means on the day the money is received or, if that is not possible, on the next working day.

The following should be particularly noted.

Money which must be withheld from client account

(a) Money may not be paid into a client account if the client has asked for it not to be paid into a client account. Such a request from the client should be in writing, or confirmed in writing by the solicitor.

(b) Where a solicitor agrees to hold a cheque 'to the order' of a third party, the cheque should not be paid into a client account until it is released by the third party, as until that point it does not become the client's money.

Record keeping for accounts held jointly with outsiders

Where two firms of solicitors place stakeholder money in an account in their joint names, this is subject to limited compliance with the rules, records must be kept, statements and passbooks retained and it is subject to monitoring and inspection by reporting accountants and the Law Society. If the stakeholder money is in the sole control of one firm it is clients' money and must be paid into client account.

Agreed fees

Money which is received for or towards the payment of the solicitor's costs may not be paid into a client account. Thus, if a fee is agreed or a bill of costs delivered to the client and afterwards money is received from the client in respect of the costs or agreed fee, the money must be paid into office account.

Treatment of money received for unpaid professional disbursements

A solicitor's bill of costs may include the charges of a professional third party instructed by the solicitor on the client's behalf, for example, counsel, an expert witness or an agent. These liabilities to third parties are excluded from the definition of 'costs' and so, unless the third-party liability has already been discharged by the solicitor when the client pays the bill, the part of the payment representing counsel's fees, etc. must be paid into a client account. For example, a solicitor delivers a bill showing profit costs £200, VAT £35 and counsel's fees £117.50. When the client pays the bill the solicitor has not paid counsel's fees. The solicitor must do one of the following:

(a) Pay the cheque into client account and then transfer £235 for the costs and VAT to office account within 14 days of receipt.

(b) Split the cheque, by paying £235 for costs and VAT into office account and £117.50 for counsel's fees into client account. When the solicitor subsequently pays counsel's fees it will be by way of a cheque drawn on client account.

BASIC SOLICITORS' ACCOUNTS

(c) If the payment consists of office money and client money in the form of unpaid professional disbursements, pay the entire sum into office account and by the end of the second working day following receipt either the unpaid professional disbursement is paid or the relevant sum transferred to client account.

There are also special rules relating to the treatment of monies received from the Legal Aid Board and payments from a third party in respect of legal aid work (see **7.2.5** and **7.2.6**).

Money received from client on account

Money paid generally on account of costs and disbursements is clients' money and must be paid into client account.

Partners' money is office money

Money belonging to a principal solicitor or one of his partners cannot be treated as clients' money and must always be paid into office account. For example, if the firm acts for one of the partners in the purchase of a house in his sole name, free of mortgage, and the partner hands a cheque for the deposit to the firm's cashier, the cheque must be paid into office account. Note the following, however:

(a) If the firm is acting for a partner and that partner's spouse (who is not a partner), any moneys received will be held on behalf of both as trustees and must be treated as clients' money.

(b) If the firm is acting for a partner in the purchase of a property with the aid of a mortgage, the mortgage advance is clients' money.

(c) If the firm is acting for an assistant solicitor, a consultant or a non-solicitor employee, or in the case of a recognised body, a director, they will be regarded as clients even if dealing with the matter personally.

Money which may be paid into client account

The following 'non-client' money may be paid into a client account:

(a) Controlled trust moneys (see **7.2.8**).

(b) The solicitor's own money required to open or maintain the account.

(c) An advance from the solicitor to find a payment on behalf of a client or controlled trust in excess of funds held for that client or controlled trust, the sum becomes client money or controlled trust money on payment into the account.

(d) Money to replace that withdrawn in contravention of the rules.

(e) A sum in lieu of interest paid into client account.

(f) Cheques which the solicitor would be entitled to 'split' but does not (i.e., mixed office/client money).

Money which may be withheld from client account

A solicitor is not obliged to pay into a client account, clients' money held or received:

(a) in cash, which is, without delay, paid in cash, in the ordinary course of business, to the client or on the client's behalf to a third party; or

BASIC SOLICITORS' ACCOUNTS

(b) in the form of a cheque or banker's draft received which is endorsed over in the ordinary course of business to the client or on the client's behalf to a third party; or

(c) which is paid into a separate bank account or building society account opened in the name of the client or a third party designated in writing by the client or acknowledged in writing by the solicitor.

Note: if a solicitor negotiates cash or endorses a cheque made out to him, then the solicitor has handled clients' money and must make entries in the account to show the receipt and payment of clients' money. Note also that many cheques are now non-endorseable (see **7.3.5**).

If a solicitor receives a cheque made payable to a third party which the solicitor passes on to that third party then the solicitor has not handled clients' money and should not record a receipt and payment of clients' money in the accounts. It is, however, advisable to record the fact that the cheque has been received and passed on. This can be done by a file note and/or an entry on the client's ledger account by way of memorandum.

7.2.5 PAYMENTS FROM THE LEGAL AID BOARD

An advance payment in anticipation of work to be carried out, although client money, may be placed in office account provided the Board instructs in writing that this may be done. A payment for costs, interim or final, may be paid into office account, although it may include client money re advance payments for fees of disbursements or money for unpaid professional disbursements provided all money for payment of disbursements is transferred to client account or the disbursements paid within 14 days of receipt.

7.2.6 LEGAL AID — PAYMENTS FROM A THIRD PARTY

If the Legal Aid Board has paid any costs to a solicitor or paid professional disbursements direct and costs are later settled by a third party the entire third party settlement must be paid into client account (either the individual's client account or a separate account in the Board's name). Any balance belonging to the solicitor must be transferred to office account within 14 days of the solicitor sending a report of the details of the payment to the Board. A sum representing the payments made by the Board must be retained in client account until the Board notifies the solicitor that it has recouped an equivalent sum from subsequent legal aid payments due to the solicitor, when the retained sum should be transferred to office account.

7.2.7 WITHDRAWALS FROM A CLIENT ACCOUNT

The following, in particular, should be noted with regard to the withdrawal of money from a client account:

(a) Clients' money can be used to make payments only if enough money is held in client account for the particular client on whose behalf it is desired to make the payment.

(b) If insufficient money is held in client account for the particular client the solicitor may either:

(i) pay the disbursement out of office account (the solicitor may then transfer the balance held on client account, to office account); or

(ii) draw two cheques, one on client account for the balance held and one on office account for the remainder.

Note also that the solicitor may advance money to fund a payment on behalf of a client in excess of funds held for that client.

BASIC SOLICITORS' ACCOUNTS

(c) Rule 22, **Withdrawals from a client account** states that: **client money** can be withdrawn if:

(i) Properly required for a payment to or on behalf of the client.

(ii) Properly required for payment of a disbursement on behalf of the client.

(iii) Properly required in full or partial reimbursement of money spent by the solicitor on behalf of the client. Money is spent by the solicitor at the time when the solicitor dispatches a cheque unless the cheque is to be held to the solicitor's order. Money is also spent by the use of a credit account, for example, search fees or taxi fares.

(iv) Transferred to another client account.

(v) Withdrawn on the client's instructions provided the instructions are for the client's convenience and are given in writing or confirmed by the solicitor in writing.

(vi) A refund to the solicitor of an advance no longer required to fund a payment on behalf of a client.

(vii) Money which has been paid into the account in breach of the rules (e.g., money paid into the wrong separate designated client account or interest wrongly credited to a general client account).

(viii) Money withdrawn from the account on the written authorisation of the Law Society.

Office money can be withdrawn if it is:

(i) Money which had properly been paid in to open or maintain the account.

(ii) Money properly required for payment of the solicitors' costs, where a bill of costs or other written notification of the costs incurred has been given to the client. Once the solicitor has done this the money must be transferred out of client account within 14 days.

(iii) The whole or part of payment re legal aid payment paid in.

(iv) Part of a mixed office/client payment previously paid in.

Note that similar rules apply to controlled trust money.

(d) It is possible to draw against an uncleared cheque under the rules.

However, a solicitor should use discretion in drawing against an uncleared cheque. If the cheque is not met then other client's money will have been used to make the payment in breach of the rules and the breach must be remedied. A solicitor may be able to avoid a breach of the rules by instructing the bank or building society to charge all unpaid credits to the solicitor's office or personal account.

7.2.8 CONTROLLED TRUSTS

A solicitor may hold money as a 'controlled trustee'. A solicitor will be a controlled trustee if a sole trustee or the only other trustees are his or her partners or employees. If a solicitor is a trustee with an outside third party then the solicitor is not a controlled trustee.

Normally controlled trust money should be paid without delay into a client account under Rule 15. This is subject to the same exceptions as client money, for example, cash received and without delay paid in cash in the execution of the trust to a beneficiary or third party (see para **7.2.4** (i) previously) and, in accordance with the trustee's powers, it may be paid into or retained in an account of the trustee which is not a client account (e.g., a building society share account or an account outside England and Wales) or properly retained in cash in the performance of the trustee's duties. The general law requires a solicitor to act in the best interests of a controlled trust and not to benefit personally from it. Note that the rules as to interest on client money do not apply to controlled trust money. A solicitor must obtain the best reasonably obtainable rate of interest for the controlled trust money and must account to the relevant controlled trust for all the interest earned, whether the controlled trust money is held in a separate designated client account or in a general client account. To ensure that all interest is accounted for, solicitors may set up a general client account just for controlled trust money or can set up a designated account for each controlled trust. When controlled trust money is held in a general client account, interest will be credited to the office account in the normal way, but all interest must be promptly allocated to each controlled trust — either by transfer to the general client account or to separate designated client accounts for the particular trust or by payment to each trust in some other way.

Solicitors must also consider whether they have received any indirect benefit from controlled trust money at the expense of the controlled trust. For example, the bank might charge a reduced overdraft rate on office account by reference to the total funds (including controlled trust money) held by the solicitors on client account in return for paying a lower rate of interest on those funds. The solicitor may have to do more for the trust than merely account for such interest earned in these circumstances.

Note that if controlled trust money is invested in the purchase of assets other than money, e.g., stocks and shares, it is no longer controlled trust money, but it will become controlled trust money again when the investments are later sold.

There is a special provision that controlled trustees may delegate to an outside manager the day-to-day keeping of accounts of the business or property portfolio of an estate or trust, provided the manager keeps and retains appropriate accounting records which are available for inspection by the Law Society.

Contrast the above with the position where the solicitor is trustee with others outside the firm and is not a controlled trustee. In such circumstances moneys held will be normal client account money and the normal rules will apply, including the rules as to interest payable.

7.2.9 NOTE ALSO THE FOLLOWING UNDER THE SAR 1998

Liquidators, trustees in bankruptcy and Court of Protection receivers are now included in the rules, limited to record keeping requirements, and subject to monitoring and inspection by the Law Society and reporting accountants, to protect the clients and the profession from claims on the Solicitors' Indemnity and Compensation Funds.

Solicitors operating a client's account, e.g., under a power of attorney, should receive all statements and passbooks and retain these, as they will be subject to monitoring and inspection by the Law Society and reporting accountants.

7.3 Basic Entries

Note that office and client columns are separate. An entry in the client column of one account must have its corresponding double entry in the client column of another account. The same obviously applies also to office account entries. In the following examples no balances will be shown on the Cash Book as this will include all client money.

BASIC SOLICITORS' ACCOUNTS

7.3.1 RECEIPT OF OFFICE MONEYS

The firm must pay money owed to it into office account. The entries to record this are:

(a) Credit clients' ledger account — office column.

(b) Debit cash account — office column.

Example On 1 February the solicitor receives £100 in respect of disbursements already paid out of office account for his client, Black.

BLACK

Date	Details	Office account			Client account		
		Dr £	Cr £	Balance £	Dr £	Cr £	Balance £
Feb 1	Balance Cash		100	100 Dr —			

CASH ACCOUNT

Date	Details	Office account			Client account		
		Dr £	Cr £	Balance £	Dr £	Cr £	Balance £
Feb 1	Black	100					

7.3.2 PAYMENTS OF OFFICE MONEYS

The firm must pay disbursements out of office account if there is insufficient money in client account for that particular client, unless the solicitor decides to transfer office moneys to client account (see **7.2.4**). The entries to record a payment of office moneys are:

(a) Debit client's ledger account — office column.

(b) Credit cash account — office column.

Example Brown's solicitors are acting on his behalf with regard to a personal injury claim. They are not holding any money on Brown's behalf and pay £100 to counsel for an opinion on liability on 1 March.

BROWN: RE PERSONAL INJURY ACTION

Date	Details	Office account			Client account		
		Dr £	Cr £	Balance £	Dr £	Cr £	Balance £
Mar 1	Cash: counsel	100		100 Dr			

CASH ACCOUNT

Date	Details	Office account			Client account		
		Dr £	Cr £	Balance £	Dr £	Cr £	Balance £
Mar 1	Brown — counsel		100				

The client's ledger account should generally show a debit balance or a nil balance on office account. A credit balance indicates a breach of the Solicitors' Accounts Rules. The only exception to this is in respect of agreed fees (see **7.5.2**) and mixed monies, including unpaid professional disbursements.

If there is money held in client account but not enough to pay the particular disbursements, so that the whole payment is made out of office account, the solicitor may transfer the money held in client account to office account once the disbursement has been paid. As an alternative, two cheques could be drawn to pay the disbursement, one on client account for the amount held and the remainder on office account. In practice this is rarely done.

7.3.3 RECEIPT OF CLIENTS' MONEY

Once it has been decided that money received is clients' money it must be paid into client account promptly. The entries are:

(a) Credit client's ledger account — client column.

(b) Debit cash account — client column.

Example On 1 April the firm receives a cheque for £2,000 from the Bramchester Building Society to be used as a deposit on the purchase of Blackacre by the firm's client, White.

WHITE: RE PURCHASE OF BLACKACRE

Date	Details	Office account			Client account		
		Dr £	Cr £	Balance £	Dr £	Cr £	Balance £
Apr 1	Cash: Bramchester Building Society					2,000	2,000 Cr

CASH ACCOUNT

Date	Details	Office account			Client account		
		Dr £	Cr £	Balance £	Dr £	Cr £	Balance £
Apr 1	White: Bramchester Building Society				2,000		

If money is received from a third party on behalf of a client, as in the preceding example, the receipt is recorded in the ledger account of the client on whose behalf the money is received. An account is not opened for the third party.

Remember the solicitor must not pay the following into client account:

(a) The solicitor's own or a partner's money (except as allowed by the rules).

(b) Money received to pay costs after a bill has been delivered.

(c) Money the client asks him or her not to pay into client account.

BASIC SOLICITORS' ACCOUNTS

7.3.4 PAYMENT OF CLIENTS' MONEY

Before making a payment out of client account, the solicitor should check:

(a) That sufficient money is held in client account for the client on whose behalf the payment is being made.

(b) That the payment is permissible within the Solicitors' Accounts Rules 1998.

The bookkeeping entries are:

(a) Debit the client's ledger account — client column.

(b) Credit the cash account — client column.

Example On 7 April the firm pays the £2,000 deposit received from the Bramchester Building Society for White, to Fleecems the seller's solicitors.

WHITE: RE PURCHASE OF BLACKACRE

Date	Details	Office account Dr £	Cr £	Balance £	Client account Dr £	Cr £	Balance £
Apr 1	Cash: Bramchester Building Society					2,000	2,000 Cr
Apr 7	Cash: Fleecems re deposit				2,000		—

CASH ACCOUNT

Date	Details	Office account Dr £	Cr £	Balance £	Client account Dr £	Cr £	Balance £
Apr 1	White: Bramchester Building Society				2,000		
Apr 7	White: Fleecems re deposit					2,000	

7.3.5 ENDORSED CHEQUES AND CHEQUES MADE PAYABLE TO THIRD PARTIES

Note s. 81(a), Bills of Exchange Act 1882 as inserted by s. 1, Cheques Act 1992. A cheque that is crossed with the words 'account payee' is not transferable but remains a valid cheque as between the parties only. Any purported endorsement would be of no effect. In practice many cheque books are now preprinted 'account payee' unless some arrangement is made.

However, you should appreciate that if you do endorse a cheque made payable to the firm without paying it through your bank account, you have handled clients' money. This requires entries for the receipt and payment of clients' money. The details column should show that the cheque has been endorsed to avoid problems when the bookkeeper prepares the client account bank reconciliation statement, as the receipt and payment will not be shown on the firm's bank statement.

BASIC SOLICITORS' ACCOUNTS

Example The firm acts for Yellow with regard to the sale of Blackacre and the purchase of Whiteacre. Completion of the sale and purchase takes place on 1 December. On completion of the sale of Blackacre, the firm receives a banker's draft for £90,000 from the purchaser's solicitors. The firm endorses the banker's draft in favour of the solicitors acting for the seller of Whiteacre.

YELLOW: SALE OF BLACKACRE, PURCHASE OF WHITEACRE

Date	Details	Office account			Client account		
		Dr £	Cr £	Balance £	Dr £	Cr £	Balance £
Dec 1	Cash: sale of Blackacre (draft endorsed)					90,000	90,000 Cr
	Cash: purchase of Whiteacre (draft endorsed)				90,000		—

CASH ACCOUNT

Date	Details	Office account			Client account		
		Dr £	Cr £	Balance £	Dr £	Cr £	Balance £
Dec 1	Yellow: cash sale of Blackacre (draft endorsed)				90,000		90,000 Dr
	Yellow: cash: purchase of Whiteacre (draft endorsed)					90,000	—

You may also be required to show that you appreciate that when you hand over to a third party a cheque made payable to the third party, you have not handled clients' money. You can do this by making no entry at all in the accounts. Alternatively, you can make what is known as a memorandum entry. If you do this, remember; no entry is made in the cash account at all, no balance column entry is made in the client's ledger account and the details column should show clearly that the entry is by way of memorandum only.

Example You act for Charles to recover a debt owed to him by Janis. On 1 February Janis sends you a cheque for £250 made payable to Charles.

CHARLES: RE DEBT COLLECTION

Date	Details	Office account			Client account		
		Dr £	Cr £	Balance £	Dr £	Cr £	Balance £
Feb 1	Cheque received from Janis payable to Charles memorandum entry only				[250	250]	

BASIC SOLICITORS' ACCOUNTS

7.4 Payments out of Petty Cash — Office Account

Small disbursements paid on behalf of clients, for example, commissioner's fees, may be paid in cash rather than by cheque.

The solicitor maintains a petty cash float by drawing money out of office account at the bank. Any petty cash payments must therefore be made from the office account.

To record dealings with petty cash, a petty cash account is used, or a petty cash book if the ledger system is operated.

To record the transfer of money from the office bank account to the petty cash float the following entries are made:

(a) Credit the cash account in the office column.

(b) Debit the petty cash account.

Example On 10 January a solicitor draws £500 out of office account for petty cash.

PETTY CASH ACCOUNT
OFFICE ACCOUNT

Date	Details	Dr £	Cr £	Balance £
Jan 10	Cash	500		500 Dr

Only office money can be held in petty cash, therefore only office account columns are necessary.

CASH ACCOUNT

Date	Details	Office account Dr £	Office account Cr £	Office account Balance £	Client account Dr £	Client account Cr £	Client account Balance £
Jan 10	Balance say Petty cash		500	2,000 Dr 1,500 Dr			

As payments made out of petty cash are always office account payments, even if there is money in client account, a petty cash payment must be recorded as coming out of office account.

To record the payment of a petty cash disbursement on a client's behalf the following entries are made in the accounts:

(a) Debit the client's ledger account in the office column.

(b) Credit the petty cash account.

BASIC SOLICITORS' ACCOUNTS

> **Example** On 15 January the firm pays £40 out of petty cash for local advertisements in the administration of Kate's estate.
>
> ### KATE DECEASED: ADMINISTRATION OF ESTATE
>
> | Date | Details | Office account | | | Client account | | |
> |------|---------|----|----|----|----|----|----|
> | | | Dr £ | Cr £ | Balance £ | Dr £ | Cr £ | Balance £ |
> | Jan 15 | Petty cash: local advertisements | 40 | | 40 Dr | | | |
>
> ### PETTY CASH ACCOUNT
> ### OFFICE ACCOUNT
>
> | Date | Details | Dr £ | Cr £ | Balance £ |
> |------|---------|------|------|-----------|
> | Jan 10 | Cash | 500 | | 500 Dr |
> | Jan 15 | Kate deceased | | 40 | 460 Dr |

7.5 Profit Costs

7.5.1 DELIVERY OF BILLS OF COSTS

When a solicitor delivers a bill of costs to the client, a central record or file of copies of bills must be kept. This is in addition to the entries shown below.

When a bill of costs is delivered to a client the following entries are made in the accounts:

(a) Debit client ledger account office column with profit costs and VAT (on separate lines).

(b) Credit the profit costs account with profit costs.

(c) Credit the Customs and Excise account with VAT.

The profit costs account and Customs and Excise accounts only record dealings with office money and therefore only have office columns.

> **Example** On 15 June 2001 the firm delivers a bill of costs to Beryl, for whom it has acted in divorce proceedings, for £100 plus £17.50 VAT.
>
> ### BERYL: RE DIVORCE
>
> | Date | Details | Office account | | | Client account | | |
> |------|---------|----|----|----|----|----|----|
> | | | Dr £ | Cr £ | Balance £ | Dr £ | Cr £ | Balance £ |
> | 2001 June 15 | Profit costs VAT | 100 17.50 | | 117.50 Dr | | | |

BASIC SOLICITORS' ACCOUNTS

PROFIT COSTS ACCOUNT

Date	Details	Dr £	Cr £	Balance £
2001 June 15	Beryl		100	100 Cr

CUSTOMS AND EXCISE ACCOUNT

Date	Details	Dr £	Cr £	Balance £
2001 June 15	Beryl		17.50	17.50 Cr

Entries are made to record the delivery of the bill of costs on the date of delivery regardless of the date of payment. When payment of the bill is made entries are made in the accounts to record a receipt of office moneys.

Example Beryl pays her bill on 1 July.

Date	Details	Office account Dr £	Cr £	Balance £	Client account Dr £	Cr £	Balance £
2001 June 15	Profit costs	100		100 Dr			
	VAT	17.50		117.50 Dr			
July 1	Cash you		117.50	—			

Debit the cash account — office column, £117.50.

7.5.2 AGREED FEES

A solicitor and client may agree a fee for work which the solicitor has done or is to do on the client's behalf. When the solicitor receives the agreed fee it must be paid into office account notwithstanding that a bill of costs is not delivered until a later date. The agreed fee must be evidenced in writing. It is not necessary to draw a bill when a fee is agreed.

Example On 10 July 2001 the firm receives £70.50 from Jill in respect of a fee agreed at the beginning of the month for work done by the firm on Jill's behalf in connection with a tenancy dispute. A bill is delivered on receipt of the fee.

JILL: RE HOUSING

Date	Details	Office account Dr £	Cr £	Balance £	Client account Dr £	Cr £	Balance £
2001 July 10	Cash you		70.50	70.50 Cr			
	Profit costs (agreed fee)	60		10.50 Cr			
	VAT	10.50		—			

Note:

(a) It would be a breach of the Solicitors' Accounts Rules to pay money, expressly paid in respect of an agreed fee, into client account.

(b) The tax point for VAT arises when the fee is received, not when a bill is subsequently delivered.

7.6 Transfers

7.6.1 TRANSFERS FROM CLIENT TO OFFICE ACCOUNT

A transfer may be made from client to office account if it is permissible, within the Solicitors' Accounts Rules 1998, to withdraw money from client account.

A solicitor may wish to transfer money from client to office account if:

(a) Disbursements have been paid out of office account on the client's behalf.

(b) A bill of costs has been delivered to the client and the solicitor wishes to obtain payment of costs by transferring money held in client account.

(c) A split cheque has been paid into client account.

The bookkeeping entries to record a transfer from client to office account are:

(1) The entries to record a payment out of clients' money (see **7.3.4**).

(2) The entries to record a receipt of office money (see **7.3.1**).

Example On 2 December 2001 the firm delivered a bill of costs to its client Green, showing profit costs of £200 and VAT £35. The firm is holding £500 in client account for Green. On 5 December the firm transfers £235 from client to office account.

GREEN

Date	Details	Office account			Client account		
		Dr £	Cr £	Balance £	Dr £	Cr £	Balance £
2001	Balance						500 Cr
Dec 2	Profit costs	200					
	VAT	35		235 Dr			
Dec 5	Cash: transfer			—	235(1)		265 Cr
	Cash: transfer		235(2)				

Double entry payment in   Double entry payment out

CASH ACCOUNT

Date	Details	Office account			Client account		
		Dr £	Cr £	Balance £	Dr £	Cr £	Balance £
2001	Green				500		500 Dr
Dec 5	Cash: transfer					235(1)	265 Dr
	Cash: transfer	235(2)		235 Dr			

Note:

(1) Payment of client's money.

(2) Receipt of office money.

BASIC SOLICITORS' ACCOUNTS

7.6.2 TRANSFER FROM OFFICE ACCOUNT TO CLIENT ACCOUNT

A solicitor must make an immediate transfer from office account to client account if he or she has breached the Solicitors' Accounts Rules 1998 by overdrawing on client account, for example, by drawing against an uncleared cheque which is subsequently dishonoured.

The bookkeeping entries to record a transfer of money from office account to client account are as follows:

(1) Entries to record a payment of office money (see **7.3.2**).

(2) Entries to record a receipt of clients' money (see **7.3.3**).

Example Brown has a credit balance on client account of £50. On 20 October her solicitor inadvertently pays counsel's fee of £70 out of client account. She makes an immediate transfer from office to client account to rectify the breach.

BROWN

Date	Details	Office account Dr £	Cr £	Balance £	Client account Dr £	Cr £	Balance £
Oct 20	Balance Cash: counsel Cash: transfer Cash: transfer	20[1]		20 Dr	70	20[2]	50 Cr 20 Dr —

| | | Double entry payment out | | | Double entry payment in | | |

CASH ACCOUNT

Date	Details	Office account Dr £	Cr £	Balance £	Client account Dr £	Cr £	Balance £
Oct 20	Brown Cash: counsel: Brown Cash: transfer: Brown Cash: transfer: Brown		20[1]	20 Cr	50 20[2]	70	50 Dr 20 Cr —

Note:

(1) Entries to record payment of office money.

(2) Entries to record receipt of clients' money.

7.6.3 TRANSFERS BETWEEN CLIENT ACCOUNTS

Money is not moved from one bank account to another and therefore no entries are made in the cash account.

BASIC SOLICITORS' ACCOUNTS

A transfer can be made from one client ledger account to another client ledger account if:

(a) It is permissible within the rules to withdraw money from the account of client A.

(b) It is permissible within the rules to pay money into the account of client B.

When a transfer is made from one client ledger account to another, a separate record must be made. This may be, for example, in a journal if the ledger system is used, or on a transfer sheet if a card system is used.

The bookkeeping entries to record transfers between client accounts are as follows:

(a) Debit the ledger account of the client from whose account the transfer is being made. (Make a separate record.)

(b) Credit the ledger account of the client to whose account the transfer is being made. (Make a separate record.)

Example The firm is holding £10,000 in client account for its client Blue. The firm also acts for Blue's son-in-law, Red, with regard to his house purchase. Blue is making a gift to Red of the deposit of £8,000 and asks the firm to pay Red's deposit on 7 April out of the money held for him.

BLUE

Date	Details	Office account			Client account		
		Dr £	Cr £	Balance £	Dr £	Cr £	Balance £
Apr 7	Balance Red: transfer sheet				8,000		10,000 Cr 2,000 Cr

RED

Date	Details	Office account			Client account		
		Dr £	Cr £	Balance £	Dr £	Cr £	Balance £
Apr 7	Blue: transfer sheet Cash: deposit paid				8,000	8,000	8,000 Cr —

Note: a transfer may be made from the client account of one client to the office account of another or vice versa. For example, if one client has agreed to moneys being taken from his or her client account to discharge another client's liability for costs. If this is done the four entries used to make a transfer from client to office account or vice versa must be shown (see **7.6.1** and **7.6.2**).

BASIC SOLICITORS' ACCOUNTS

Example The firm acts for the executors of Alexander. It also acts for Olivia, Alexander's daughter and the sole beneficiary. There is a balance of £12,000 on Alexander's account. The firm has acted for Olivia in her divorce proceedings and a bill has been delivered to Olivia for £1,000 plus VAT. The executors agree to this being paid out of the estate.

EXECUTORS OF ALEXANDER DECEASED

Date	Details	Office account			Client account		
		Dr £	Cr £	Balance £	Dr £	Cr £	Balance £
	Balance						12,000 Cr
	Cash — Olivia				1,175		10,825 Cr

OLIVIA: RE DIVORCE

Date	Details	Office account			Client account		
		Dr £	Cr £	Balance £	Dr £	Cr £	Balance £
	Profit costs	1,000					
	VAT	175		1,175 Dr			
	Cash — Alexander		1,175	—			

CASH ACCOUNT

Date	Details	Office account			Client account		
		Dr £	Cr £	Balance £	Dr £	Cr £	Balance £
	Alexander — transfer to Olivia					1,175	
	Olivia — transfer from Alexander	1,175					

The Solicitors' Accounts Rules 1998 restrict inter-client transfers in repect of private loans. Rule 30(2) states that no sum in respect of a private loan shall be paid out of funds held on account of the lender, either:

(a) directly to the borrower; or

(b) by means of a payment from one client account to another or by a paper transfer from the ledger of the lender to that of the borrower without the prior written authority of **both** clients.

A private loan on standard terms is defined as meaning a loan other than one provided by an institution which provides loans in the normal course of its activities. The solicitor should keep a register of authorities for transactions of this type.

7.6.4 SPLIT CHEQUES

A split cheque is one which contains part office money and part clients' money.

When a solicitor receives a split cheque the alternatives are:

(a) pay the cheque into client account and then make a transfer from client to office account of the office money; or

(b) split the cheque by paying the client's money into client account and the office money into office account.

If the payment consists of office money and client money in the form of unpaid professional disbursements the entire sum may be paid into office account and by the end of the second working day following receipt either the unpaid professional disbursement should be paid or the relevant sum transferred to client account.

There are also special rules relating to the treatment of monies received from the Legal Aid Board and payments from a third party in respect of legal aid work (see **7.2.5**).

Example Pink sends a cheque for £250 to his solicitor on 1 March. The cheque represents £200 owed by Pink to a creditor and £50 costs owed to the solicitor in respect of which a bill was delivered to Pink on 1 February.

(a) If the cheque is split the entries in Pink's account will be:

PINK ACCOUNT

Date	Details	Office account			Client account		
		Dr £	Cr £	Balance £	Dr £	Cr £	Balance £
Mar 1	Balance Cash: you		50	50 Dr —		200	200 Cr

(b) If the cheque is not split, the entries in Pink's account will be:

PINK ACCOUNT

Date	Details	Office account			Client account		
		Dr £	Cr £	Balance £	Dr £	Cr £	Balance £
	Balance Cash: you			50 Dr		250	250 Cr

When the £50 in respect of costs is transferred to office account, entries will be made in Pink's account and the cash account to record a transfer from client to office account (see **7.6.1**).

BASIC SOLICITORS' ACCOUNTS

7.7 Exercises on Basic Ledger Entries

1 The firm acts for Algernon with regard to the recovery of debts. The following events take place:

1 September	Algernon sends a cheque for £20 on account of disbursements.
2 September	Proceedings are issued in the county court against X and a court fee of £10 is paid.
4 September	Proceedings are issued against Y and a court fee of £15 is paid.
5 September	Z pays £25 in cash to settle his debt to Algernon. Algernon calls at the office the same day and the £25 cash is handed to him.
12 September	A cheque for £150 is received from Y in settlement of the debt he owes Algernon and court costs.
22 September	The firm receives a cheque for £100 from X. The cheque is made payable to Algernon and is handed to him.
30 September	The firm sends a bill of costs to Algernon for £100 plus £17.50 VAT. Costs due to the firm are transferred from client to office account. A cheque is sent to Algernon for the balance due to him.

Prepare Algernon's account to record the above transactions.

2 The firm's client, Smith, asks the firm to carry out a number of transactions whilst he is abroad. Smith promises to send a cheque for £800 to cover expenditure. The following events take place with regard to Smith's account.

1 June	Pay £30 to enquiry agent.
2 June	Pay £60 for newspaper advertisements.
3 June	Pay surveyor's bill £230.
4 June	Pay counsel's fee £115.
8 June	Receive Smith's cheque for £800. The cheque is to be split between office and client account.
9 June	Send a bill of costs to Smith for £60 plus £10.50 VAT and account to Smith for the balance due to him.

Prepare Smith's account to record the above transactions.

3 Prepare clients' ledger accounts to record the following transactions.

(a) Pay counsel's fee £47 on behalf of Nigel. Deliver a bill for £60 plus £10.50 VAT and disbursement. Receive payment.

(b) You act for Mary. Pay search fee £10 by cash. Pay for office copy entries by cheque £15. Receive £100 from Mary on account of disbursements.

(c) Lynn pays you £75 on account. Pay £5 out of petty cash on Lynn's behalf for inspection of deeds. Deliver a bill of costs for £100 plus VAT. Receive payment of balance from Lynn and close her account.

(d) Receive £235 from John in respect of an agreed fee for conveyancing work, which includes VAT.

(e) Margaret's account shows a balance in hand of £500. Margaret asks you to transfer £300 to Daphne, another client of the firm.

(f) Keith asks you to pay a premium of £75 to the Star Insurance Co. for whom you act. He pays £75 to you one week later, by agreement.

(g) You act for Alan, pay counsel's fee £60 plus VAT £10.50. Deliver a bill of costs to Alan for £100 plus VAT. Receive moneys due from Alan.

(h) You act for Carol: 1 September pay counsel's fee £40 plus VAT £7, 19 September receive £200 from Carol; 23 September pay disbursement £20 plus VAT £3.50; 30 September deliver a bill of costs £60 plus VAT £10.50. Transfer sum due from client to office account. Pay balance due to Carol.

4   Your firm is acting for John Brown who is purchasing a house for £90,000. The following events occur:

4 September	Pay search fee £15.
20 September	Receive cheque for £9,000 from client for deposit.
21 September	Contracts exchanged — pay deposit of £9,000 to vendor's solicitor.
29 September	Pay search fee £4.
9 October	Deliver a bill for £200 plus VAT.
13 October	Receive a cheque from client for £81,254, the balance of the purchase money and costs.
14 October	Complete purchase — pay £81,000 to vendor's solicitors. Transfer profit costs.

Prepare the client ledger card for John Brown and the cash account to record the above transactions. The cash account need not be balanced.

5   Your firm is acting for the executors of Olive White in the administration of her estate. The following events occur:

5 October	Pay probate fees of £80.
31 October	Receive £1,000 from the Longlife Insurance Company in respect of a policy which the deceased held with them. Pay £535 to the executors' bank to repay the loan.
5 November	Receive £2,000 from the deceased's building society account.
6 November	Receive £400 from sale of household contents. Pay legacy of £1,500.
10 November	Deliver a bill of costs £240 plus VAT.
11 November	Pay residuary beneficiary £1,003. Transfer £362 from client to office account.

Prepare the ledger account for the executors of Olive White and the cash account to record the above. The cash account need not be balanced.

BASIC SOLICITORS' ACCOUNTS

7.8 Suggested Answers to Exercises on Basic Ledger Entries

1 ALGERNON: DEBT RECOVERY

Date	Details	Office account Dr £	Office account Cr £	Office account Balance £	Client account Dr £	Client account Cr £	Client account Balance £
Sept 1	Cash: you					20	20 Cr
Sept 2	Cash: court fee				10		10 Cr
Sept 4	Cash: court fee	15		15 Dr			
Sept 5	Cash: Z (paid direct to you)					25	35 Cr
	Cash: you (from Z, paid direct to you)				25		10 Cr
Sept 12	Cash: Y					150	160 Cr
Sept 22	Cheque from X handed direct to you. (Note that this entry is by way of a memorandum. There is no double entry in the cash book.)				[100	100]	
Sept 30	Profit costs	100					
	VAT	17.50		132.50 Dr			
	Cash: transfer: profit costs				132.50		27.50 Cr
	Cash: transfer: profit costs		132.50	—			
	Cash: you				27.50		—

2 SMITH

Date	Details	Office account Dr £	Office account Cr £	Office account Balance £	Client account Dr £	Client account Cr £	Client account Balance £
June 1	Cash: enquiry agent	30		30 Dr			
June 2	Cash: newspaper advertisements	60		90 Dr			
June 3	Cash: surveyor	230		320 Dr			
June 4	Cash: counsel	115		435 Dr			
June 8	Cash: you		435	—		365	365 Cr
June 9	Profit costs	60					
	VAT	10.50		70.50 Dr			
	Cash: transfer: profit costs				70.50		294.50 Cr
	Cash: transfer: profit costs		70.50	—			
	Cash: you				294.50		—

BASIC SOLICITORS' ACCOUNTS

3 (a)   NIGEL

Date	Details	Office account			Client account		
		Dr £	Cr £	Balance £	Dr £	Cr £	Balance £
1999	Cash: counsel's fee	47		47 Dr			
	Profit costs	60					
	VAT	10.50		117.50 Dr			
	Cash: you		117.50	—			

3 (b)   MARY

Date	Details	Office account			Client account		
		Dr £	Cr £	Balance £	Dr £	Cr £	Balance £
1999	Petty cash: search fee	10		10 Dr			
	Cash: office copies	15		25 Dr			
	Cash: you		25	—		75	75 Cr

3 (c)   LYNN

Date	Details	Office account			Client account		
		Dr £	Cr £	Balance £	Dr £	Cr £	Balance £
1999	Cash: you					75	75 Cr
	Petty cash: inspection fee	5		5 Dr			
	Profit costs	100					
	VAT	17.50		122.50 Dr			
	Cash: you		47.50	75 Dr			
	Cash: transfer: profit costs				75		—
	Cash: transfer: profit costs		75	—			

3 (d)   JOHN

Date	Details	Office account			Client account		
		Dr £	Cr £	Balance £	Dr £	Cr £	Balance £
	Profit costs (agreed fee)	200					
	VAT	35		235 Dr			
	Cash: you		235	—			

3 (e)   MARGARET

Date	Details	Office account			Client account		
		Dr £	Cr £	Balance £	Dr £	Cr £	Balance £
	Balance						500 Cr
	Daphne: transfer (transfer sheet)				300		200 Cr

BASIC SOLICITORS' ACCOUNTS

DAPHNE

Date	Details	Office account Dr £	Cr £	Balance £	Client account Dr £	Cr £	Balance £
	Margaret: transfer (transfer sheet)					300	300 Cr

3 (f) KEITH

Date	Details	Office account Dr £	Cr £	Balance £	Client account Dr £	Cr £	Balance £
	Cash: transfer premium to Star Insurance Co.	75		75 Dr			
	Cash: you		75				

STAR INSURANCE CO.

Date	Details	Office account Dr £	Cr £	Balance £	Client account Dr £	Cr £	Balance £
	Cash: Keith: transfer premium					75	75 Cr

3 (g) ALAN

Date	Details	Office account Dr £	Cr £	Balance £	Client account Dr £	Cr £	Balance £
	Cash: counsel's fee	70.50		70.50 Dr			
	Profit costs	100					
	VAT	17.50		188 Dr			
	Cash: you		188				

3 (h) CAROL

Date	Details	Office account Dr £	Cr £	Balance £	Client account Dr £	Cr £	Balance £
Sept 1	Cash: counsel's fee	47		47 Dr			
Sept 19	Cash: you					200	200 Cr
Sept 23	Cash: disbursement				23.50		176.50 Cr
Sept 30	Profit costs	60					
	VAT	10.50		117.50 Dr			
	Cash: transfer: profit costs				117.50		59 Cr
	Cash: transfer: profit costs		117.50	—			
	Cash: you				59		—

4   JOHN BROWN:
MATTER: CONVEYANCING

Date	Details	Office account			Client account		
		Dr £	Cr £	Balance £	Dr £	Cr £	Balance £
Sept 4	Cash: search fee	15		15 Dr			
Sept 20	Cash: you					9,000	9,000 Cr
Sept 21	Cash: deposit				9,000		—
Sept 29	Cash: search fee	4		19 Dr			
Oct 9	Profit costs	200		219 Dr			
	VAT	35		254 Dr			
Oct 13	Cash: you					81,254	81,254 Cr
Oct 14	Cash: completion				81,000		254 Cr
	Cash: transfer profit costs		254	—	254		—

CASH ACCOUNT

Date	Details	Office account			Client account		
		Dr £	Cr £	Balance £	Dr £	Cr £	Balance £
Sept 4	Brown: search fee		15				
Sept 20	Brown				9,000		
Sept 21	Brown: deposit					9,000	
Sept 29	Brown: search fee		4				
Oct 13	Brown				81,254		
Oct 14	Brown: completion					81,000	
	Brown: transfer profit costs	254				254	

5   EXECUTORS OF OLIVE WHITE DECEASED

Date	Details	Office account			Client account		
		Dr £	Cr £	Balance £	Dr £	Cr £	Balance £
Oct 5	Cash: probate fees	80		80 Dr			
Oct 31	Cash: Longlife Insurance Co.					1,000	1,000 Cr
	Cash: bank loan				535		465 Cr
Nov 5	Cash: Building Society					2,000	2,465 Cr
Nov 6	Cash: sale of household contents					400	2,865 Cr
	Cash: legacy				1,500		1,365 Cr
Nov 10	Profit costs	240		320 Dr			
	VAT	42		362 Dr			
	Cash: residuary beneficiary				1,003		362 Cr
	Cash: transfer profit costs		362	—	362		—

BASIC SOLICITORS' ACCOUNTS

CASH ACCOUNT

Date	Details	Office account			Client account		
		Dr £	Cr £	Balance £	Dr £	Cr £	Balance £
Oct 5	Olive White: probate fee		80				
Oct 31	Olive White: Longlife Insurance Co.				1,000		
	Olive White: bank loan					535	
Nov 5	Olive White: Building Society				2,000		
	Olive White: re household contents				400		
	Olive White: legacy					1,500	
Nov 11	Olive White: legacy					1,003	
	Olive White: transfer profit costs	362				362	

7.9 Value Added Tax

7.9.1 REGISTERING FOR VAT

A solicitor whose annual taxable supplies exceed the limit set by the Value Added Tax Act 1994 (currently £54,000) must register for VAT purposes. The limit is changed from time to time to take account of inflation. In practice, all solicitors register.

A solicitor's taxable supplies consist mainly of the supply of services to clients but also include supplies of goods in the course of business, for example, the sale of office equipment.

The effect of being registered for VAT is that the solicitor must collect VAT at the standard rate (currently 17.5%) on profit costs billed or on the sale of a business asset.

VAT becomes payable when a bill of costs is delivered to a client regardless of whether the client pays the bill. In the case of agreed fees the tax point is when the fee is received, regardless of whether or when a bill is subsequently delivered. Note that there is a discretion for small and medium sized firms. In their case VAT can be payable only on bills paid, i.e., cash.

Generally, provided a solicitor delivers a bill of costs to the client within three months of completion of the work, the date of delivery of the bill is the tax point. The tax point determines the date on which the solicitor must account to Customs and Excise for VAT charged.

A solicitor must provide a tax invoice to clients who themselves are registered for VAT. In practice, solicitors usually supply invoices to all their clients. When tax invoices are supplied, they are usually attached to the bottom of the bill of costs delivered to the client.

Example of a tax invoice

Name Invoice No.
Address Date

VAT No. (the solicitor's VAT registration number)

To supply of legal services £
VAT at 17.5% £
 ─────
 Total £
 ─────

7.9.2 CHARGING OUTPUT TAX

A solicitor will charge output tax on supply of professional services — thus, when a bill of costs is delivered to the client, VAT must be charged at 17.5% on the profit costs figure. In **7.5.1** we saw that when a solicitor delivers a bill of costs the costs are debited in the client ledger account office column and credited in the profit costs account. To record the VAT on the delivery of a bill:

(a) Debit the client's ledger account — office column.

(b) Credit the Customs and Excise account.

When a solicitor makes a taxable supply other than of professional services, for example, on the sale of second-hand office equipment, the following entries will be made in the accounts:

(a) Credit the appropriate asset disposal account with the tax-exclusive price charged.

(b) Credit the Customs and Excise account with VAT charged on the supply of goods.

(c) Debit the cash account — office column, with the price charged and the VAT.

Example The firm sells a second-hand typewriter for £400 plus VAT £70 on 30 September 2001.

ASSET DISPOSAL (OFFICE EQUIPMENT) ACCOUNT

Date	Details	Dr £	Cr £	Balance £
Sept 30	Cash (typewriter)		400	400 Cr

CUSTOMS AND EXCISE ACCOUNT

Date	Details	Dr £	Cr £	Balance £
Sept 30	Cash (typewriter) (office equipment)		70	70 Cr

CASH ACCOUNT

Date	Details	Office account Dr £	Office account Cr £	Office account Balance £	Client account Dr £	Client account Cr £	Client account Balance £
Sept 30	Asset disposal (Office equipment) Customs and Excise	400 70		470 Dr			

7.9.3 PAYING INPUT TAX

When solicitors pay VAT on supplies made to them the following entries will be made in the accounts:

BASIC SOLICITORS' ACCOUNTS

(a) Debit the Customs and Excise account with VAT paid.

(b) Debit the appropriate real or nominal account with the tax-exclusive price paid.

(c) Credit the cash account office column.

Example The firm buys a word processor on 1 April and pays £1,175 which includes £175 VAT.

OFFICE EQUIPMENT ACCOUNT

Date	Details	Dr	Cr	Balance
		£	£	£
Apr 1	Cash (word processor)	1,000		1,000 Dr

CUSTOMS AND EXCISE ACCOUNT

Date	Details	Dr	Cr	Balance
		£	£	£
Apr 1	Cash: word processor	175		175 Dr

CASH ACCOUNT

Date	Details	Office account Dr £	Cr £	Balance £	Client account Dr £	Cr £	Balance £
Apr 1	Office equipment (word processor)		1,000				
	Customs and Excise (word processor)		175	1,175 Cr			

7.9.4 ACCOUNTING TO CUSTOMS AND EXCISE FOR VAT

Solicitors who are registered for VAT must account to Customs and Excise for the balance on the Customs and Excise account, i.e., tax charged on supplies of services and goods (output tax being tax on goods or services going out of the firm) less tax paid by the solicitors on services supplied to them (input tax, being tax on goods or services coming into the firm).

Tax is normally paid to Customs and Excise quarterly. Within one month of the end of the quarterly period, the solicitor must send a completed return form and remittance to Customs and Excise. However, small and medium sized firms may account yearly.

When VAT is paid to Customs and Excise, the following entries are made in the accounts:

(a) Debit Customs and Excise account.

(b) Credit cash account office column.

7.9.5 VAT AND PAYMENT OF DISBURSEMENTS

Some disbursements paid on behalf of a client do not attract VAT, for example, search fees, Land Registry fees and stamp duty. The solicitor must not charge a client VAT on these disbursements when delivering a bill to that client.

When disbursements do attract VAT, for example, counsels' fees, the VAT may be dealt with using the agency method or the principal method.

7.9.5.1 The agency method

The **agency method** is used when the tax invoice is made out to the client. When the agency method is used, the supply is made from the supplier to the client and the solicitor acts as an intermediary in making payment on the client's behalf. If money is held in client account for the client on whose behalf the disbursement is paid, payment can be made out of client account.

When a disbursement is paid on the agency method, the following entries are made in the accounts:

(a) Debit the client's ledger account with the tax-inclusive value of the disbursement.

(b) Credit the cash account with the tax inclusive value of the disbursement.

> **Example** On 8 May the firm pays an estate agent's account for its client, Brown. The estate agent's account is in Brown's name and is for £2,000 plus £350 VAT. The firm holds £15,000 in client account for Brown, following completion of the sale.
>
> BROWN
>
> | Date | Details | Office account | | | Client account | | |
> |---|---|---|---|---|---|---|---|
> | | | Dr £ | Cr £ | Balance £ | Dr £ | Cr £ | Balance £ |
> | | Balance | | | | | | 15,000 Cr |
> | May 8 | Cash: estate agent | | | | 2,350 | | 12,650 Cr |
>
> (No entry is made in the Customs and Excise account of the solicitor.)

7.9.5.2 The principal method

The **principal method** is used when the tax invoice is made out in the solicitor's name. The input is to the solicitor and the solicitor must therefore pay the disbursement (including VAT) out of office account.

The following entries are made in the accounts when a disbursement is paid using the principal method:

(a) Debit the client's ledger account office column with the tax-exclusive value of the disbursement.

(b) Debit the Customs and Excise account with VAT paid on the disbursement.

(c) Credit the cash account office account showing the disbursement and VAT separately.

Example Using the principal method of treatment, a solicitor pays counsel's fee of £200 plus VAT £35 on 2 June on behalf of a client Smith.

SMITH

Date	Details	Office account Dr £	Office account Cr £	Office account Balance £	Client account Dr £	Client account Cr £	Client account Balance £
June 2	Cash: counsel	200		200 Dr			

CUSTOMS AND EXCISE

Date	Details	Dr £	Cr £	Balance £
June 2	Cash: Smith	35		35 Dr

CASH ACCOUNT

Date	Details	Office account Dr £	Office account Cr £	Office account Balance £	Client account Dr £	Client account Cr £	Client account Balance £
June 2	Smith — Counsel (fees)		200				
June 2	Customs and Excise (Smith — VAT on counsel's fees)		35	235 Cr			

When a bill of costs is sent to the client, the solicitor will treat the disbursement as an output from himself or herself to the client along with profit costs charged to the client. The solicitor will charge the client VAT on the total output (i.e., profit costs and disbursement).

Continuing the example, on 30 June the firm delivers a bill of costs to Smith, charging profit costs of £300 plus VAT:

SMITH

Date	Details	Office account Dr £	Office account Cr £	Office account Balance £	Client account Dr £	Client account Cr £	Client account Balance £
June 2	Cash: counsel	200		200 Dr			
June 30	Profit costs	300					
	VAT	87.50		587.50 Dr			

(VAT is £52.50 on profit costs plus £35 on supply of disbursement.)

BASIC SOLICITORS' ACCOUNTS

Agency method — summary

(a) The invoice is made out to the client.

(b) Office or client account may be used.

(c) On payment show the total figure paid, including the VAT. Do not show the VAT separately, as the VAT (Customs and Excise) account is not used.

Principal method — summary

(a) The invoice is made out to the firm of solicitors.

(b) Office account must be used.

(c) On the client ledger card show the net amount paid only. (The VAT will be shown on the VAT (Customs and Excise) account). Charge the VAT on the amount paid when the bill is sent to the client.

7.10 Exercises on Ledger Accounts Including VAT

1 You are acting in litigation for your client Jenny Green. You instruct a consulting engineer to prepare a report. The engineer sends you a bill for £200 plus VAT £35 addressed to your firm. You are holding £300 in client account for Jenny Green. On 23 September you pay the engineer's bill. In November the case is concluded and on 21 November you send a bill of costs to Jenny Green of £100 plus VAT.

Show Jenny Green's ledger account and the cash account to record the above.

2 You are acting for Lucy Blue. A surveyor has been instructed to prepare a report. The surveyor sends a bill addressed to Lucy Blue for £100 plus VAT £17.50. You are holding £200 on account of costs and disbursements in client account. On 7 November you pay the surveyor's bill. On 1 December you deliver a bill of costs to Lucy for £200 plus VAT.

Show Lucy Blue's ledger account.

3 You are acting for Lyndon Tree. In the month of October the following events occur:

1 October	Pay enquiry agent's fee £75. The enquiry agent is not registered for VAT.
3 October	Pay surveyor's fee £100 plus £17.50 VAT. The bill is made out to Lyndon Tree.
4 October	Pay counsel's fee £200 plus £35 VAT. The fee note is made out to you.
8 October	Receive a payment on account of costs and disbursements of £500 from Lyndon Tree.
9 October	Deliver a bill of costs to Lyndon Tree of £60 plus £10.50 VAT. Transfer moneys due to you from client to office account and account to Lyndon Tree for the balance.

Show Lyndon Tree's ledger account to record the above transactions.

7.11 Suggested Answers to Exercises on Ledger Accounts Including VAT

1 JENNY GREEN ACCOUNT

Date	Details	Office account Dr £	Office account Cr £	Office account Balance £	Client account Dr £	Client account Cr £	Client account Balance £
	Balance					300	300 Cr
Sept 23	Cash: engineer (VAT £35)	200		200 Dr			
Nov 21	Profit costs	100					
	VAT (£17.50 + £35)	52.50					

CASH ACCOUNT

Date	Details	Office account Dr £	Office account Cr £	Office account Balance £	Client account Dr £	Client account Cr £	Client account Balance £
Sept 23	Jenny Green: engineer's fee		200				
	Customs and Excise (J.G.)		35	235 Cr			

2 LUCY BLUE ACCOUNT

Date	Details	Office account Dr £	Office account Cr £	Office account Balance £	Client account Dr £	Client account Cr £	Client account Balance £
	Balance					200	200 Cr
Nov 7	Cash: surveyor				117.50		82.50 Cr
Dec 1	Profit costs	200					
	VAT	35		235 Dr			

3 LYNDON TREE ACCOUNT

Date	Details	Office account Dr £	Office account Cr £	Office account Balance £	Client account Dr £	Client account Cr £	Client account Balance £
Oct 1	Cash: enquiry agent	75		75 Dr			
Oct 3	Cash: surveyor's fee	117.50		192.50 Dr			
Oct 4	Cash: counsel (VAT £35)	200		392.50 Dr			
Oct 8	Cash: you					500	500 Cr
Oct 9	Profit costs	60					
	VAT (£10.50 + £35)	45.50		498 Dr			
	Cash: transfer costs		498	—	498		2.00 Cr
	Cash: you				2.00		—

EIGHT

FINANCIAL STATEMENTS AND CONVEYANCING TRANSACTIONS

8.1 Financial Statements to Clients

Solicitors dealing with receipts of money and payments out on behalf of clients will have to account to the client for such receipts and payments. These will be shown on a financial statement, or statement of account, which will often be sent to the client at the same time as the bill of costs. This is common in, e.g., conveyancing transactions, or probate or trust matters. Other examples would be in respect of debt collection for a client, or any matter where funds have been received and held for a client.

Although there is no set form for such statements of account, they must be clear, contain a record of all receipts and payments, be relatively easy for the client to understand and show at the end the amount due to or from the client.

In conveyancing transactions it is a good idea to show a clear distinction between receipts and payments regarding the purchase of property, and receipts and payments regarding the sale of property. In probate and trust matters, a clear distinction between capital and interest should be made.

Later in this chapter some examples are given of financial statements in respect of conveyancing transactions.

8.2 Conveyancing Transactions

Note that where a client is selling one property and buying another, rather than have two ledger cards for the client, one for the sale and one for the purchase, it is usually more convenient to deal with both purchase and sale on one client ledger card, as the proceeds of sale will be used towards the purchase of the new property. A summary of the most common financial transactions found in respect of a client's sale and purchase is set out below. This is a guide only, as obviously these will vary.

(a) Discuss finance with the client, giving details of solicitor's own charges, disbursements, e.g., search fees, stamp duty, land registry fees, estate agent's commission. If there is a mortgage on the property to be sold, obtain details of the amount required to pay off the mortgage. If there is a mortgage on the purchase, discover how much will be available, less any costs.

(b) Money may be received from the client on account of costs generally.

(c) Pay any search fees, fees for office copy entries, etc.

FINANCIAL STATEMENTS AND CONVEYANCING TRANSACTIONS

(d) If the client has instructed a surveyor to check the property in respect of the purchase, surveyor's fees may be paid.

(e) Money may be received from the client or a third party, e.g., the bank, to meet the deposit payable on the purchase.

(f) On exchange of contracts, a deposit will be received in respect of the sale. This may be held as stakeholder, when a separate stakeholder client ledger card will be opened — it cannot be used towards the deposit payable regarding the purchase — or it may be held as agent for the seller, when it may be credited direct to the client ledger card and can be used towards the deposit payable regarding the purchase. Note that a solicitor should now account for interest on stakeholder money held, where appropriate. See **Chapter 9** on deposit interest generally.

Payment of a deposit on the purchase will be made to the seller's solicitors, either as agent for the seller, or as stakeholder.

(g) Completion statements will be sent in respect of the sale and the purchase, showing how much money will be required on completion, taking account of the deposit already paid, and any other adjustments, e.g., additional amounts in respect of carpets, fittings, etc. Note that these are merely for information — no entries will be made on the accounts until the sale and purchase are completed.

(h) A financial statement will be sent to the client, showing all the receipts and payments out in respect of the sale and purchase, together with the solicitor's bills of costs and the amount that will be due to the client, or needed from the client to complete. Note that at this stage, as the bills have been sent out, the solicitor's costs and VAT will be debited to the client ledger card. All other disbursements, receipts, etc. are entered only when actually paid or received.

(i) Any mortgage money in respect of the purchase will be received before completion and any money required from the client, if applicable.

(j) Complete the sale first, receive the net proceeds, i.e., the purchase price less any deposit paid, together with any other adjustments regarding fittings, etc.

If the deposit on the sale was held as stakeholder, the money should be transferred from the stakeholder account to the client ledger card. This should also be separately recorded on a transfer sheet or journal.

Pay out the amount needed to redeem the mortgage.

Complete the purchase. Ensure that mortgage moneys are available before paying out the amount required to complete the purchase, again less the deposit which has been paid, and take account of any other adjustments needed.

(k) Pay the estate agent's commission on sale. There should be sufficient money on client account to do this.

(l) Pay stamp duty regarding purchase, again from client account if the money is available.

(m) Pay Land Registry fees, from client account if possible.

(n) Transfer costs and disbursements due to the firm from client account to office account.

(o) Pay any balance to the client.

8.3 Receipt of Deposit on Exchange of Contracts

A solicitor receiving a deposit on behalf of a client may hold the deposit as:

(a) agent; or

(b) stakeholder.

8.3.1 RECEIPT OF DEPOSIT AS AGENT

If a solicitor receives a deposit on exchange of contracts which is to be held as agent, it is held on behalf of the client seller. To record the receipt of a deposit as agent, the solicitor will make entries in the accounts to record a receipt of clients' money on behalf of the client seller.

Example The firm acts for White, the seller of Whiteacre, which is being sold for £70,000. On 23 September the firm receives a 10% deposit to hold as agents.

WHITE: SALE OF WHITEACRE

Date	Details	Office account Dr £	Cr £	Balance £	Client account Dr £	Cr £	Balance £
Sept 23	Cash: purchaser's solicitor, deposit					7,000	7,000 Cr

CASH ACCOUNT

Date	Details	Office account Dr £	Cr £	Balance £	Client account Dr £	Cr £	Balance £
Sept 23	White Cash: purchaser's solicitor, deposit				7,000		7,000 Dr

8.3.2 RECEIPT OF DEPOSIT AS STAKEHOLDER

When a solicitor receives a deposit as stakeholder, it is not held on deposit for the client seller, or for the buyer, therefore the receipt of a stakeholder deposit should not be recorded in the client seller's ledger account.

A separate account, the stakeholder account, is opened to record dealings with deposits held by a solicitor as stakeholder. The deposit is held in the stakeholder account until completion, when it belongs to the seller.

The stakeholder account only records dealings with clients' money; the money belongs to the client(s) not the solicitor.

When the firm receives a deposit as stakeholder, the following entries are made:

(a) Credit the stakeholder ledger account.

(b) Debit the cash account client column.

Note the position where money is held on joint stake (see **7.2.4**).

FINANCIAL STATEMENTS AND CONVEYANCING TRANSACTIONS

> **Example** Assume that in the example in **8.3.1** the firm receives the 10% deposit as stakeholder.
>
> STAKEHOLDER ACCOUNT
>
> | Date | Details | Office account Dr £ | Cr £ | Balance £ | Client account Dr £ | Cr £ | Balance £ |
> |---|---|---|---|---|---|---|---|
> | Sept 23 | Cash: deposit re White sale of Whiteacre | | | | | 7,000 | 7,000 Cr |

The double entry will be in the cash account as in the example in **8.3.1**.

On completion of the sale the deposit is transferred from the stakeholder account to the client seller's account. The bookkeeping entries are those to record a transfer from one client ledger account to another.

> **Example** Continuing the example, assume that completion takes place on 23 October.
>
> STAKEHOLDER ACCOUNT
>
> | Date | Details | Office account Dr £ | Cr £ | Balance £ | Client account Dr £ | Cr £ | Balance £ |
> |---|---|---|---|---|---|---|---|
> | Sept 23 | Cash: deposit re White sale of Whiteacre | | | | | 7,000 | 7,000 Cr |
> | Oct 23 | White: transfer sheet | | | | 7,000 | | — |
>
> WHITE: RE SALE OF WHITEACRE
>
> | Date | Details | Office account Dr £ | Cr £ | Balance £ | Client account Dr £ | Cr £ | Balance £ |
> |---|---|---|---|---|---|---|---|
> | Oct 23 | Stakeholder: transfer sheet | | | | | 7,000 | 7,000 Cr |

8.4 Mortgage Advances

8.4.1 ACTING FOR MORTGAGEE AND PURCHASER

Rule 32(6) of the Solicitors' Accounts Rules 1998 provides that a solicitor acting for a borrower and lender on a mortgage advance in a conveyancing transaction shall not be required to open separate ledger accounts for the borrower and lender provided that:

FINANCIAL STATEMENTS AND CONVEYANCING TRANSACTIONS

(a) the funds belonging to each client are clearly identifiable; and

(b) the lender is an institutional lender which provides mortgages on standard terms in the normal course of its business, for example, a building society or bank.

Thus, if the solicitor is acting for a buyer and a building society provides the mortgage, the transactions can all be recorded in the client buyer's ledger account, without the need to open a separate ledger account for the building society.

If the solicitor is acting for a buyer and a private lender, separate ledger accounts must be opened for each.

In (a) above, 'clearly identifiable' requires the solicitor to ensure that the buyer's ledger account states unambiguously the nature and owner of the mortgage. Care therefore needs to be taken in completing the details entry. For example, if the Branchester Building Society makes an advance of £50,000 to Smith who is purchasing Greenacre, Smith's ledger account should state, when the advance is received:

'Cash: mortgage advance from Branchester Building Society: £50,000.'

Note that the mortgage money credited to the account still belongs to the lender, not the borrower, until completion takes place.

Example (institutional lender) The firm acts for Red who is purchasing Cosy Villa for £150,000. Red has obtained a mortgage advance of £100,000 from the High Finance Building Society for which the firm also acts. Red is providing the balance from his own funds. The firm receives the mortgage advance on 16 October 2000, with the usual instruction that the cheque is not to be negotiated until completion. Red has been informed that he will be required to pay £50,517 prior to completion. He brings a cheque to the office on 17 October. Completion takes place on 18 October and on the same date the firm sends two bills of costs to Red, one for £400 plus VAT for the conveyancing and one for £40 plus VAT for acting on behalf of the building society. The transactions will be recorded as follows.

RED: RE PURCHASE OF COSY VILLA

Date	Details	Office account Dr £	Cr £	Balance £	Client account Dr £	Cr £	Balance £
2000							
Oct 17	Cash: you					50,517	50,517 Cr
Oct 18	Cash: mortgage advance from High Finance Building Society					100,000	150,517 Cr
	Cash: seller's solicitor				150,000		517 Cr
	Profit costs	400					
	VAT	70		470 Dr			
	Profit costs (High Finance Building Society re mortgage)	40					
	VAT	7		517 Dr			
	Cash: transfer costs		517	—		517	—

211

FINANCIAL STATEMENTS AND CONVEYANCING TRANSACTIONS

Example (private lender) In the above example assume that Red is borrowing £100,000 from Uncle Black, for whom the firm also acts. On 16 October 2000 Uncle Black pays the firm £100,000 and gives written authority for that money to be used towards Red's purchase of Cosy Villa. The transactions will be recorded as follows:

RED: RE PURCHASE OF COSY VILLA

Date	Details	Office account			Client account		
		Dr £	Cr £	Balance £	Dr £	Cr £	Balance £
2000 Oct 18	Cash: you					50,517	50,517 Cr
	Uncle Black: transfer mortgage advance					100,000	150,517 Cr
	Cash: seller's solicitors				150,000		517 Cr
	Profit costs	400					
	VAT	70		470 Dr			
	Uncle Black: transfer costs	47		517 Dr			
	Cash: transfer costs		517	—	517		—

UNCLE BLACK: RE MORTGAGE ADVANCE

Date	Details	Office account			Client account		
		Dr £	Cr £	Balance £	Dr £	Cr £	Balance £
2000 Oct 16	Cash: you					100,000	100,000
Oct 18	Profit costs	40					
	VAT	7		47 Dr			
	Red: transfer sheet mortgage advance				100,000		
	Red: transfer costs		47	—			—

When this method is used the lender's costs are transferred from the buyer's account to the lender's account by making the following entries:

(a) Debit purchaser's ledger card office account with costs and VAT.

(b) Credit lender's ledger card office account with costs and VAT.

As an alternative to transferring the gross advance from Uncle Black to Red, the solicitor could have either:

(a) Transferred the net advance, after deducting costs, in which case Uncle Black's account would have appeared as follows:

FINANCIAL STATEMENTS AND CONVEYANCING TRANSACTIONS

UNCLE BLACK: RE MORTGAGE ADVANCE

Date	Details	Office account			Client account		
		Dr £	Cr £	Balance £	Dr £	Cr £	Balance £
2000							
Oct 16	Cash: you					100,000	100,000 Cr
Oct 18	Profit costs	40					
	VAT	7		47 Dr			
	Red: transfer net advance				99,953		47 Cr
	Cash: transfer costs		47	—	47		—

Or:

(b) Paid the net advance to the seller's solicitors out of Uncle Black's account. No entry will be made in Red's account in respect of the payment of the net advance.

8.4.2 SOLICITOR ACTING FOR MORTGAGEE ONLY

The accounting entries when the solicitor acts for the mortgagee only are:

(a) The solicitor opens an account for the mortgagee.

(b) When the mortgage advance is received, the solicitor makes entries in the mortgagee's account to record a receipt of client money.

(c) On completion, the solicitor makes entries in the mortgagee's account to record the delivery of a bill of costs to the mortgagee.

(d) On completion, the solicitor pays the net advance to the purchaser's solicitor and records this in the mortgagee's account as a payment of clients' money.

(e) Following completion, the solicitor transfers the costs from client to office account.

> **Example** The firm acts for the High Finance Building Society which is making a mortgage advance of £100,000 to Red in connection with his purchase of Cosy Villa. Red's solicitors are Bagnets. The firm's costs for acting for the building society are £100 plus £17.50 VAT. The mortgage advance is received on 16 October and completion takes place on 18 October. Costs are transferred on 18 October.
>
> ## HIGH FINANCE BUILDING SOCIETY
>
> | Date | Details | Office account ||| Client account |||
> |---|---|---|---|---|---|---|---|
> | | | Dr £ | Cr £ | Balance £ | Dr £ | Cr £ | Balance £ |
> | 2000 | | | | | | | |
> | Oct 16 | Cash: you | | | | | 100,000 | 100,000 Cr |
> | Oct 18 | Profit costs | 100 | | | | | |
> | | VAT | 17.50 | | 117.50 Dr | | | |
> | | Cash: Bagnets | | | | 99,882.50 | | 117.50 Cr |
> | | Cash: transfer: costs | | | | 117.50 | | — |
> | | Cash: transfer: costs | | 117.50 | — | | | |

FINANCIAL STATEMENTS AND CONVEYANCING TRANSACTIONS

8.4.3 SOLICITOR ACTING FOR BUYER/BORROWER ONLY

The accounting entries when the solicitor acts for the buyer/borrower only are:

(a) An account is opened for the buyer. No account is opened for the mortgagee because the mortgagee is not a client.

(b) On completion the firm records the receipt of the net advance as a receipt of client's money, in the buyer's ledger account.

(c) On completion the firm records the payment of the net advance to the seller's solicitor, as a payment of clients' money, in the buyer's ledger account.

(d) Entries are made in the cash account and the buyer's ledger account to record receipt and payment of clients' money, even if the cheque from the mortgagee is endorsed in favour of the seller's solicitor.

Example The firm acts for Red with regard to his purchase of Cosy Villa. Red is obtaining a mortgage advance of £100,000 from the High Finance Building Society. The solicitors acting for the building society have intimated that their costs, which are to be paid by Red, will be £100 plus £17.50 VAT. It has been agreed that these costs will be deducted from the mortgage advance. On completion on 18 October, the building society's cheque for £99,882.50 is received by the firm and a cheque for that amount is paid to Gallops, the seller's solicitor.

RED

Date	Details	Office account Dr £	Cr £	Balance £	Client account Dr £	Cr £	Balance £
2000 Oct 18	Cash: High Finance Cash: Gallops				99,882.50	99,882.50	99,882.50 —

8.5 Mortgage Redemption

8.5.1 ACTING FOR THE SELLER AND A LENDER

Rule 32(6) of the Solicitors' Accounts Rules 1998 may not apply on redemption of a mortgage. Thus, if the solicitor acts for the seller and a lender, separate accounts will need to be opened for the seller and the lender. NB: this will be uncommon in practice.

(a) Entries on completion. When completion takes place the sale proceeds belong to the seller and are shown as a receipt of client's money in the client seller's account.

FINANCIAL STATEMENTS AND CONVEYANCING TRANSACTIONS

Example The firm acts for George with regard to the sale of Somehut. Completion takes place on 28 January when £140,000 is received.

GEORGE: RE SALE OF SOMEHUT

Date	Details	Office account			Client account		
		Dr £	Cr £	Balance £	Dr £	Cr £	Balance £
Jan 28	Cash: sale proceeds					140,000	140,000 Cr

(b) Costs. The solicitor's costs for acting on the redemption will be recorded in the lender's account, although in practice they will be paid by the seller client.

Example The firm's costs for acting on behalf of Andover Building Society, which has a mortgage on Somehut, of £55,000, and for whom the firm also acts, are £40 plus VAT £7.

ANDOVER BUILDING SOCIETY: RE MORTGAGE REDEMPTION (GEORGE)

Date	Details	Office account			Client account		
		Dr £	Cr £	Balance £	Dr £	Cr £	Balance £
Jan 28	Profit costs VAT	40 7		47 Dr			

As the redemption costs will be paid by the borrower, a transfer of the costs and VAT will be made from the borrower's account to the lender's account. The transfer will be effected by making the following entries in the accounts.

(i) Debit the seller's ledger account office column.

(ii) Credit the lender's ledger account office column.

(c) Redemption. When the mortgage is redeemed a transfer of the redemption money is made from the seller's account to the lender's account. The payment of the redemption money to the lender is then shown as a payment of client money from the ledger account.

FINANCIAL STATEMENTS AND CONVEYANCING TRANSACTIONS

Example The firm's costs for acting for George on the sale of Somehut are £200 plus VAT £35. The redemption figure for the mortgage is £55,000. The mortgage is redeemed and costs transferred on 28 January. On the same date a cheque is sent to George for the balance due to him. The entries in the ledger accounts for George and Andover Building Society will be as follows:

GEORGE: RE SALE OF SOMEHUT

Date	Details	Office account Dr £	Cr £	Balance £	Client account Dr £	Cr £	Balance £
Jan 28	Cash: sale proceeds					140,000	140,000 Cr
	Andover: transfer mortgage redemption				55,000		85,000 Cr
	Profit costs	200					
	VAT	35		235 Dr			
	Andover: transfer costs	47		282 Dr			
	Cash: transfer costs					282	84,718 Cr
	Cash: transfer costs		282	—			
	Cash: you				84,718		—

ANDOVER: RE MORTGAGE REDEMPTION (GEORGE)

Date	Details	Office account Dr £	Cr £	Balance £	Client account Dr £	Cr £	Balance £
Jan 28	Profit costs	40					
	VAT	7		47 Dr			
	George: transfer redemption money					55,000	55,000 Cr
	George: transfer costs		47	—			
	Cash: you (mortgage redemption)				55,000		—

8.6 Completion

8.6.1 FINANCIAL STATEMENT

Prior to the completion of a sale or purchase on behalf of a conveyancing client, a financial statement will be sent to the client. This will show the amount which the client will have to provide for completion or the balance due to the client following completion. There is no set form of financial statement, but whichever form is used it is essential that the statement should show all moneys received from and on behalf of the client and all payments made on his or her behalf.

The following is a suggested method of presentation of a financial statement when a solicitor is acting for a client selling and buying property simultaneously.

FINANCIAL STATEMENTS AND CONVEYANCING TRANSACTIONS

FINANCIAL STATEMENT

To: A. Client.
Re: Sale of Blackacre
    Purchase of Whiteacre

		£	£	£
Sale of Blackacre				
Receipts:	Deposit	X		
	Balance of sale price	X	X	
Less payments:				
	Estate agent's fee	X		
	Mortgage redemption	X		
	Costs on sale	X		
	VAT thereon	X	X	
	Net sale proceeds			X
Purchase of Whiteacre				
Payments:	Deposit	X		
	Balance of purchase money	X		
	Stamp duty	X		
	Land Registry fees	X		
	Search fees	X		
	Mortgage costs (incl VAT)	X		
	Purchase costs	X		
	VAT thereon	X	X	
Less:	Receipts			
	Paid by you on account	X		
	Mortgage advance	X	X	
	Required to complete purchase			X
Amount required to complete purchase				X
Less amount due from sale				X
Balance due from you prior to completion				X

8.6.2 EXERCISES ON FINANCIAL STATEMENTS

1. You act for Virgil who is selling 'Olympus' for £50,000. On 1 April you receive a 10% deposit as stakeholder, Olympus is subject to a mortgage of £15,000. You receive an account from the estate agent for £600 plus VAT £105. Your costs for acting on the sale are £200 plus VAT £35. Prepare a financial statement for Virgil.

2. You act for Samuel who is buying 'The Temple' for £80,000. He is borrowing £40,000 from the building society for whom you also act. Your local search costs £75. You receive a bridging loan of £8,000 from your client's bank for the deposit. You exchange contracts and pay the deposit. You pay bankruptcy search fee £1. Your costs for acting for the building society are £60 plus VAT and these are to be paid by Samuel. Your costs are £400 plus VAT £70, land registry fee £90 and stamp duty £800. Samuel's bank informs you that the interest on the bridging loan is £75. Prepare a financial statement for Samuel.

FINANCIAL STATEMENTS AND CONVEYANCING TRANSACTIONS

8.6.3 ANSWERS TO EXERCISES ON FINANCIAL STATEMENTS

1   FINANCIAL STATEMENT

To: Virgil
Re: Sale of 'Olympus'

		£	£	£
Receipts:	Deposit	5,000		
	Balance of sale price	45,000	50,000	
Less payments:				
	Estate agent inc VAT	705		
	Mortgage redemption	15,000		
	Costs on sale	200		
	VAT thereon	35	15,940	
Balance due to you from sale				34,060

2   FINANCIAL STATEMENT

To: Samuel
Re: Purchase of 'The Temple'

		£	£	£
Payments:	Deposit	8,000		
	Balance of purchase money	72,000	80,000	
	Stamp duty	800		
	Land Registry fees	90		
	Search fees	76		
	Bank loan interest	75		
	Mortgage costs (£60 + £10.50)	70.50		
	Purchase costs	400		
	VAT thereon	70	1,581.50	
			81,581.50	
Less:	Receipts:			
	Mortgage advance		40,000	
Balance due from you prior to completion				41,581.50

8.6.4 SALE COMPLETIONS

The solicitor's accounts must reflect all the transactions involved in completing the sale of a property on the client's behalf. The following entries will usually have to be made on the completion of a sale:

FINANCIAL STATEMENTS AND CONVEYANCING TRANSACTIONS

(a) Entries to record the delivery of a bill of costs to the client for acting on the client's behalf with regard to the sale.

Example The firm acts for Ali with regard to the sale of 'Church Cottage' at a price of £60,000. On 3 May a bill of costs is delivered to Ali in the sum of £200 plus £35 VAT. Ali's account will appear as follows:

ALI

Date	Details	Office account			Client account		
		Dr £	Cr £	Balance £	Dr £	Cr £	Balance £
May 3	Profit costs VAT	200 35		235 Dr			

(b) Entries to record the receipt of the sale proceeds from the purchaser's solicitor (i.e., entries to record a receipt of clients' money).

Continuing the example:

Completion of Ali's sale takes place on 3 May. The firm receives a bank draft for £54,000. A deposit of £6,000 was paid to the firm as stakeholders on 3 April. Ali's account will appear as follows:

ALI

Date	Details	Office account			Client account		
		Dr £	Cr £	Balance £	Dr £	Cr £	Balance £
May 3	Profit costs VAT Cash: purchaser's solicitor on completion	200 35		235 Dr		 54,000	 54,000 Cr

---

(c) Entries to record the transfer of the deposit from stakeholder account to the client's ledger account if the deposit was paid to the seller's solicitor as stakeholder on exchange of contracts.

FINANCIAL STATEMENTS AND CONVEYANCING TRANSACTIONS

Continuing the example:

STAKEHOLDER ACCOUNT

Date	Details	Office account Dr £	Cr £	Balance £	Client account Dr £	Cr £	Balance £
Apr 3	Cash: deposit re Ali					6,000	6,000 Cr
May 3	Ali: transfer sheet				6,000		—

ALI

Date	Details	Office account Dr £	Cr £	Balance £	Client account Dr £	Cr £	Balance £
May 3	Profit costs	200					
	VAT	35		235 Dr			
	Cash: purchaser's solicitor on completion					54,000	54,000 Cr
	Stakeholder: transfer sheet					6,000	60,000 Cr

(d) Entries to record the redemption of a mortgage.

Continuing the example:

Assume that there is a mortgage to the Timberwell Building Society on 'Church Cottage'. The mortgage of £18,000 is redeemed on 4 May. Ali's account would appear as follows:

ALI

Date	Details	Office account Dr £	Cr £	Balance £	Client account Dr £	Cr £	Balance £
May 3	Profit costs	200					
	VAT	35		235 Dr			
	Cash: purchaser's solicitor					54,000	54,000 Cr
	Stakeholder: transfer					6,000	60,000 Cr
May 4	Cash: Timberwell Building Society				18,000		42,000 Cr

(e) Entries to record the payment of any outstanding disbursements, e.g., estate agent's fees.

FINANCIAL STATEMENTS AND CONVEYANCING TRANSACTIONS

Continuing the example:

Assume that on 6 May the firm pays an estate agent's charges of £705. Ali's account would appear as follows:

ALI

Date	Details	Office account			Client account		
		Dr £	Cr £	Balance £	Dr £	Cr £	Balance £
May 3	Profit costs	200					
	VAT	35		235 Dr			
	Cash: purchaser's solicitor					54,000	54,000 Cr
	Stakeholder: transfer					6,000	60,000 Cr
May 4	Cash: Timberwell Building Society: redemption				18,000		42,000 Cr
May 6	Cash: estate agent				705		41,295 Cr

(f) Entries to record the transfer of costs from client to office account and to record the payment to the client of any balance owed.

Continuing the example:

Assume that on 6 May costs are transferred and the balance remaining in client account is paid to Ali.

Ali's account will appear as follows:

ALI

Date	Details	Office account			Client account		
		Dr £	Cr £	Balance £	Dr £	Cr £	Balance £
May 3	Profit costs	200					
	VAT	35		235 Dr			
	Cash: purchaser's solicitor					54,000	54,000 Cr
	Stakeholder: transfer					6,000	60,000 Cr
May 4	Cash: Timberwell Building Society: redemption				18,000		42,000 Cr
May 6	Cash: estate agent				705		41,295 Cr
	Cash: transfer: costs				235		41,060 Cr
	Cash: transfer: costs		235	—			
	Cash: you				41,060		—

FINANCIAL STATEMENTS AND CONVEYANCING TRANSACTIONS

8.6.5 PURCHASE COMPLETIONS

The solicitor's accounts must reflect all the transactions involved in completing the purchase of a property on the client's behalf. The following entries will usually have to be made on the completion of a purchase.

(a) Entries to record the delivery of a bill of costs to the client for acting with regard to the purchase.

Example The firm acts for Alfred with regard to the purchase of 'Costa Bit' at a price of £45,000. On 3 May a bill of costs is delivered to Alfred in the sum of £300 plus VAT £52.50. The firm also acted for the mortgagee, Tall Trees Building Society, and its costs are £60 plus VAT £10.50. Alfred's account will appear as follows:

ALFRED

Date	Details	Office account			Client account		
		Dr £	Cr £	Balance £	Dr £	Cr £	Balance £
2000 May 3	Profit costs VAT Profit costs: building society VAT	300 52.50 60 10.50		352.50 Dr 423 Dr			

(b) Entries to record the receipt of the balance of the purchase money from the client, if required, as shown on the financial statement.

Continuing the example:

A financial statement has been delivered to Alfred, showing a balance due from him on completion of £11,023. On 3 May Alfred pays the sum of £11,023 to the firm. Alfred's account will appear as follows:

ALFRED

Date	Details	Office account			Client account		
		Dr £	Cr £	Balance £	Dr £	Cr £	Balance £
2000 May 3	Profit costs VAT Profit costs: building society VAT Cash: you	300 52.50 60 10.50		352.50 Dr 423 Dr		 11,023	 11,023 Cr

(c) Entries to record the receipt of the mortgage advance from the building society. Note: if the mortgage was from a private lender for whom the firm was acting, a separate ledger account would be opened for the lender and the mortgage advance would be shown as a transfer from the lender's account.

Continuing the example:

Alfred has obtained a mortgage advance of £30,000 from the Tall Trees Building Society for whom the firm also acts.

ALFRED

Date	Details	Office account			Client account		
		Dr £	Cr £	Balance £	Dr £	Cr £	Balance £
May 3	Profit costs VAT Profit costs: building society VAT Cash: Tall Trees Building Society, mortgage advance	300 52.50 60 10.50		352.50 Dr 423 Dr		11,023 30,000	11,023 Cr 41,023 Cr

---

(d) Entries to record the payment of the balance of the purchase moneys to the seller's solicitors.

Continuing the example:

Completion takes place on 3 May. On 3 April a 10% deposit had been paid to the seller's solicitors, Redhen and Co. The balance payable to Redhen and Co. on completion is £40,500. Alfred's account would appear as follows:

ALFRED

Date	Details	Office account			Client account		
		Dr £	Cr £	Balance £	Dr £	Cr £	Balance £
May 3	Profit costs VAT Profit costs: building society VAT Cash you Cash: Tall Trees Building Society, mortgage advance Cash: Redhen & Co.	300 52.50 60 10.50		352.50 Dr 423 Dr	 40,500	11,023 30,000	11,023 Cr 41,023 Cr 523 Cr

---

(e) Entries to record the payment of any disbursements after completion, e.g., stamp duty or Land Registry fees.

FINANCIAL STATEMENTS AND CONVEYANCING TRANSACTIONS

Continuing the example:

On 5 May the firm pays Land Registry fees of £100. Alfred's account will appear as follows:

ALFRED

Date	Details	Office account			Client account		
		Dr £	Cr £	Balance £	Dr £	Cr £	Balance £
May 3	Profit costs	300					
	VAT	52.50					
	Profit costs: building society	60					
	VAT	10.50		423 Dr			
	Cash you					11,023	11,023 Cr
	Cash: Tall Trees Building Society, mortgage advance					30,000	41,023 Cr
	Cash: Redhen & Co.				40,500		523 Cr
May 5	Cash: Land Registry fees				100		423 Cr

(f) Entries to record the transfer of costs from client to office account.

Continuing the example:

Costs are transferred to office account on 7 May. Alfred's account will appear as follows:

ALFRED

Date	Details	Office account			Client account		
		Dr £	Cr £	Balance £	Dr £	Cr £	Balance £
May 3	Profit costs	300		352.50 Dr			
	VAT	52.50					
	Profit costs: building society	60					
	VAT	10.50		423 Dr			
	Cash you					11,023	11,023 Cr
	Cash: Tall Trees Building Society, mortgage advance					30,000	41,023 Cr
	Cash: Redhen & Co.				40,500		523 Cr
May 5	Cash: Land Registry fees				100		423 Cr
May 7	Cash: transfer: costs				423		—
	Cash: transfer: costs		423	—			

FINANCIAL STATEMENTS AND CONVEYANCING TRANSACTIONS

8.6.6 SIMULTANEOUS SALE AND PURCHASE

When acting for a client with regard to a simultaneous sale and purchase, entries will be made in the accounts as in **8.6.4** and **8.6.5**.

8.6.6.1 Question

Swift & Co., solicitors, acted for Gulliver in the purchase of 'Lilliput' for £350,000 and sale of 'Lagado' for £300,000 and for the Academy Building Society in respect of an advance. The following events took place.

2001

2 September	Paid search fees of £65 in respect of the purchase of 'Lilliput' by Gulliver.
9 September	Paid survey fee of £940 including VAT in respect of the purchase of 'Lilliput'.
10 September	The Academy Building Society instructed the firm to act in respect of an advance of £125,000.
15 September	Received from Yahoo Limited a cheque for £35,000, being a bridging loan in respect of 'Lilliput'.
17 September	Exchanged contracts for the sale of Gulliver's house, 'Lagado', the deposit of 10% (£30,000) having been paid to the estate agent by the buyer. On the same day contracts were exchanged for the purchase of 'Lilliput' and the deposit of £35,000 was paid to the seller's solicitor to hold as stakeholder.
24 September	Received completion statement from the seller's solicitor in respect of 'Lilliput', showing £315,000 due on completion.
27 September	Sent completion statement to the solicitors acting for the buyer of 'Lagado', showing the balance due of £270,000.
2 October	Received cheque for £125,000 from the building society. The profit costs to be charged regarding the advance are £120 plus VAT.
5 October	Sent financial statement to Gulliver showing the balance of money required from him on completion of the sale and purchase, together with bills of costs in respect of the sale, purchase and mortgage advance. The statement includes, *inter alia*, the following information:

Solicitor's costs on sale	£400 plus VAT
Solicitor's costs on purchase	£600 plus VAT
Estate agent's commission inc VAT	£7,050
Stamp duty	£10,500
Land Registry fees	£250
Amount to redeem mortgage	£60,500

7 October	Cheque received from Gulliver, being the balance of purchase money and payment of costs.
12 October	Completed the sale and purchase. The amount due to redeem the mortgage is paid the same day. A cheque for £22,950 is received from the estate agents, being the deposit less their charges.
14 October	The bridging loan of £35,000 is paid to Yahoo Limited. Gulliver has paid the interest due on the loan direct to Yahoo Limited.
15 October	Paid stamp duty.
25 October	Paid Land Registry fees. Transferred costs and disbursements from client account to office account.

Draw up the ledger account of Gulliver, showing all entries necessary to deal with the above events, and prepare a financial statement, suitable for presentation to Gulliver on 5 October 2001, showing the balance due from him on completion.

FINANCIAL STATEMENTS AND CONVEYANCING TRANSACTIONS

FINANCIAL STATEMENT

5 October 2001
To: Gulliver
Re: Sale of 'Lagado'
    Purchase of 'Lilliput'

Sale of 'Lagado'

	£	£	£
Receipts:			
Deposit on sale	30,000		
Balance of sale price	270,000		
		300,000	
Less payments:			
Estate agent (inc VAT)	7,050		
Mortgage redemption	60,500		
Costs	400		
VAT on costs	70		
		68,020	
Net proceeds of sale		231,980	
Purchase of 'Lilliput'			
Payments:			
Deposit	35,000		
Balance of purchase price	315,000		
		350,000	
Add:			
Survey fee	940		
Search fees	65		
Stamp duty	10,500		
Land Registry fees	250		
Cost re mortgage advance inc VAT	141		
Costs on purchase inc VAT	705		
		12,601	
			362,601
Less: Mortgage advance			125,000
Amount required to complete purchase			237,601
Less net sale proceeds			231,980
Balance required from you to complete			5,621

FINANCIAL STATEMENTS AND CONVEYANCING TRANSACTIONS

GULLIVER
SALE OF 'LAGADO': PURCHASE OF 'LILLIPUT'

Date	Details	Office account Dr £	Office account Cr £	Office account Balance £	Client account Dr £	Client account Cr £	Client account Balance £
2001							
Sept 2	Cash search fee	65		65 Dr			
Sept 9	Cash survey fee	940		1,005 Dr			
Sept 15	Cash: Yahoo Ltd re deposit					35,000	35,000 Cr
Sept 17	Cash: deposit on purchase				35,000		—
Oct 2	Cash: mortgage advance Academy Building Society					125,000	125,000 Cr
Oct 5	Costs on sale	400					
	VAT	70		1,475 Dr			
	Costs on purchase	600					
	VAT	105		2,180 Dr			
	Costs re advance	120					
	VAT	21		2,321 Dr			
Oct 7	Cash: you to complete					5,621	130,621 Cr
Oct 12	Cash balance proceeds sale					270,000	400,621 Cr
	Cash: estate agent's deposit on sale less their commission					22,950	423,571 Cr
	Cash: re purchase				315,000		108,571 Cr
	Transfer re redemption				60,500		48,071 Cr
Oct 14	Cash: bridging loan				35,000		13,071 Cr
Oct 15	Cash: stamp duty				10,500		2,571 Cr
Oct 25	Cash: Land Registry fee				250		2,321 Cr
	Cash: transfer costs and disbursements		2,321	—	2,321		—

8.7 Exercises on Conveyancing Transactions

1 Guppy and Jobling, solicitors, acted for Smallweed in respect of the purchase of a house 'The Badgers' and the sale of his existing house 'Chesney'. 'The Badgers' was being purchased for £180,000 and 'Chesney' was to be sold for £140,000.

2001
8 May   Paid local search fees of £50.
14 May   Instructions received from the Dedlock Building Society to act in connection with the advance to Smallweed of £28,000 regarding 'The Badgers'.
20 May   Received £18,000 from Smallweed, being the deposit on 'The Badgers'.
25 May   Exchanged contracts for the sale of 'Chesney' and received 10% deposit as stakeholder. Also exchanged contracts for purchase of 'The Badgers' and paid 10% deposit to the seller as stakeholder.
10 June   Seller's solicitors sent completion statement showing the balance of purchase money due, being the purchase price less the deposit paid.
15 June   Sent financial statement to Smallweed, showing the amount due from him on completion, together with bills of costs in respect of the sale and the purchase. Costs on sale were £280 plus VAT, costs on the purchase were £360 plus VAT, costs in respect of the mortgage advance were £80 plus VAT.

FINANCIAL STATEMENTS AND CONVEYANCING TRANSACTIONS

23 June	Smallweed sent a cheque for the amount shown as due on the financial statement.
24 June	Paid petty cash search fees of £10.
25 June	Received advance cheque from the Dedlock Building Society.
27 June	Completed the sale and purchase of the properties.
30 June	Paid the estate agent's charges, being £2,800 plus VAT. Paid stamp duty of £1,800.
10 July	Paid Land Registry fees of £400. Transferred costs and disbursements from client account to office account.

Draw up the financial statement for Smallweed and the client ledger card.

2 Mick, Mike Michael and Co. acted for Jones in the sale of his house 'Nibblers' for £50,000 and for the Expandant Building Society who were owed £15,000 by way of mortgage on the house. The following events took place:

2001

8 May	Received cheque for £45,000 from the buyer's solicitors, being the balance of purchase moneys. The amount required to redeem the mortgage including interest is £15,325. The amount due to the building society is paid by cheque.
9 May	Noe de Lay and Co., estate agents, acting for Jones, send a cheque for £3,590, being the deposit less their commission of £1,200 plus VAT £210.
10 May	Sent cheque for £594 including VAT to I. Repare in respect of pre-sale repairs to the property.
13 May	Bill of costs sent to Jones for £220 plus VAT.
15 May	Costs and disbursements are transferred to office account and the balance due to Jones is paid to him.

Write up the client's ledger account for Jones, showing all necessary entries to record the above transactions. VAT is to be calculated at 17.5%.

(Law Society Final Examination, updated.)

3 Edward has recently retired and wishes to sell his house The Larches for £250,000 and purchase Rose Cottage for £140,000. There is a mortgage on The Larches of £25,000. He instructs Able and Co, solicitors, to act on the sale and purchase.

The following events and transactions take place and you are required to draw up a financial statement for Edward and to show the ledger card of Edward on the books of Able and Co, making all the necessary entries to deal with the events and transactions. Both the sale and purchase should be dealt with on one ledger account for Edward.

The rate of VAT is to be taken at 17.5%.

2001

6 February	Received cheque from Edward for £200 on account of costs generally.
11 February	Local land charges search fee of £80 is paid from client account re Rose Cottage.
20 February	The survey fee re Rose Cottage is paid from office account, amounting to £400 plus VAT. The invoice is made out to Edward. The balance on client account is transferred to office account.
22 February	As Edward has no readily available cash for the deposit on Rose Cottage a bridging loan is arranged with his bank, Village Bank PLC. The bank forward a cheque for £14,000 to be used for the deposit.

FINANCIAL STATEMENTS AND CONVEYANCING TRANSACTIONS

3 March   Contracts are exchanged for the sale of The Larches, the deposit of £25,000 being paid to Able and Co as stakeholders. Contracts are also exchanged on the purchase of Rose Cottage and a cheque for the deposit of £14,000 is forwarded to the seller's solicitors, who are also holding as stakeholder.

20 March   A completion statement is sent to the buyer's solicitors in respect of the sale of The Larches showing the balance due being £225,000. The solicitors for the seller of Rose Cottage confirm that the balance due on completion will be £126,000.

23 March   An invoice is received from the estate agent acting for Edward, showing commission due of £4,000 plus VAT.

29 March   Bills of costs in respect of the sale and purchase are sent to Edward, being £680 plus VAT in respect of the sale of The Larches and £360 plus VAT in respect of the purchase of Rose Cottage.

2 April   Completed sale of The Larches and purchase of Rose Cottage. The bridging loan is repaid to the Village Bank PLC together with interest of £80. The mortgage of The Larches is redeemed, being £24,500, taking into account payments made and including interest due.
Stamp duty of £1,400 is paid.

8 April   Paid the estate agent's commission plus VAT. Paid the Land Registry fees of £120. Transfer costs and disbursements from client account to office acccount, having received confirmation that Edward agrees the costs. Edward has also asked that the firm retain the balance in respect of the transactions until he decides where to invest it. Interest allowed of £110 is transferred to client account before the firm transfers the balance to a designated deposit account.

4 Your firm acts for Andrew Arbuthnot who is purchasing 'Holywell House' for £60,000 with a private mortgage of £30,000 from Lancelot Lake for whom the firm also acts. The following events take place:

2000
2 December   Pay search fee £18.
16 December   Receive cheque for £6,000 from Andrew for the deposit.
17 December   Contracts exchanged. Paid £6,000 to the seller's solicitors.
20 December   Receive completion statement from seller's solicitors showing £54,000 payable on completion.
31 December   Send statement to Andrew showing amount required for completion including:

Costs on sale: £120 plus VAT
Costs on mortgage: £40 plus VAT
Search fee: £18
Bill of costs also sent.

2001
12 January   Receive mortgage advance and Andrew's cheque for the balance of the completion money.
15 January   Complete the purchase.
16 January   Transfer costs and disbursements to office account.

Prepare the ledger accounts for Andrew and Lancelot Lake and the cash account, together with the financial statement sent to Andrew on 31 December. It is not necessary to balance the cash account.

FINANCIAL STATEMENTS AND CONVEYANCING TRANSACTIONS

5   Team Players & Co act for Mr and Mrs Plum in respect of the sale of their property 8 Pleasant Avenue for £450,000 and the purchase of Top Hole for £600,000. There is a mortgage of approximately £100,000 on 8 Pleasant Avenue, due to the Trusty Building Society.

The High Flyers Bank Limited has agreed to advance £200,000 in respect of the new purchase. The bank will also assist with bridging finance in respect of the deposit due on the purchase. The balance required for the purchase will come from a bonus that Mr Plum is expecting.

2001

1 June	Local land charge search fee £100 paid.
9 June	Bridging loan in respect of the balance required for the deposit on the purchase is received in the sum of £15,000.
14 June	Contracts are exchanged in respect of the sale of 8 Pleasant Avenue the deposit of £45,000 being received as agents for the sellers. Contracts are also exchanged in respect of the purchase of Top Hole and a cheque for £60,000 is forwarded to the solicitors for the sellers who are holding as stakeholders.
20 June	A completion statement is sent to the buyers solicitors in respect of the sale of 8 Pleasant Avenue showing the balance due of £405,000 and a sum of £10,000 in respect of carpets, curtains and furnishings. The solicitors acting for the seller of Top Hole confirm that the balance due on the purchase will be £540,000.
21 June	An invoice is received from the estate agents acting for Mr and Mrs Plum showing the commission due to them of £9,000 plus VAT.
24 June	The firm sends bills of costs in respect of the sale and purchase to Mr and Mrs Plum. Profit costs on the purchase are £1,200 plus VAT, profit costs on the sale are £800 plus VAT. Profit costs in respect of the mortgage advance amount to £200 plus VAT.
25 June	Mr Plum sends a a cheque to cover the balance required on purchase and all costs and disbursements. The High Flyers Bank Ltd send a draft for £200,000 in respect of the mortgage advance.
4 July	Completed sale of 8 Pleasant Avenue and purchase of Top Hole. The bridging loan is repaid to the bank, together with interest of £140. The mortgage on 8 Pleasant Avenue is redeemed in the sum of £99,500. Costs and disbursements due are transferred from client account to office account. Stamp duty of £24,000 is paid.
10 July	Paid the estate agent's commission plus VAT. Paid the Land Registry fees of £300.

Draw up a financial statement showing the amount required from Mr and Mrs Plum to complete the transactions, and show the account of Mr and Mrs Plum.

6   You act for Dinah Dobbs in the sale of 'Green Trees' and the purchase of 'Red Roofs'. The sale price of 'Green Trees' is £40,000 and the purchase price of 'Red Roofs' is £80,000. She is purchasing 'Red Roofs' with a mortgage of £55,000 from the Lendalot Building Society. 'Green Trees' is mortgaged to a private lender, her nephew Charles. You have also received instructions from the Lendalot Building Society and Charles. The following events occur:

2001

2 August	Pay search fee £18 out of petty cash.
5 August	Receive instructions from the Lendalot Building Society in connection with the mortgage.
16 August	A bridging loan is obtained from the Mid-West Bank for £8,000 and that sum is transferred by the bank into Dinah's client account.

FINANCIAL STATEMENTS AND CONVEYANCING TRANSACTIONS

19 August	Exchange contracts. Receive deposit of £4,000 on 'Green Trees' as stakeholder. Pay £8,000 deposit on 'Red Roofs'.
23 August	Receive invoice from Sellalot estate agents for their commission, £400 plus VAT. The invoice is addressed to Dinah. Receive completion statement from seller's solicitors showing amount due to complete purchase of 'Red Roofs'.
30 August	Send completion statement of purchaser's solicitors showing balance of £36,000 due on completion of sale of 'Green Trees'.
2 September	Charles informs you that the amount required to redeem the mortgage on 'Green Trees' will be £10,425. Your costs will be £40 plus VAT, payable by Dinah. You ascertain from the Mid-West Bank the interest on the bridging loan is £83.
4 September	Send a financial statement together with bills of costs to Dinah showing: costs on sale £120 plus VAT, on the purchase £400 plus VAT and on the mortgage advance £60 plus VAT; stamp duty £800; Land Registry fee £175.
12 September	Receive mortgage advance, held to order until 16 September.
16 September	Complete sale and purchase. Send cheques to Charles to redeem mortgage and to the Mid-West Bank to pay the bridging loan and interest.
17 September	Pay stamp duty, land registry fees and estate agent's commission. Send balance due to Dinah and transfer costs and disbursements.

Prepare the financial statement sent to Dinah on 4 September and make the necessary entries in Dinah's ledger account, Charles's ledger account and the cash account to record the above transactions. It is not necessary to balance the cash account. VAT is assumed to be 17.5%.

8.8 Suggested Answers to Exercises on Conveyancing Transactions

1 Guppy and Jobling

FINANCIAL STATEMENT

To: Smallweed
Re: Sale of 'Chesney'
 Purchase of 'The Badgers'

	£	£	£
Sale of 'Chesney'			
Receipts: Deposit	14,000		
Balance of sale price	126,000	140,000	
Less: Payments:			
Estate agent's fee inc VAT	3,290		
Costs	280		
VAT (17.5%)	49	3,619	
Net sale proceeds		136,381	

FINANCIAL STATEMENTS AND CONVEYANCING TRANSACTIONS

Less: Purchase of 'The Badgers'			
Payments: Deposit		18,000	
Balance of purchase money		162,000	180,000
Costs		360	
VAT thereon at 17.5%		63	
Search fees		60	
Stamp duty		1,800	
Land Registry fees		400	
Mortgage costs		80	
VAT		14	2,777
			182,777
Less: Receipts:			
Paid by you on account		18,000	
Mortgage advance		28,000	46,000

Required to complete purchase   136,777
Less: Due from sale   136,381

Balance required from you prior to completion   396

SMALLWEED:
RE SALE OF 'CHESNEY' AND PURCHASE OF 'THE BADGERS'

Date	Details	Office account Dr £	Cr £	Balance £	Client account Dr £	Cr £	Balance £
2001							
May 8	Cash: local search fee	50		50 Dr			
May 20	Cash: you re deposit					18,000	18,000 Cr
May 25	Cash: deposit on sale				18,000		—
June 15	Costs on sale	280		330 Dr			
	VAT	49		379 Dr			
	Costs on purchase	360		739 Dr			
	VAT	63		802 Dr			
	Costs re advance	80		882 Dr			
	VAT	14		896 Dr			
June 23	Cash: you to complete					396	396 Cr
June 24	Petty cash search fees	10		906 Dr			
June 25	Cash: mortgage advance Dedlock Building Society					28,000	28,396 Cr
June 27	Cash: sale proceeds					126,000	154,396 Cr
	Transfer stakeholder					14,000	168,396 Cr
	Transfer sheet Cash: seller's solicitors				162,000		6,396 Cr
June 30	Cash: estate agents inc VAT				3,290		3,106 Cr
	Cash: stamp duty				1,800		1,306 Cr
July 10	Cash: Land Registry fees				400		906 Cr
	Cash: transfer from client to office	906		—	906		—

FINANCIAL STATEMENTS AND CONVEYANCING TRANSACTIONS

2 Mick, Mike Michael and Co.

JONES: RE SALE OF 'NIBBLERS'

Date	Details	Office account			Client account		
		Dr £	Cr £	Balance £	Dr £	Cr £	Balance £
2001							
May 8	Cash: sale proceeds					45,000	45,000 Cr
	Cash: Expandant Building Society: mortgage redemption				15,325		29,675 Cr
May 9	Cash: Noe de Lays (less commission £1,410)					3,590	33,265 Cr
May 10	Cash: I. Repare				594		32,671 Cr
May 13	Costs	220					
	VAT	38.50		258.50 Dr			
May 15	Cash: transfer: costs					258.50	32,412.50 Cr
	Cash: transfer: costs		258.50	—			
	Cash: you				32,412.50		—

3 FINANCIAL STATEMENT

To: Edward
Re: Sale of The Larches
     Purchase of Rose Cottage

		£	£	£
Sale of The Larches				
Receipts:	Deposit	25,000		
	Balance of sale price	225,000	250,000	
		————		
Less: Payments:				
	Estate agent's fees including VAT	4,700		
	Mortgage redemption	24,500		
	Sale costs	680		
	VAT thereon (17.5%)	119	29,999	
		————	————	
Net sale proceeds				220,001
Purchase of Rose Cottage				
Payments:	Deposit	14,000		
	Balance of purchase price	126,000	140,000	
		————		
	Search fees	80		
	Survey fee including VAT	470		
	Stamp duty	1,400		
	Land Registry fees	120		
	Interest on bridging loan	80		
	Cost on purchase	360		
	VAT thereon	63	2,573	

FINANCIAL STATEMENTS AND CONVEYANCING TRANSACTIONS

Amount required		142,573
Less paid on account		200
		142,373
Due from sale	220,001	
Less required on purchase:	142,373	
Due to you	77,628	
Add interest allowed	110	
Total due to you	77,738	

CLIENT: EDWARD

MATTER: SALE OF THE LARCHES AND PURCHASE OF ROSE COTTAGE

Note transferred £77,738 to deposit April 8

Date	Details	Office account Dr £	Cr £	Balance £	Client account Dr £	Cr £	Balance £
2001							
Feb 6	Cash: on account of costs					200	200 Cr
Feb 11	Cash: search fee				80		120 Cr
Feb 20	Cash: survey fee	470		470 Dr			
	Cash transfer balance due		120	350 Dr	120		—
Feb 22	Cash Village Bank: deposit					14,000	14,000 Cr
Mar 3	Cash: deposit on purchase				14,000		—
Mar 29	Costs on sale	680		1,030 Dr			
	VAT	119		1,149 Dr			
	Costs on purchase	360		1,509 Dr			
	VAT	63		1,572 Dr			
Apr 2	Cash: balance on sale					225,000	225,000 Cr
	Stakeholder transfer sheet					25,000	250,000 Cr
	Cash: balance on purchase				126,000		124,000 Cr
	Cash: repay bridging loan plus interest				14,080		109,920 Cr
	Cash: mortgage redemption				24,500		85,420 Cr
	Cash: stamp duty				1,400		84,020 Cr
Apr 8	Cash: Estate agents				4,700		79,320 Cr
	Cash: Land Registry fees				120		79,200 Cr
	Cash: transfer costs from client to office account		1,572	—	1,572		77,628 Cr
	Cash interest allowed					110	77,738 Cr

4 FINANCIAL STATEMENT

To: Andrew Arbuthnot
Re: Purchase of Holywell House

		£	£
Payments:	Deposit	6,000	
	Balance of purchase money	54,000	60,000
	Cost on purchase	120	
	VAT at 17.5%	21	
	Costs on mortgage	40	
	VAT at 17.5%	7	
	Search fees	18	206
			60,206
Less: Receipts			
Deposit paid by you		6,000	
Mortgage advance		30,000	36,000
Balance required from you before completion			24,206

CLIENT: ANDREW ARBUTHNOT
MATTER: PURCHASE OF HOLYWELL HOUSE

Date	Details	Office account			Client account		
		Dr £	Cr £	Balance £	Dr £	Cr £	Balance £
2000							
Dec 2	Cash: search fee	18		18 Dr			
Dec 16	Cash: you					6,000	6,000 Cr
Dec 17	Cash: deposit				6,000		—
	Costs (purchase)	120					
	VAT	21		159 Dr			
2001							
Jan 12	Cash: you					24,206	24,206 Cr
Jan 15	Lancelot Lake						
	transfer advance					30,000	54,206 Cr
	Cash: completion				54,000		206 Cr
	Lancelot Lake						
	transfer costs	47		206 Dr			
	Cash: transfer costs		206	—	206		—

LANCELOT LAKE

Date	Details	Office account			Client account		
		Dr £	Cr £	Balance £	Dr £	Cr £	Balance £
2000							
Dec 31	Costs	40					
	VAT	7		47 Dr			
2001							
Jan 12	Cash: you					30,000	30,000 Cr
Jan 15					30,000		
	Arbuthnot: transfer costs		47				—

FINANCIAL STATEMENTS AND CONVEYANCING TRANSACTIONS

CASH ACCOUNT

Date	Details	Office account Dr £	Cr £	Balance £	Client account Dr £	Cr £	Balance £
2000 Dec 2	Arbuthnot: search fee		18				
Dec 16	Arbuthnot				6,000		
Dec 17	Arbuthnot: deposit					6,000	
2001 Jan 12	Lancelot Lake mortgage advance Arbuthnot				30,000 24,206		
Jan 15	Arbuthnot: completion					54,000	
Jan 16	Arbuthnot: transfer: costs	206				206	

5 FINANCIAL STATEMENT

To: Mr and Mrs Plum
Re: Sale of 8 Pleasant Avenue
　　Purchase of Top Hole

	£	£
Sale of 8 Pleasant Avenue		
Receipts: Deposit	45,000	
Balance of sale price	405,000	450,000
Add: Payment re carpets curtains etc.		10,000
		460,000
Less: Payments:		
Estate agent's fees including VAT	10,575	
Mortgage redemption	99,500	
Sale costs	800	
VAT at (17.5%)	140	111,015
Net sale proceeds		348,985
Purchase of Top Hole		
Payments: Deposit	60,000	
Balance of purchase price	540,000	600,000
Search fees	100	
Stamp duty	24,000	
Land Registry fees	300	
Interest on bridging loan	140	
Costs on purchase	1,200	
VAT thereon	210	
Mortgage costs inc VAT	235	26,185
Amount required to complete purchase		626,185
Less: Mortgage advance		200,000
		426,185
Less: due from sale		348,985
Due from you prior to completion		77,200

236

CLIENT: MR AND MRS PLUM
MATTER: SALE OF 8 PLEASANT AVENUE AND PURCHASE OF TOP HOLE

Date	Details	Office account Dr £	Cr £	Balance £	Client account Dr £	Cr £	Balance £
2001							
June 1	Cash: search fee	100		100 Dr			
June 9	Cash: High Flyers Bank: deposit					15,000	15,000 Cr
June 14	Cash: deposit on sale					45,000	60,000 Cr
	Cash: deposit on purchase				60,000		—
June 24	Costs on purchase	1,200		1,300 Dr			
	VAT	210		1,510 Dr			
	Costs on sale	800		2,310 Dr			
	VAT	140		2,450 Dr			
	Costs on mortgage	200		2,650 Dr			
	VAT	35		2,685 Dr			
June 25	Cash: you balance due					77,200	77,200 Cr
	Cash: mortgage advance					200,000	277,200 Cr
July 4	Cash: balance on sale					415,000	692,200 Cr
	Cash: balance on purchase				540,000		152,200 Cr
	Cash: repay bridging loan plus interest				15,140		137,060 Cr
	Cash: mortgage redemption				99,500		37,560 Cr
	Cash: stamp duty				24,000		13,560 Cr
	Cash: transfer costs from client to office account		2,685	—	2,685		10,875 Cr
July 10	Cash: Estate agents				10,575		300 Cr
	Cash: Land Registry fee				300		—

FINANCIAL STATEMENTS AND CONVEYANCING TRANSACTIONS

6   CLIENT: DINAH DOBBS
MATTER: SALE OF 'GREEN TREES': PURCHASE OF 'RED ROOFS'
FINANCIAL STATEMENT

Sale of 'Green Trees':

		£	£
Receipts:	Deposit	4,000	
	Balance of sale price	36,000	40,000
Less: Payments:			
	Estate agent's fees	470	
	Mortgage redemption	10,425	
	Redemption costs	47	
	Sale costs	120	
	VAT at 17.5%	21	11,083
Due from sale			28,917

Less: Purchase of 'Red Roofs'

Payments:	Deposit	8,000	
	Balance of purchase price	72,000	80,000
		80,000	
	Search fees	18	
	Bridging loan interest	83	
	Purchase costs	400	
	VAT	70	
	Mortgage advance costs	60	
	VAT	10.50	
	Stamp duty	800	
	Land Registry fee	175	1,616.50
			81,616.50
Less mortgage advance			55,000
Required to complete purchase			26,616.50
Due from sale		28,917	
Required to complete purchase		26,616.50	
Balance due to you following completion		2,300.50	

FINANCIAL STATEMENTS AND CONVEYANCING TRANSACTIONS

CLIENT: DINAH DOBBS
MATTER: SALE OF 'GREEN TREES'; PURCHASE OF 'RED ROOFS'

Date	Details	Office account			Client account		
		Dr £	Cr £	Balance £	Dr £	Cr £	Balance £
2001							
Aug 2	Petty cash: search fees	18		18 Dr			
Aug 16	Cash: bridging loan					8,000	8,000 Cr
Aug 19	Cash: deposit paid				8,000		—
Sept 4	Costs: sale	120		138 Dr			
	VAT	21		159 Dr			
	Purchase	400		559 Dr			
	VAT	70		629 Dr			
	Costs: mortgage advance	60		689 Dr			
	VAT	10.50		699.50 Dr			
Sept 16	Cash: sale proceeds					36,000	36,000 Cr
	Stakeholder Transfer					4,000	40,000 Cr
	Cash: Lendalot Building Society mortgage advance					55,000	95,000 Cr
	Cash: purchase				72,000		23,000 Cr
	Charles: transfer mortgage redemption				10,425		12,575 Cr
	Cash: Mid-West Bank: repay loan				8,083		4,492 Cr
Sept 17	Cash: stamp duty				800		3,692 Cr
	Cash: Land Registry				175		3,517 Cr
	Cash: estate agent				470		3,047 Cr
	Charles: transfer: redemption costs	47		746.50 Dr			
	Cash: transfer costs				746.50		2,300.50 Cr
	Cash: transfer costs		746.50	—			
	Cash: you				2,300.50		—

CLIENT: CHARLES
MATTER: MORTGAGE REDEMPTION

Date	Details	Office account			Client account		
		Dr £	Cr £	Balance £	Dr £	Cr £	Balance £
2001							
Sept 4	Costs	40		47 Dr			
	VAT	7					
Sept 16	Dinah: transfer: redemption money					10,425	10,425 Cr
	Cash: you (redemption)				10,425		—
Sept 17			47	—			

239

CASH ACCOUNT

Date	Details	Office account Dr £	Cr £	Balance £	Client account Dr £	Cr £	Balance £
2001							
Aug 16	Dinah: bridging loan				8,000		
Aug 19	Stakeholder re Dinah deposit				4,000		
	Dinah: deposit paid					8,000	
Sept 12	Dinah: mortgage advance (Lendalot Building Society)				55,000		
Sept 16	Dinah: sale proceeds				36,000		
	Dinah: purchase					72,000	
	Charles: mortgage redemption					10,425	
	Dinah: loan repayment					8,083	
	Dinah: stamp duty					800	
	Dinah: Land Registry fees					175	
	Dinah: estate agent's fees					470	
	Dinah: transfer: costs	746.50				746.50	
	Dinah: payment of balance					2,300.50	

NINE

DEPOSIT INTEREST AND PROBATE TRANSACTIONS

9.1 Paying Interest to the Client

9.1.1 THE RULES

Where a solicitor holds money on behalf of a client then:

(a) Where money is held in a separate designated deposit account the solicitor must account to his or her client for the interest earned.

(b) If the money is not held in a designated deposit account a sum in lieu of interest is payable but not if:

   (i) the amount calculated is £20 or less;

   (ii) the sum of money held does not exceed the amount shown below for a time not exceeding the period shown:

   £1,000 held for 8 weeks.

   £2,000 held for 4 weeks.

   £10,000 held for 2 weeks.

   £20,000 held for 1 week.

   If a sum of money exceeding £20,000 is held for one week or less, there is no need to account for a sum in lieu unless it is fair and reasonable to do so having regard to all the circumstances.

   (iii) on money held for the payments of counsel's fees, once counsel has requested a delay in settlement;

   (iv) on money held for the Legal Aid Board;

   (v) on an advance from the solicitor to fund a payment for the client in excess of funds held for that client; or

DEPOSIT INTEREST AND PROBATE TRANSACTIONS

(vi) if there is an agreement to contract out of the requirement to pay interest. This must be by written agreement with the client. NB: contracting out is never appropriate if it is against the client's interests.

(c) The amount of interest should be a reasonable rate of interest on money held on separate designated deposit account or a fair sum in lieu of interest, i.e., equivalent to the higher of the rate earned on separate designated deposit or the rate payable if placed on deposit on similar terms by a member of the business community.

(d) A client may apply to the Law Society (the Office for the Supervision of Solicitors) for a certificate as to whether or not interest should have been paid and, if so, the amount and if the Law Society certifies interest should have been paid, this should be paid by the solicitor.

(e) These provisions in respect of interest do not apply to controlled trust money, as solicitors must account for all interest earned and not benefit themselves from the trust monies (see **7.2.6**.)

If the solicitor is a trustee with others outside the firm and holds money by virtue of a retainer as trust solicitor then the normal rules as to interest will apply.

(f) Where interest should be paid to a client, the solicitor may either:

(i) place the client's money on deposit in a separate designated deposit account in the client's name and pay the client the interest earned — to do this the solicitor must anticipate the need to pay interest; or

(ii) pay the client, out of the solicitor's own money, the amount which would have been earned as interest if the client's money had been placed on deposit.

9.1.2 DESIGNATED DEPOSIT

If a client's money is placed on designated deposit, the solicitor asks the bank to transfer the client's money from current client account to a deposit account in the client's name.

The bookkeeping entries to record the transfer to a deposit account are:

(a) Credit the cash account in the client column.

(b) Debit the designated deposit account cash account (only shows dealings with client's money).

DEPOSIT INTEREST AND PROBATE TRANSACTIONS

Example The firm acts for Brown with regard to the sale of 'Costa Packet'. On completion on 7 November, the firm holds £50,000 for Brown and decides to transfer the balance to a designated deposit account, opened on Brown's behalf.

CASH ACCOUNT

Date	Details	Office account			Client account		
		Dr £	Cr £	Balance £	Dr £	Cr £	Balance £
2000 Nov 7	Cash: Brown: sale proceeds Designated deposit: cash: transfer (Brown)				50,000	50,000	50,000 Dr ———

DESIGNATED DEPOSIT CASH ACCOUNT

Date	Details	Office account			Client account		
		Dr £	Cr £	Balance £	Dr £	Cr £	Balance £
2000 Nov 7	Cash: transfer (Brown)				50,000		50,000 Dr

No entry is made in the client's account but a note should be made at the top of the client ledger card.

BROWN

Designated deposit account
Opened 7 November 2000
Closed . . . .

Date	Details	Office account			Client account		
		Dr £	Cr £	Balance £	Dr £	Cr £	Balance £
2000 Nov 7	Cash: sale proceeds					50,000	50,000 Cr

When a client's money has been placed on deposit, the money is not available for the payment of disbursements on the client's behalf. Money must be transferred back to current account before payment can be made on the client's behalf.

When the solicitor asks the bank to close the designated deposit account, the bank will calculate the interest due and will notify the solicitor. The solicitor will make the following entries in the accounts to record the interest.

(a) Credit the client's ledger account in the client column.

(b) Debit the designated deposit cash account.

DEPOSIT INTEREST AND PROBATE TRANSACTIONS

Continuing the example:

Assume that interest of £500 is allowed on the account at 1 January 2001.

BROWN

Designated deposit account
Opened 7 November 2000

Date	Details	Office account			Client account		
		Dr £	Cr £	Balance £	Dr £	Cr £	Balance £
2000 Nov 7	Cash: sale proceeds					50,000	50,000 Cr
2001 Jan 1	Deposit: cash: interest					500	50,500 Cr

DESIGNATED DEPOSIT CASH ACCOUNT

Date	Details	Office account			Client account		
		Dr £	Cr £	Balance £	Dr £	Cr £	Balance £
2000 Nov 7	Cash: transfer (Brown)				50,000		50,000 Dr
2001 Jan 1	Brown: interest				500		50,500 Dr

When the client's money is taken off designated deposit account, the following bookkeeping entries are made.

(a) Credit the designated deposit cash account client column with the amount placed on deposit plus interest allowed.

(b) Debit the cash account client column.

Continuing the example:

Assume that the designated deposit account is closed on 1 January.

DESIGNATED DEPOSIT CASH ACCOUNT

Date	Details	Office account			Client account		
		Dr £	Cr £	Balance £	Dr £	Cr £	Balance £
2000 Nov 7	Cash: transfer (Brown)				50,000		50,000 Dr
2001 Jan 1	Brown: interest Cash: transfer (Brown)				500	50,500	50,500 Dr ———

DEPOSIT INTEREST AND PROBATE TRANSACTIONS

CASH ACCOUNT

Date	Details	Office account			Client account		
		Dr £	Cr £	Balance £	Dr £	Cr £	Balance £
2000 Nov 7	Cash: Brown: sale proceeds				50,000		50,000 Dr
	Designated deposit: cash: transfer (Brown)					50,000	———
2001 Jan 1	Deposit: cash: transfer (Brown)				50,500		50,500 Dr

No entry is made in the client's ledger account when money is transferred off deposit but a note should be put on the top of the ledger account to show that the designated deposit account has been closed.

Continuing the example:

BROWN

Designated deposit account
Opened 7 November 2000
Closed 1 January 2001

Date	Details	Office account			Client account		
		Dr £	Cr £	Balance £	Dr £	Cr £	Balance £
2000 Nov 7	Cash: sale proceeds					50,000	50,000 Cr
2001 Jan 1	Deposit: cash: interest					500	50,500 Cr

9.1.3 PAYMENT OF A SUM OF MONEY IN LIEU OF INTEREST

If a solicitor does not place a client's money on deposit and is required by the Solicitors' Accounts Rules 1998 to pay interest to the client, then the solicitor must pay a sum out of office account at least equal to that which the client would have received had that money been placed on deposit.

If a solicitor pays a sum out of office account in lieu of interest, a business expense has been paid. To record payments in lieu of interest, a nominal expense account, the interest payable account, is opened. This is an office account only.

When a solicitor pays a client a sum in lieu of interest only and does not, at the same time, account to the client for money held in client account on the client's behalf, the bookkeeping entries will be:

(a) Debit the interest payable account with the sum paid in lieu of interest.

(b) Credit the cash account office column.

DEPOSIT INTEREST AND PROBATE TRANSACTIONS

Example On 19 September 2001 the firm pays £20 in lieu of interest to its client Grey by sending Grey an office account cheque.

INTEREST PAYABLE ACCOUNT
OFFICE ACCOUNT

Date	Details	Dr	Cr	Balance
2001 Sept 19	Cash: Grey	£ 20	£	£ 20 Dr

CASH ACCOUNT

Date	Details	Office account			Client account		
		Dr £	Cr £	Balance £	Dr £	Cr £	Balance £
2001 Sept 19	Interest payable: re Grey		20	20 Cr			

A note should be made at the top of the client's ledger account to show that a sum in lieu of interest has been paid. No entry is made in the account itself.

GREY

Note: £20 in lieu of interest paid 19 September 2001

Date	Details	Office account	Client account

When a solicitor pays a sum in lieu of interest and at the same time accounts to the client for money held in client account on the client's behalf, the solicitor may either:

(a) send the client two cheques, one drawn on office account for the payment in lieu of interest and one drawn on client account; or

(b) send one cheque drawn on client account.

If the solicitor decides to send one cheque, drawn on client account, the following three sets of entries in the accounts will be made:

(a) Entries to record the payment of a sum in lieu of interest out of office account.

(b) Entries to record a receipt of client's money.

The entries in (a) and (b) above record the transfer of money to be paid in lieu of interest, from office account to client account.

(c) Entries to record a payment to the client, of the sum held on the client's behalf plus the sum paid in lieu of interest, out of client account.

DEPOSIT INTEREST AND PROBATE TRANSACTIONS

Example The firm holds £1,000 in its client account for its client Black. On 17 March 2001 the firm pays Black the £1,000 plus £40 in lieu of interest.

BLACK'S ACCOUNT

Date	Details	Office account			Client account		
		Dr £	Cr £	Balance £	Dr £	Cr £	Balance £
2001 Mar 17	Balance Cash: interest payable Cash: you				1,040	40[2]	1,000 Cr 1,040 Cr ———

CASH ACCOUNT   Double entry IN

Date	Details	Office account			Client account		
		Dr £	Cr £	Balance £	Dr £	Cr £	Balance £
2001 Mar 17	Black Interest payable: re Black Black: in lieu of interest Black		40[1]	40 Cr	1,000 40[2]	1,040	1,000 Dr 1,040 Dr ———

Double entry OUT

INTEREST PAYABLE ACCOUNT
OFFICE ACCOUNT

Date	Details	Dr	Cr	Balance
		£	£	£
Mar 17	Cash (Black)	40[1]		40 Dr

At the end of the financial year the balance on the interest payable account is transferred to the profit and loss account as a practice expense.

9.2 Earning Interest on Clients' Money

A solicitor is entitled to transfer a proportion of the money held in the client general current account to a deposit account, including a building society account.

The solicitor is entitled to keep any interest earned on the client deposit account. There is no need to account to clients for the interest earned, subject to the rules in **9.1**.

When a solicitor transfers clients' money from current account to deposit account the following entries in the accounts are made:

(a) Credit the cash account client column.

(b) Debit the deposit cash account client column.

DEPOSIT INTEREST AND PROBATE TRANSACTIONS

Example The firm has a balance of £100,000 on its client current account. The partners decide to place £30,000 of this on deposit on 9 September 2000.

CASH ACCOUNT

Date	Details	Office account			Client account		
		Dr £	Cr £	Balance £	Dr £	Cr £	Balance £
2000 Sept 9	Balance Deposit cash: general deposit					30,000	100,000 Dr 70,000 Dr

DEPOSIT CASH ACCOUNT

Date	Details	Office account			Client account		
		Dr £	Cr £	Balance £	Dr £	Cr £	Balance £
2000 Sept 9	Cash: general deposit, clients' money				30,000		30,000 Dr

Interest earned on the general deposit account is practice income and the firm will open a nominal income account, the interest receivable account, to record this income.

When the bank notifies the firm that interest has been earned on the client deposit account, the following bookkeeping entries will be made:

(a) Credit the interest receivable account.

(b) Debit the cash account office column.

Example On 8 May 2001 the bank credits £1,000 interest to office account on money held on general deposit.

INTEREST RECEIVABLE ACCOUNT
OFFICE ACCOUNT

Date	Details	Dr	Cr	Balance
2001 May 8	Cash (general deposit)	£	£ 1,000	£ 1,000 Cr

CASH ACCOUNT

Date	Details	Office account			Client account		
		Dr £	Cr £	Balance £	Dr £	Cr £	Balance £
2001 May 8	Cash (general deposit): interest receivable	1,000		1,000 Dr			

At the end of the financial year the interest receivable account is closed and the balance on the account is transferred to the profit and loss account as a practice income.

9.3 Example on Deposit Interest

Swanning, who intended to go on extended holiday, deposited the sum of £100,000 with the solicitor on 1 May 2001, with instructions that this sum was to be remitted to Taxhaven Ltd on 1 November 2001 to be held on Swanning's account. The solicitor decided to use a designated deposit account for the money and the sum of £105,000 was transferred to client current account on 31 October 2001.

The same firm of solicitors also acted for Martin in the collection of a debt due to him, amounting to the sum of £4,000. The debtor gave two cheques for the debt, each being £2,000. The first cheque was dated 1 July 2001 and the second was dated 1 September 2001. Both cheques were duly presented and met and the total amount due, after deduction of costs (£60 plus VAT £10.50) was paid to Martin by client account cheque on 5 September 2001. The firm has agreed to pay Martin the sum of £33 in lieu of interest.

The general deposit account for the firm earned £11,250 in interest for the six months ended 31 December 2001. Record the above transactions in the ledger accounts of the firm.

(Law Society Final Examination, updated and amended.)

9.4 Suggested Answer to Example on Deposit Interest

SWANNING

Designated deposit account opened
1 May 2001. Closed 31 October 2001

Date	Details	Office account			Client account		
		Dr £	Cr £	Balance £	Dr £	Cr £	Balance £
2001 May 1	Deposit: cash: you					100,000	100,000 Cr
Oct 31	Deposit: cash: interest					5,000	105,000 Cr
Nov 1	Cash: Taxhaven				105,000		

MARTIN

Date	Details	Office account			Client account		
		Dr £	Cr £	Balance £	Dr £	Cr £	Balance £
2001 July 1	Cash: debtor					2,000	2,000 Cr
Sept 1	Cash: debtor					2,000	4,000 Cr
Sept 5	Costs	60					
	VAT	10.50		70.50 Dr			
	Cash: interest					33	4,033 Cr
	Cash: transfer: costs				70.50		3,962.50 Cr
	Cash: transfer: costs		70.50	—			
	Cash: you				3,962.50		—

DEPOSIT INTEREST AND PROBATE TRANSACTIONS

INTEREST PAYABLE ACCOUNT
OFFICE ACCOUNT

Date	Details	Dr	Cr	Balance
2001 Sept 5	Cash: Martin	£ 33	£	£ 33 Dr

INTEREST RECEIVABLE ACCOUNT

Date	Details	Dr	Cr	Balance
2001 Dec 31	Cash: interest credited by bank on client general deposit account	£	£ 11,250	£ 11,250 Cr

9.5 Probate Transactions

These occur when a firm acts in connection with the administration of an estate. A summary of some common financial transactions is set out below:

(a) A grant of probate or letters of administration will be required, probate fees will be paid and, where applicable, inheritance tax. It may be necessary to obtain a loan from the bank to the executors in respect of the inheritance tax payable. This may be paid direct from the loan account to the Inland Revenue, or the money may be paid into the firm's client account before payment is made to the Inland Revenue.

(b) Payments will be made regarding advertisements.

(c) Once probate has been obtained the firm will use it to collect all the assets of the deceased, for example bank account moneys, building society moneys, life policy proceeds. Some of this may be used to pay back the bank loan for inheritance tax, together with any interest due on the loan.

(d) Property belonging to the deceased may be sold, e.g., house and household contents.

(e) Debts due from the estate of the deceased will be paid, as will funeral expenses.

(f) Pecuniary legacies will be paid.

(g) The firm will charge costs (plus VAT) regarding administration and any sale of property, and transfer such costs from client account to office account with the agreement of the executors.

(h) The balance of the estate will be distributed to the beneficiary/beneficiaries, together with any interest due from the firm, either from moneys held on designated deposit or interest in lieu.

9.6 Exercises on Probate Transactions

1 Olde, Bayley & Co., solicitors, are instructed by the executors of Passway, deceased, to administer the estate on their behalf. The gross value of the estate amounts to £62,000 and consists

of a house valued at £45,000 (subject to a mortgage of £12,000) and personalty valued at £17,000. There are sundry debts due by the estate amounting to £1,892. The following events take place:

2001

7 October	Probate fees of £50 are paid by the firm's cheque.
15 October	A cheque for £16 is drawn in respect of the statutory advertisements, the cost of the local advertisement (£8) being met by a payment out of petty cash.
18 October	The balance remaining in the Standoff Building Society (£223) is paid into client account.
21 October	Proceeds of life policy received, the whole amount (£5,000) being placed in a designated deposit account.
28 October	The household contents are sold and a cheque for £5,890 is received from the auctioneer. Commission of £620 had already been deducted.
4 November	Contracts for the sale of the house (£44,500) are exchanged, and a deposit of £4,450 is received by Olde, Bayley & Co., for them to hold as stakeholders.
18 November	Debts amounting to £1,927 are paid.
25 November	Paid funeral expenses £432.
4 December	The sale of the house is completed and a bank draft (£40,050) for the balance of the purchase money is received. The mortgage is redeemed by the payment of £12,367 which is inclusive of accrued interest.
11 December	A pecuniary legacy of £5,000 is paid to a legatee.
12 December	Bill of costs re sale of the house is prepared and agreed with the executors, profit costs being £440 plus VAT, and cash disbursements £20 (no VAT) are paid. Paid estate agents their commission £700 plus VAT.
16 December	Bill of costs for the administration of the estate, profit costs £580 (plus VAT) and disbursements, rendered to executors, and after receiving their agreement, all moneys due to the firm from the estate are transferred to office account.
17 December	The balance of moneys now held by Olde, Bayley & Co., on behalf of the executors, is paid over to Rich, the residuary legatee, in accordance with their instructions. Interest earned on the designated deposit account amounted to £107, whilst the interest to be allowed on other moneys held by the firm on behalf of the executors is £208.

Show the client ledger card of the executors of Passway deceased. The rate of VAT is to be taken as 17.5%.

2   The following balances appeared on the relevant clients' ledger accounts of Milky Way & Co., solicitors, as at 7 March 2001:

Saturn	Office account	£75 Dr	Client account	£1,294 Cr
Neptune	Office account	£15 Dr	Client account	£ nil

The firm is informed that Saturn died on 26 February 2001, and the executors appointed in the will instruct the firm to act in the administration of the estate generally. The estate consists of a house 'Eudestar' valued at £70,000 and personalty valued at £47,500. There are sundry debts due by the estate (£1,500) together with a loan from an insurance company (secured on a life insurance policy) amounting to £5,000. The residue of the estate has been left to Neptune, a nephew who is in the process of purchasing a cottage, 'The Wild Leap', a matter which is being dealt with by the firm.

During the administration, the following events take place:

DEPOSIT INTEREST AND PROBATE TRANSACTIONS

2001

8 March	House insurance premium (£95) on 'Eudestar', now due, and the firm debits the executors' account, the amount being transferred to the account of the insurance company, for whom the firm acts.
14 March	Probate fees of £70 are paid by cheque.
19 March	The grant is received and registered with the bank.
26 March	The amount invested by the deceased with the Constellation Building Society is, after registration of the grant, withdrawn, the balance amounting to £590 being paid into client account.
27 March	With the executors' concurrence, the net amount outstanding in Saturn deceased's account at 7 March 2001, is transferred to the executors' account. The firm draws a cheque in respect of statutory advertisements (£22), and pays £12 out of petty cash in respect of the local advertisement.
29 March	Received cheque from the Pluto Insurance Co. Ltd, for the sum of £6,342, being the net sum receivable from the company after the deduction of £5,158 in respect of the loan together with accrued interest.
1 April	Debts amounting to £1,500, together with funeral expenses of £1,000, are paid out of client account.
	The executors have agreed to an interim distribution of £4,000 to Neptune, which is transferred to Neptune's client account. The firm then sends a cheque (£4,000) to the solicitors acting for the vendor of the cottage 'The Wild Leap', for them to hold as stakeholders, contracts being exchanged the same day.
5 April	Exchanged contracts for the sale of 'Eudestar', the deposit of £7,000 having been received by the firm for them to hold as stakeholders.
12 April	Sundry fees (£3) paid from office account re the transmission of shares to Virgo, a beneficiary in the estate of Saturn, deceased.
26 April	Received completion statement in respect of 'The Wild Leap', showing £36,000 due, being the balance of purchase money. Sent financial statement to Neptune same day, showing profit costs of £300 excluding VAT (as per bill of costs attached thereto), Land Registry fees £70 and search fees £16, of which £15 had been expended prior to 7 March 2001. Paid £1 from petty cash, in respect of bankruptcy search.
30 April	Completed purchase of 'The Wild Leap', the balance of purchase moneys being received by the firm from the Bank of Aries as a loan, an undertaking having been given that the sum would be repaid to them from the proceeds of sale of 'Eudestar'. The executors had previously agreed to this arrangement.
2 May	Completed sale of 'Eudestar', receiving a bank draft (£63,000) in respect of the balance of purchase moneys. Paid Land Registry fees re 'The Wild Leap'.
9 May	The firm agrees the bills of cost for the sale of the house and the administration of the estate with the executors. Profit costs with regard to the sale amount to £440 (excluding VAT), and with regard to the administration £700 (excluding VAT), together with disbursements in both cases. With the executors' agreement, a sum amounting to £36,146 is transferred from the account of the executors to the account of Neptune, and a cheque for this amount is sent to the Bank of Aries in accordance with the firm's undertaking.
16 May	All moneys due to the firm from the estate are transferred to office account.
17 May	The balance of moneys held by the firm on behalf of the executors is transferred to the account of Neptune at the request of the executors, such sum being inclusive of interest allowed by the firm of £567.
	All moneys due to the firm from Neptune are transferred to office account, the balance due to Neptune being held pending further instructions.

DEPOSIT INTEREST AND PROBATE TRANSACTIONS

You are required to show the ledger accounts of:

(i) Neptune;

(ii) the executors of Saturn, deceased.

The rate of VAT is to be taken as 17.5%.

In making the necessary entries, it is important that the account in which the corresponding entry would be made is clearly identified by the appropriate entry in the details column.

(Solicitors' Final Examinations, updated.)

9.7 Suggested Answers to Exercises on Probate Transactions

1   EXECUTORS OF PASSWAY DECEASED

Designated deposit account
Opened 21 October 2001
Closed 17 December 2001

Date	Details	Office account Dr £	Cr £	Balance £	Client account Dr £	Cr £	Balance £
2001							
Oct 7	Cash: probate fees	50		50 Dr			
Oct 15	Cash: advertisements	16		66 Dr			
	Petty cash: advertisements	8		74 Dr			
Oct 18	Cash: Standoff Building Society					223	223 Cr
Oct 21	Deposit cash: life policy					5,000	5,223 Cr
Oct 28	Cash: auctioneer (less commission £620)					5,890	11,113 Cr
Nov 18	Cash: debts				1,927		9,186 Cr
Nov 25	Cash: funeral expenses				432		8,754 Cr
Dec 4	Cash: sale proceeds					40,050	48,804 Cr
	Stakeholder: transfer					4,450	53,254 Cr
	Cash: mortgage redemption				12,367		40,887 Cr
Dec 11	Cash: legacy				5,000		35,887 Cr
Dec 12	Costs: sale	440					
	VAT	77		591 Dr			
	Petty cash: disbursements	20		611 Dr			
	Cash: estate agent				822.50		35,064.50 Cr
Dec 16	Costs: re estate	580					
	VAT	101.50		1,292.50 Dr			
	Cash: transfer: costs				1,292.50		33,772 Cr
	Cash: transfer: costs		1,292.50	—			
Dec 17	Deposit cash: interest					107	33,879 Cr
	Cash: in lieu of interest					208	34,087 Cr
	Cash: Rich				34,087		—

253

DEPOSIT INTEREST AND PROBATE TRANSACTIONS

2   EXECUTORS OF SATURN DECEASED RE ADMINISTRATION OF ESTATE

Date	Details	Office account Dr £	Cr £	Balance £	Client account Dr £	Cr £	Balance £
2001 Mar 8	Cash: transfer: insurance premium: client account: Eudestar	95		95 Dr			
Mar 14	Cash: probate fees	70		165 Dr			
Mar 26	Cash: Constellation Building Society					590	590 Cr
Mar 27	Saturn: transfer: net balance					1,219	1,809 Cr
	Cash: statutory advertisement				22		1,787 Cr
	Petty cash: local advertisement	12		177 Dr			
Mar 29	Cash: Pluto Insurance Co. Ltd					6,342	8,129 Cr
Apr 1	Cash: debts				1,500		6,629 Cr
	Cash: funeral expenses				1,000		5,629 Cr
	Neptune: transfer				4,000		1,629 Cr
Apr 12	Cash: fees: transmission of shares to Virgo	3		180 Dr			
May 2	Cash: purchaser's of Eudestar					63,000	64,629 Cr
	Stakeholder: transfer sheet					7,000	71,629 Cr
May 9	Costs: sale	440					
	VAT	77		697 Dr			
	Costs: administration	700					
	VAT	122.50		1,519.50 Dr			
	Neptune: transfer				36,146		35,483 Cr
May 16	Cash: transfer: costs		1,519.50	—	1,519.50		33,963.50 Cr
May 17	Cash: transfer: from office account in lieu of interest					567	34,530.50 Cr
	Neptune: transfer residue				34,530.50		—

NEPTUNE: RE PURCHASE OF 'WILD LEAP'

Date	Details	Office account Dr £	Cr £	Balance £	Client account Dr £	Cr £	Balance £
2001 Mar 7	Balance			15 Dr			
Apr 1	Executors of Saturn deceased: transfer					4,000	4,000 Cr
	Cash: deposit re 'The Wild Leap'				4,000		—
Apr 26	Costs	300					
	VAT	52.50					
	Petty cash: bankruptcy search	1		368.50 Dr			
Apr 30	Cash: Bank of Aries					36,000	36,000 Cr
	Cash: purchase of 'The Wild Leap'				36,000		—

Date	Details	Office account			Client account		
		Dr £	Cr £	Balance £	Dr £	Cr £	Balance £
2001							
May 2	Cash: Land Registry	70		438.50			
May 9	Executors of Saturn deceased: transfer					36,146	36,146 Cr
	Cash: Bank of Aries				36,146		—
May 17	Executors of Saturn deceased: transfer: residue					34,530.50	34,530.50 Cr
	Cash: transfer: costs		438.50	—	438.50		34,092 Cr

Although not specifically asked to do so, it would be advisable to place the sum of £34,092 on designated deposit.

9.8 Test 1 on Probate Transactions

Allow approximately 1 hour to complete this test.

Tulip, Crocus & Co., solicitors, are instructed by the executors of Daffodil, deceased, to act in the administration of the estate generally. The whole of the net estate has been left to the widow of Daffodil, and consists of a house valued at £50,000 and personalty valued at £42,000. There are sundry debts due by the estate, amounting to £1,496, together with a bank loan of £5,000 which is secured on the house. During the administration the following events take place:

2001

1 March	Probate fees of £50 are paid by cheque.
4 March	Grant received and registered with the bank, which transfers all moneys due by it to the deceased, amounting to £896, to the firm's bank account.
5 March	At the request of the widow of Daffodil, the executors instruct the firm to sell the house for £50,000, together with some of the contents, and, when feasible, to send a bank draft for £5,000 to a firm in Spain, which is dealing with the purchase of a villa for the widow.
8 March	Cheque drawn on a client account for £20 in respect of statutory advertisements. The cost of the local advertisement (£12) is met out of petty cash.
11 March	Proceeds of life policy (£3,500) received, together with cheque from the Pompeii Building Society for £18,000 which closes that account.
12 March	Some of the contents of the house are sold and a cheque for £3,250 is received in respect thereof.
18 March	Exchanged contracts for the sale of the house, the deposit of £5,000 having been paid to the estate agent by the prospective purchaser.
22 March	Paid sundry debts of £1,496 together with funeral expenses of £485.
29 March	Received cheque (£11,900) in respect of the sale of units held in a unit trust by the deceased.
12 April	Bank draft in respect of the widow's villa sent to firm in Spain, the full cost of the draft (£5,012) being charged to the firm's client bank account.
16 April	The sale of the house is completed and a bank draft (£45,000) for the balance of purchase money is received. The bank loan is repaid which, together with accrued interest, amounted to £5,340. Received same day, from estate agents, the balance of the deposit on the house, less commission of £1,150 (including VAT).
19 April	Bills of costs for the sale of the house, and for administration of the estate are agreed with the executors. The bill of costs for the sale of the house

DEPOSIT INTEREST AND PROBATE TRANSACTIONS

	shows profit costs of £300, and disbursements £10. VAT is to be charged on the profit costs only. The bill of costs for the administration of the estate shows profit costs of £600 (plus VAT) and disbursements.
22 April	All moneys due to the firm from the estate are transferred to office account.
23 April	The balance of moneys held by the firm, on behalf of the executors, together with interest allowed by the firm of £410, is deposited into a designated deposit account pending further instructions.
30 April	Mrs Daffodil (the residuary legatee), who is already a client of the firm, having instructed it some time previously to act for her in the purchase of a cottage, has requested that the executors pay her the sum of £2,850 on account of money due to her from the estate, this amount being the deposit on the cottage she proposes to purchase. The executors have agreed, the firm sends a cheque for that amount to the solicitors acting for the seller, for them to hold as stakeholders, the cheque being drawn on the client account.
30 April	The firm, to date, has made disbursements amounting to £180 out of office moneys, in respect of the proposed purchase of the cottage.
24 May	A financial statement and bill of costs in respect of the purchase of the cottage, had been sent to Mrs Daffodil some time previously, showing the sum of £26,194.50 due, being the balance of the purchase price £25,650, sundry disbursements £380 (including VAT where relevant) and profit costs £140 plus VAT. The sum of £26,194.50 is transferred with the agreement of the executors, from the executors' account to the account of Mrs Daffodil, and completion then takes place. The account of Mrs Daffodil is then closed.

The rate of VAT is to be taken as 17.5%. Show the accounts of the executors of Daffodil, deceased, and Mrs Daffodil.

(Law Society Final Examination, amended.)

9.9 Suggested Answer to Test 1 on Probate Transactions

THE EXECUTORS OF DAFFODIL DECEASED

30 April £2,850 taken off deposit
24 May £26,191 taken off deposit

Designated deposit account
Opened 23 April 2001

Date	Details	Office account Dr £	Cr £	Balance £	Client account Dr £	Cr £	Balance £
2001							
Mar 1	Cash: Probate fees	50		50 Dr			
Mar 4	Cash: bank					896	896 Cr
Mar 8	Cash: advertisements				20		876 Cr
	Petty cash: advertisements	12		62 Dr			
Mar 11	Cash: life policy					3,500	4,376 Cr
	Cash: Pompeii Building Society					18,000	22,376 Cr
Mar 12	Cash: house contents					3,250	25,626 Cr
Mar 22	Cash: debts				1,496		24,130 Cr
	Cash: funeral expenses				485		23,645 Cr
Mar 29	Cash: unit trust					11,900	35,545 Cr

Date	Details	Office account			Client account		
		Dr £	Cr £	Balance £	Dr £	Cr £	Balance £
2001							
Apr 12	Cash (bank draft) villa					5,012	30,533 Cr
Apr 16	Cash: sale proceeds					45,000	75,533 Cr
	Cash: bank loan repaid				5,340		70,193 Cr
	Cash: estate agent, deposit (less commission)					3,850	74,043 Cr
Apr 19	Costs: re sale	300					
	VAT	52.50					
	Petty cash: disbursements	10		424.50 Dr			
	Costs: re administration	600					
	VAT	105		1,129.50 Dr			
Apr 22	Cash: transfer: costs				1,129.50		72,913.50 Cr
	Cash: transfer: costs		1,129.50	—			
Apr 23	Cash: in lieu of interest					410	73,323.50 Cr
Apr 30	Mrs Daffodil: transfer				2,850		70,473.50 Cr
May 24	Mrs Daffodil: transfer				26,194.50		44,279 Cr

MRS DAFFODIL

Date	Details	Office account			Client account		
		Dr £	Cr £	Balance £	Dr £	Cr £	Balance £
2001							
Apr 30	Balance b/d			180 Dr			
	Executors of Daffodil: transfer					2,850	2,850 Cr
	Cash: vendor's solicitors				2,850		—
May 24	Executors of Daffodil: transfer					26,194.50	26,194.50 Cr
	Cash: purchase				25,650		544.50 Cr
	Cash: disbursements	200		380 Dr			
	Costs	140					
	VAT	24.50		544.50 Dr			
	Cash: transfer: costs				544.50		—
	Cash: transfer: costs		544.50	—			

9.10 Test 2 on Probate Transactions

Allow approximately 1 hour to complete this test.

Only Mortal & Co., solicitors, are instructed by the executors of Styx, deceased, to administer the estate on their behalf. The estate consists of a house valued at £250,000 (subject to a mortgage of around £30,000) and personalty valued at £100,000. Debts due by the estate total £15,000.

The following events take place:

DEPOSIT INTEREST AND PROBATE TRANSACTIONS

2001

5 January	The inheritance tax payable in respect of the estate amounts to £28,800 and the deceased's bank agrees to advance that amount to the executors, the sum being credited to the bank account of Only Mortal & Co. The firm then issues a cheque in favour of the Inland Revenue for the same amount. Probate fees of £250 are paid by the firm's cheque.
10 January	Grant received and registered with the bank, who transfer all moneys due by them to the deceased (£16,000) to the executors' loan account.
16 January	A cheque for £150 is drawn on office account in respect of statutory advertisements, and the cost of the local advertisement, being £20, is paid from petty cash.
19 January	Proceeds of sale of shares, totalling £55,000, received by the firm and £13,000 is paid by the firm to the bank for the credit of the executors' loan account (which is then closed).
29 January	The household contents are sold and a cheque for £27,120 is received from the auctioneer. Commission of £1,800 including VAT had already been deducted.
2 February	Contracts are exchanged for the sale of the house for the sum of £250,000 and a cheque for £25,000 is received by the firm as deposit, to hold as stakeholders.
20 February	Debts totalling £15,000 are paid.
26 February	Paid funeral expenses of £2,000.
4 March	The sale of the house is completed and a bank draft is received for the balance of the purchase money. The mortgage is redeemed by the payment of £30,200, which includes accrued interest.
14 March	Legacies are paid, being £10,000 to Greenpeace and £5,000 to the NSPCC.
16 March	A bill of costs re the sale is prepared, and agreed with the executors; profit costs are £600 plus VAT. The estate agents are paid £5,000 plus VAT by cheque. The amount due to the firm is transferred from client account to office account.
17 March	Elysium, the sole residuary beneficiary, who is already a client of the firm, has instructed the firm to act for her in her purchase of a house. She has asked that the executors pay her the sum of £15,000 on account of the money due to her from the estate, this sum being the deposit on the house she is purchasing. After the executors have agreed to this, Only Mortal & Co. send a cheque for this amount to the solicitors acting for the seller of the house, for them to hold as stakeholders.
21 March	A bill of costs for the administration of the estate, agreed at £800 plus VAT, is sent to the executors and after receiving their agreement, the amount due is transferred to office account.
30 March	Interest allowed of £1,500 is transferred to client account. By agreement between Elysium and the executors, the balance of moneys now held by Only Mortal & Co. on behalf of the executors, is transferred to the account of Elysium.

Show the ledger accounts of the executors of Styx deceased and Elysium, as they would appear in the books of Only Mortal & Co.

9.11 Suggested Answer to Test 2 on Probate Transactions

EXECUTORS OF STYX

Date	Details	Office account Dr £	Office account Cr £	Office account Balance £	Client account Dr £	Client account Cr £	Client account Balance £
2001							
Jan 5	Cash: advance bank re inheritance tax					28,800	28,800 Cr
Jan 5	Cash: Inland Revenue re inheritance tax				28,800		—
	Cash: probate fees	250		250 Dr			
Jan 16	Cash: Statutory adverts	150		400 Dr			
Jan 16	Petty cash: local adverts	20		420 Dr			
Jan 19	Cash: sale of shares					55,000	55,000 Cr
Jan 19	Cash: bank loan account				13,000		42,000 Cr
Jan 29	Cash: auctioneer					27,120	69,120 Cr
Feb 20	Cash: debts				15,000		54,120 Cr
Feb 26	Cash: funeral expenses				2,000		52,120 Cr
Mar 4	Cash: balance purchase money re sale of house					225,000	277,120 Cr
Mar 4	Transfer sheet: stakeholder					25,000	302,120 Cr
Mar 4	Cash redeem mortgage				30,200		271,920 Cr
Mar 14	Cash: legacy to Greenpeace				10,000		261,920 Cr
	Cash: legacy to NSPCC				5,000		256,920 Cr
Mar 16	Pofit costs re sale house	600		1,020 Dr			
	Customs & Excise VAT	105		1,125 Dr			
	Cash: estate agents				5,875		251,045 Cr
	Cash: transfer costs from client to office account		1,125	—	1,125		249,920 Cr
Mar 17	Transfer sheet to Elysium on account				15,000		234,920 Cr
Mar 21	Profit costs re admin of estate	800		800 Dr			
	Customs & Excise VAT	140		940 Dr			
	Cash: transfer costs		940	—	940		233,980 Cr
Mar 30	Cash: interest allowed					1,500	235,480 Cr
	Transfer sheet: Elysium				235,480		—

DEPOSIT INTEREST AND PROBATE TRANSACTIONS

ELYSIUM RE PURCHASE OF HOUSE

Date	Details	Office account			Client account		
		Dr £	Cr £	Balance £	Dr £	Cr £	Balance £
2001 Mar 17	Transfer sheet Exors Styx Cash deposit on purchase				15,000	15,000	15,000 Cr —
Mar 30	Transfer sheet from Exors Styx					235,480	235,480 Cr

Note: The firm should consider placing moneys held for Elysium on a designated deposit account.

TEN

FURTHER TRANSACTIONS

The following transactions are further examples of the operation of the Solicitors' Accounts Rules 1998, the Solicitors' Practice Rules 1990 and the Solicitors' Investment Business Rules 1995. Note that the Investment Business Rules will change shortly.

10.1 Commissions

A solicitor may receive commission from a building society or insurance company for introducing business or, in the case of an insurance company, for collecting premiums.

Rule 10 of the Solicitors' Practice Rules 1990 deals with commission and provides as follows:

(a) Where a solicitor receives a commission exceeding £20, this must be accounted for to the client unless the solicitor has disclosed to the client in writing the amount or basis of the calculation of the commission or, if neither the amount nor the basis can be ascertained, an approximation, and the client has agreed to the solicitor retaining the commission.

(b) Where the commission actually received materially exceeds the amount or basis or approximation disclosed to the client, the solicitor must account to the client for the excess.

(c) Rule 10 does not apply where a member of the public deposits money with a solicitor in the solicitor's capacity as agent for a building society or other financial institution and the solicitor has not advised that member of the public as a client about the disposition of the money. So solicitors who operate building society agencies will generally be able to retain the commission paid to them by the building society.

As a general rule, therefore, unless the solicitor has the client's prior written authority to retain commission, it is clients' money and must be paid into a client account upon receipt. Where there is no authority to retain the commission, the entries made in the accounts when it is received will be:

(a) Debit cash account client column.

(b) Credit the ledger account of the client entitled to the commission, client column.

There is nothing in the rules to prevent the solicitor from using the commission for or towards any bill of costs delivered to the client. If the commission does not exceed £20 or if the client

FURTHER TRANSACTIONS

gives written authority for the solicitor to retain it, the commission will be practice income and a nominal income account, the 'commission receivable account', will be opened.

When the commission is received the following entries will be made:

(a) Debit cash account office column.

(b) Credit insurance commission receivable account.

Example The High Risk Insurance Co. pays the firm £100 for introducing its client Jones. The firm has already obtained Jones's written consent to retain the commission.

INSURANCE COMMISSION RECEIVABLE ACCOUNT

Date	Details	Dr	Cr	Balance
		£	£	£
	Cash (High Risk)		100	100 Cr

CASH ACCOUNT

Date	Details	Office account				Client account		
		Dr £	Cr £	Balance £	Dr £	Cr £	Balance £
	Insurance commission receivable (High Risk)	100		100 Dr			

If a solicitor collects insurance premiums on behalf of an insurance company, then a client ledger account must be opened in the name of that insurance company.

To record the receipt of premiums, the solicitor will make entries in the accounts to record the receipt of clients' money.

Example The firm collects miscellaneous premiums of £500 for the High Risk Insurance Co. from non-clients.

HIGH RISK INSURANCE CO.

Date	Details	Office account			Client account		
		Dr £	Cr £	Balance £	Dr £	Cr £	Balance £
Jan	Cash: miscellaneous: premiums					500	500 Cr

When the firm charges the insurance company commission it makes the following entries in its accounts:

FURTHER TRANSACTIONS

(a) Debit the insurance company's ledger account office column.

(b) Credit the insurance commission receivable account.

Continuing the example:

The firm charges the High Risk Insurance Co. £50 commission.

HIGH RISK INSURANCE CO.

Date	Details	Office account			Client account		
		Dr £	Cr £	Balance £	Dr £	Cr £	Balance £
Jan	Cash: miscellaneous: premiums					500	500 Cr
	Commission receivable	50		50 Dr			

INSURANCE COMMISSION RECEIVABLE ACCOUNT

Date	Details	Dr	Cr	Balance
		£	£	£
	High Risk Insurance Co. (commission charged)		50	50 Cr

When commission is to be deducted from premiums collected for the insurance company, a transfer of the commission is made from client to office account.

Continuing the example:

On 31 January commission is transferred to office account.

HIGH RISK INSURANCE CO.

Date	Details	Office account			Client account		
		Dr £	Cr £	Balance £	Dr £	Cr £	Balance £
Jan	Cash: miscellaneous: premiums					500	500 Cr
	Commission receivable	50		50 Dr			
Jan 31	Cash: transfer: commission				50		450 Cr
	Cash: transfer: commission		50	—			

When the net premium is paid to the insurance company, entries are made in the accounts to record a payment of client money.

FURTHER TRANSACTIONS

Continuing the example:

The net premium is paid to the High Risk Insurance Co.

HIGH RISK INSURANCE CO.

Date	Details	Office account			Client account		
		Dr £	Cr £	Balance £	Dr £	Cr £	Balance £
Jan	Cash: miscellaneous: premiums					500	500 Cr
	Commission receivable	50		50 Dr			
Jan 31	Cash: transfer: commission					50	450 Cr
	Cash: transfer: commission		50	—			
	Cash: you				450		—

The above example is on the basis that the solicitor is taking money as an agent for a financial institution from someone who has not been advised as a client or that the solicitor has the client's written authority to retain the commission. If that were not the case and the solicitor was obliged to account to the client for commission, the commission would be shown as a transfer from the client account of the insurance company to the client account of the client entitled to the commission. No entries would be made in the commission receivable account because the firm has not received any income. So in the example below assume that the firm receives £300 from client Smith, being a premium payable to the High Risk Insurance Co. Commission on the premium totals £30. Smith has not agreed to the firm retaining the commission.

HIGH RISK INSURANCE CO.

Date	Details	Office account			Client account		
		Dr £	Cr £	Balance £	Dr £	Cr £	Balance £
	Smith: Cash premium due					300	300 Cr
	Smith: transfer commission transfer sheet				30		270 Cr

SMITH

Date	Details	Office account			Client account		
		Dr £	Cr £	Balance £	Dr £	Cr £	Balance £
	High Risk Insurance Co.: transfer sheet (commission)					30	30 Cr

FURTHER TRANSACTIONS

10.2 Agency

10.2.1 ACTING AS AGENT

If a solicitor is instructed by another solicitor to act as agent, a client ledger account will be opened in the name of the instructing solicitor.

When a bill of costs is sent to the instructing solicitor entries will be made in the ledger account to record the delivery of a bill of costs.

If the agent solicitor allows the instructing solicitor commission/reduction in the bill, the agent solicitor's bill of costs will show gross costs less commission. VAT will be charged on the net costs.

Example Brown & Co., solicitors, in Newcastle, instruct the firm to represent their client Simple in matrimonial proceedings. The firm's costs for acting as Brown & Co.'s agents are £180. Commission of £20 is allowed to Brown & Co. The bill which the firm delivers to Brown & Co. will be as follows:

	£
To professional fees	180
Less: commission	20
	160
VAT (17.5%)	28
	188

The net costs and VAT on the net costs will be recorded in the instructing solicitor's account when the bill of costs is delivered to the instructing solicitors.

Continuing the example:

The entries in the firm's accounts to record delivery of the bill of costs to Brown & Co. on 2 December 2001 will appear as follows:

BROWN & CO. RE AGENCY (MATRIMONIAL)

Date	Details	Office account			Client account		
		Dr £	Cr £	Balance £	Dr £	Cr £	Balance £
2001 Dec 2	Costs VAT	160 28		188 Dr			

When the instructing solicitor makes payment an entry will be made to record the receipt of the office moneys. Continuing the above example:

265

FURTHER TRANSACTIONS

> Assume that Brown & Co. make payment of the agency fees on 31 December.
>
> BROWN & CO. RE AGENCY (MATRIMONIAL)
>
> | Date | Details | Office account ||| Client account |||
> |---|---|---|---|---|---|---|---|
> | | | Dr £ | Cr £ | Balance £ | Dr £ | Cr £ | Balance £ |
> | 2001 Dec 2 | Costs | 160 | | | | | |
> | | VAT | 28 | | 188 Dr | | | |
> | Dec 31 | Cash— from you | | 188 | — | | | |

10.2.2 INSTRUCTING AN AGENT

When a solicitor instructs another solicitor to act as agent, the instructing solicitor treats payment of the agent solicitor's costs as a business expense. To record the payment of agency costs, the instructing solicitor opens a nominal expense account, the agency expenses account.

When the instructing solicitor pays the agent solicitor's costs and disbursements, the following entries are made in the accounts:

(a) Debit the agency expenses account with the agent's profit costs. (If the agent solicitor has allowed the instructing solicitor commission, the profit costs figure shown in the agency expenses account will be the net figure, i.e., the costs actually paid.)

(b) Debit the Customs and Excise account with VAT.

(c) Debit the ledger account of the client on whose behalf the agent was instructed with any disbursements (office account).

(d) Credit the cash account office column with the total paid to the agent solicitor. Note: these entries are made on the date on which payment is made to the agent.

> **Example** The firm instructs Burke & Hare, London solicitors, to represent its client, Knox. Burke & Hare charge £60 less commission of £6 plus VAT and have paid court fees of £10. Burke & Hare's bill is paid on 1 September 2001.
>
> CASH ACCOUNT
>
> | Date | Details | Office account ||| Client account |||
> |---|---|---|---|---|---|---|---|
> | | | Dr £ | Cr £ | Balance £ | Dr £ | Cr £ | Balance £ |
> | 2001 Sept 1 | Agency expenses | | 54 | 54 Cr | | | |
> | | VAT | | 9.45 | 63.45 | | | |
> | | Knox: disbursement | | 10 | 73.45 | | | |
>
> AGENCY EXPENSES ACCOUNT
> OFFICE ACCOUNT
>
> | Date | Details | Dr | Cr | Balance |
> |---|---|---|---|---|
> | 2001 Sept 1 | Cash: Burke & Hare: re Knox | £ 54 | £ | £ 54 Dr |
>
> The agency expenses account is a nominal expense account and therefore only has office columns.

CUSTOMS AND EXCISE ACCOUNT
OFFICE ACCOUNT

Date	Details	Dr	Cr	Balance
		£	£	£
2001 Sept 1	Cash: Burke & Hare: re Knox	9.45		9.45 Dr

KNOX

Date	Details	Office account			Client account		
		Dr	Cr	Balance	Dr	Cr	Balance
		£	£	£	£	£	£
2001 Sept 1	Cash: agent's disbursements	10		10 Dr			

When the instructing solicitor delivers a bill of costs to the client, the agent solicitor's gross profit costs will be included. The instructing solicitor does not allow the client the commission allowed by the agent solicitor, subject to the Solicitors' Practice Rules, r. 10.

Continuing the example:

The firm sends a bill of costs to Knox, showing its profit costs as £100 plus VAT. The bill is delivered on 28 November 2001

	£
To professional charges	100
Agent's charges	60
	160
VAT (17.5%)	28
	188
Disbursements	10
	198

The total costs (including the agent's gross fees) will be recorded as a delivery of a bill of costs by the firm to the client. No entry is made in respect of the agent's disbursements at this stage. The entry in respect of the agent's disbursements is, as we have seen, made when the agent's fees are paid.

KNOX

Date	Details	Office account			Client account		
		Dr	Cr	Balance	Dr	Cr	Balance
		£	£	£	£	£	£
2001 Sept 1	Cash: agent: disbursements	10		10 Dr			
Nov 28	Costs	160					
	VAT	28		198 Dr			

FURTHER TRANSACTIONS

10.3 Abatements

After a bill of costs has been delivered to the client, a solicitor may decide to reduce the profit costs.

When an abatement of costs is made, a credit note is sent to the client, showing the reduction in costs and VAT.

The solicitor will make the following entries in the accounts to record an abatement:

(a) Credit the client's ledger account office column with the reduction in costs and VAT (on separate lines).

(b) Debit the costs account with the costs abatement.

(c) Debit the Customs and Excise account with the reduction in VAT.

Example On 30 June 2001 the firm delivers a bill of costs to Charles, the executor of Fred, deceased, for £600 plus VAT. After discussing the matter with Charles, the firm agrees to reduce its bill to £400 and records the abatement in its account on 31 July 2001.

EXECUTORS OF FRED DECEASED

Date	Details	Office account Dr £	Cr £	Balance £	Client account Dr £	Cr £	Balance £
2001 June 30	Costs	600					
	VAT	105		705 Dr			
July 31	Costs: abatement		200				
	VAT: abatement		35	470 Dr			

COSTS ACCOUNT

Date	Details	Dr £	Cr £	Balance £
2001 June 30	Costs: executors of Fred deceased		600	600 Cr
July 31	Costs: abatement: executors of Fred deceased	200		400 Cr

CUSTOMS AND EXCISE ACCOUNT

Date	Details	Dr £	Cr £	Balance £
2001 June 30	Executors of Fred deceased		105	105 Cr
July 31	Executors of Fred deceased: VAT: abatement	35		70 Cr

10.4 Dishonoured Cheques

10.4.1 CHEQUE PAID INTO OFFICE ACCOUNT

If a cheque paid into office account is later dishonoured, the solicitor will make the following entries in the accounts:

(a) Debit the client ledger account office column with the value of the dishonoured cheque.

(b) Credit the cash account office column.

Example There is a debit balance of £235 on Peter's office account on 1 November 2001 in respect of costs previously charged to Peter. On 21 November Peter pays the costs by cheque. On 26 November the firm's bank notifies it that Peter's cheque has been returned by the paying banker. To record the above transactions, the following entries will be made in Peter's account.

PETER

Date	Details	Office account			Client account		
		Dr £	Cr £	Balance £	Dr £	Cr £	Balance £
2001 Nov 1	Balance b/d			235 Dr			
Nov 2	Cash: you		235	—			
Nov 26	Cash: dishonoured cheque	235		235 Dr			

The cash account will appear as follows:

CASH ACCOUNT

Date	Details	Office account			Client account		
		Dr £	Cr £	Balance £	Dr £	Cr £	Balance £
2001 Nov 21	Peter	235		235 Dr			
Nov 26	Peter (dishonoured cheque)		235	—			

10.4.2 CHEQUE PAID INTO CLIENT ACCOUNT

If a cheque paid into client account is later dishonoured, the solicitor will make the following entries in the accounts:

(a) Debit the client's ledger account client column with the value of the cheque.

(b) Credit the cash account client column.

FURTHER TRANSACTIONS

> **Example** On 4 February 2001 Jane paid the sum of £200 on account of costs and disbursements by cheque. On 7 February the firm's bankers notified it that Jane's cheque had been returned. The following entries will be made in the accounts to record these events.
>
> ### JANE
>
> | Date | Details | Office account ||| Client account |||
> |---|---|---|---|---|---|---|---|
> | | | Dr £ | Cr £ | Balance £ | Dr £ | Cr £ | Balance £ |
> | 2001 Feb 4 | Cash: you | | | | | 200 | 200 Cr |
> | Feb 7 | Cash: dishonoured cheque | | | | 200 | | — |
>
> ### CASH ACCOUNT
>
> | Date | Details | Office account ||| Client account |||
> |---|---|---|---|---|---|---|---|
> | | | Dr £ | Cr £ | Balance £ | Dr £ | Cr £ | Balance £ |
> | 2001 Feb 4 | Jane | | | | 200 | | 200 Dr |
> | Feb 7 | Jane (dishonoured cheque) | | | | | 200 | — |

10.4.3 DRAWING AGAINST UNCLEARED CHEQUES IN CLIENT ACCOUNT

The Solicitors' Accounts Rules 1998 do not prevent a solicitor from drawing against an uncleared cheque paid into client account but, if the cheque is later dishonoured, the solicitor is in breach of the Solicitors' Accounts Rules and must make an immediate transfer from office to client account of the amount by which the client account is overdrawn.

When a solicitor has drawn on client account against a cheque which is later dishonoured, the following entries will be made in the accounts:

(a) Entries to record the dishonour of a client account cheque (i.e., those entries in **10.4.2**).

(b) Entries to record the transfer from office account to client account of the amount by which client account is overdrawn.

Note: it is not necessary to transfer the full value of the cheque which has been dishonoured unless the client account is overdrawn by this amount.

Continuing the example from **10.4.2**:

Assume that on 5 February the firm drew a cheque on client account for £55 in respect of court fees.

JANE

Date	Details	Office account			Client account		
		Dr £	Cr £	Balance £	Dr £	Cr £	Balance £
2001						200	200 Cr
Feb 4	Cash: you				55		145 Cr
Feb 5	Cash: court fee						
Feb 7	Cash: dishonoured cheque				200		55 Dr
	Cash: transfer	55		55 Dr			
	Cash: transfer to remedy breach					55	—

CASH ACCOUNT

Date	Details	Office account			Client account		
		Dr £	Cr £	Balance £	Dr £	Cr £	Balance £
2001					200		200 Dr
Feb 4	Jane					55	145 Dr
Feb 5	Jane (court fee)						
Feb 7	Jane (dishonoured cheque)					200	55 Cr
	Jane (transfer to client account)		55	55 Cr			
	Jane (transfer from office account)				55		—

10.5 Small Transactions

When a solicitor does work which involves only one accounting transaction — the charging of costs, for example, for drafting a will, the solicitor may open a ledger account for the client and record the delivery of a bill of costs and receipt of payment of costs in the usual way.

Alternatively the solicitor may make entries only to record the receipt of costs, as follows:

(a) Debit the cash account office column with costs and VAT (on separate lines).

(b) Credit the costs account with costs.

(c) Credit the Customs and Excise account with VAT.

10.6 Bad Debts

If no VAT relief is available the firm will have to write off the total amount due, including VAT. If VAT relief is available (see **2.15.1**) the VAT element can be debited to Customs and Excise account, thus offsetting the VAT due to Customs and Excise.

FURTHER TRANSACTIONS

10.7 Exercises on Further Transactions

1   On 3 February 2001 a firm of solicitors receives a premium of £84 on behalf of the Fale Safe Insurance Co. for whom the firm acts and which currently owes the firm £16 commission due. On 20 February the net amount due is paid to the Fale Safe Insurance Co., being the gross premium received less commission of £8 and prior commission due. Commission due to the firm is transferred from client to office account. The firm is not required to account to any client for the commission. Prepare the account of the Fale Safe Insurance Co.

2   On 12 February 2001 a firm of solicitors receives £100 from its client Green on account of his pending divorce action costs. On 13 February the sum of £15 is paid out of moneys received from Green, to an enquiry agent. On 17 February the bank notifies the firm that the cheque from Green for £100 has been returned by the paying bankers. Green intimates that he will be in funds within the next two weeks. Prepare the account of Green.

3   Brown & Brown are acting as agents in an action for the recovery of a debt, on behalf of Green & Co. On 3 June 2001 the agents pay expert witness fee of £58 and court fees £11. On 28 June 2001 the agents forward their bill of costs to Green & Co., showing costs of £60 less agency commission of £6 plus VAT and disbursements. The bill is accompanied by an indorsed cheque for £900, being the amount recovered. On 5 July Green & Co. bill their client Herbert for their own costs, £20 agents' fee, VAT and disbursements. On 8 July a cheque is forwarded to Herbert for the balance due to him. On 8 July Green & Co. pay Brown & Brown and transfer costs and disbursements from client to office account.

(a)   Show the entries in the accounts of Green & Co. to record the above transactions.

(b)   Show the entries in the accounts of Brown & Brown to record the above transactions.

4   You act for A who is purchasing a house:

1 May   Receive a cheque for £6,000 for the deposit.
2 May   Send a cheque for £6,000 to seller's solicitors.
6 May   Bank notifies you that cheque has been returned.

Prepare the account for A and the cash account to record the above. The cash account need not be balanced.

5 (a)   On 20 January you deliver a bill of costs to Ann for £200 plus VAT £35. On 27 January you agree to reduce the cost to £160 plus VAT.

(b)   On 20 January you collect an insurance premium of £100 on behalf of Gamma Insurance Co. from Louise, since you are an agent for the Gamma Insurance Co. You retain a commission of £5, which is transferred to office account. You then send the net premium to the insurance company.

(c)   On 20 January Adam sends a cheque for £500: £117.50 is in payment of a bill you have delivered to him and the balance is for payment to the Wilshire county court for an action which he lost. On 21 January you pay the money due to the county court. On 22 January Adam's cheque is dishonoured. On 28 January Adam brings in cash to replace the dishonoured cheque.

(d)   On 20 January you repay Debra the sum of £2,000 which you have been holding for two months, with £35 paid in lieu of interest.

FURTHER TRANSACTIONS

Show the client ledger accounts and the cash account to record the above. It is not necessary to show the balances on the cash account.

6   In the month of March 2001 the following events take place:

3 March	Receive a cheque for £3,000, the deposit on the sale of a house by your client Donald, from the purchaser's solicitor. You are to hold the deposit as agent.
4 March	Receive a bill of costs from Badlot & Co., a firm of solicitors who act as your agents, for your client Neville: profit costs £200 plus VAT, and disbursements on which no VAT is payable, £25. Neville has already paid £100 on account of costs. You send a bill to Neville showing Badlot's costs and disbursements and your costs of £200 plus VAT.
5 March	You write off the sum of £117.50 which has been outstanding for some time, being costs and VAT owed by Maria, who is bankrupt.
7 March	Pay Badlot's bill by a cheque drawn on office account.
10 March	Lynne pays £90 premium due to Beta Insurance Co., for whom you act as agent. Commission due to you is currently £20.
11 March	Receive cheque from Neville in payment of his bill.
12 March	A designated deposit account opened for your client John is closed. The sum of £5,200 (inclusive of £200 interest) is sent by cheque to John.
13 March	The bank notifies you that Neville's cheque has been dishonoured.
14 March	The net amount due to the Beta Insurance Co. is paid to them. Commission charged is £5.00.
20 March	You act for Daphne in the collection of a debt of £36,000. The debtor sends two cheques of £18,000 each. One cheque dated 19 March is payable to Daphne. You have already agreed your costs of £100 plus VAT with Daphne. You retain this sum and send Daphne a cheque for the balance, the debtor's cheque and receipted bill.
28 March	Complete sale of Donald's house. Receive £27,000. Redeem mortgage of £7,221 by cheque to the High Rate Building Society. Send a bill of costs to Donald for £200 plus VAT. Pay estate agents' charges of £300 plus VAT, the bill being addressed to Donald.
31 March	Donald asks you to transfer enough money from his account to settle the indebtedness of his friend Neville. After making the necessary transfer a cheque is sent to Donald for the balance due.

Show the client ledger accounts to record the above.

7   During the month of November 2001, Teepot, Cupp & Saucer, solicitors, deal with the following events, and you are required to show all the relevant entries on the clients' ledger accounts, which are to be balanced. The rate of VAT is to be taken as 17.5%.

2001

1 November	Cheque received (£4,000) from Peter, who is not a client of the firm, being the deposit on the sale of a house by Milko, for whom the firm acts. The firm is to hold the money as stakeholders. Exchanged contracts for the sale of Milko's house, and paid petty cash disbursements of £6 (no VAT) on his behalf, on the same day.
4 November	Banker's draft received (£54,000) on completion of the sale of Lemon's house, stake money of £6,000 being transferred from stakeholder account. The mortgagee of Lemon's house, Alexander, had already instructed the firm to act on his behalf in the redemption of his charge on Lemon's house, and the redemption money (£9,675) is transferred to his account. It has been agreed that the mortgagee's costs (£40 plus VAT) will be borne by Lemon. (Assume that Alexander is not an institutional lender.)

FURTHER TRANSACTIONS

5 November — Paid by cheque the sum of £10,000 in respect of a debt which had been incurred by Lemon to Cupp, a partner in the firm, Lemon having previously agreed to this action.
The amount due to the mortgagee of Lemon's house is paid by cheque, and the estate agent's fee (£1,200 plus VAT), is paid by the firm since the invoice was addressed to them.
A bill of costs is rendered to Lemon, showing profit costs of £800 plus VAT.

8 November — Received cheque (£500) from Sucrose on account of costs generally. The firm writes off the sum of £70.50 (inclusive of VAT £10.50) as a bad debt, the amount having been owed to the firm by Smith since March 2000. Smith has now been adjudicated bankrupt.

11 November — The designated deposit account opened by the firm re Orange, in respect of an amount of £10,000 held by them for the period of six months, is closed, and a cheque for the sum, together with interest of £450 credited by the bank, is sent to Orange.

14 November — Cheque sent to Lemon in respect of balance of moneys held on his behalf, including agreed interest of £124. The amount due to the firm is transferred to office account and Lemon's account is then closed.

21 November — Bill of costs received from agent solicitors in connection with the affairs of Sucrose. The bill shows profit costs of £300 before allowing agency commission of £100 (excluding VAT) and disbursements of £80 (no VAT). The firm pays the agent's bill and now renders its own bill of costs to Sucrose, showing profit costs of £400 plus VAT and disbursements of £80 (no VAT). Both the profit costs and disbursements of the agent solicitors are included in the foregoing amounts.

25 November — Bill of costs rendered to Milko, showing profit costs (£300 plus VAT) together with disbursements already incurred.

26 November — Received from Sucrose, the balance in respect of the firm's bill of costs, the account then being closed.

29 November — The sale of Milko's house is completed, a banker's draft for £36,000 being received from the purchaser's solicitors. The amount due to the firm is transferred to office account, and a cheque for the balance due to Milko is sent to him.

(Solicitors' Final Examination, updated.)

10.8 Suggested Answers to Exercises on Further Transactions

1 Fale Safe Insurance Co. Ltd

FALE SAFE INSURANCE CO. LTD

Date	Details	Office account Dr £	Cr £	Balance £	Client account Dr £	Cr £	Balance £
2001 Feb 3	Balance b/d	16		16 Dr			
	Cash: premiums					84	84 Cr
Feb 20	Commission receivable	8		24 Dr			
	Cash: you				60		24 Cr
	Cash: transfer: commission					24	—
	Cash: transfer: commission		24	—			

274

FURTHER TRANSACTIONS

2 Green

GREEN

Date	Details	Office account			Client account		
		Dr	Cr	Balance	Dr	Cr	Balance
		£	£	£	£	£	£
2001							
Feb 12	Cash: you					100	100 Cr
Feb 13	Cash: enquiry agent				15		85
Feb 17	Cash: returned cheque				100		15 Dr
	Cash: transfer	15		15 Dr			
	Cash: transfer					15	—

3 Green & Co. ledger accounts

AGENCY EXPENSES ACCOUNT

Date	Details	Dr	Cr	Balance
		£	£	£
2001				
July 8	Cash: Brown & Brown (Herbert)	54		54 Dr

CUSTOMS AND EXCISE ACCOUNT

Date	Details	Dr	Cr	Balance
		£	£	£
2001				
July 5	Herbert		14	14 Cr
July 8	Cash: Brown & Brown (Herbert)	9.45		

HERBERT

Date	Details	Office account			Client account		
		Dr	Cr	Balance	Dr	Cr	Balance
		£	£	£	£	£	£
2001							
June 28	Cash: agents					900	900 Cr
July 5	Costs	80					
	VAT	14		94 Dr			
July 8	Cash: agency: disbursements	69		163 Dr			
	Cash: you				737		163 Cr
	Cash: transfer: costs				163		—
	Cash: transfer: costs		163	—			

CASH ACCOUNT

Date	Details	Office account			Client account		
		Dr	Cr	Balance	Dr	Cr	Balance
		£	£	£	£	£	£
2001							
July 8	Cash: Brown & Brown		132.45	132.45 Cr			

FURTHER TRANSACTIONS

Brown & Brown ledger cards

GREEN & CO. RE AGENCY

Date	Details	Office account			Client account		
		Dr £	Cr £	Balance £	Dr £	Cr £	Balance £
2001 June 3	Cash: expert witness	58		58 Dr			
	Cash: court fee	11		69 Dr			
June 28	Costs	54					
	VAT	9.45		132.45 Dr			
	Cash: indorsed cheque					900	
	Cash: you: indorsed cheque				900		
July 8	Cash: from you		132.45	—			

4 A. ACCOUNT

Date	Details	Office account			Client account		
		Dr £	Cr £	Balance £	Dr £	Cr £	Balance £
May 1	Cash: you					6,000	6,000 Cr
May 2	Cash: deposit paid				6,000		—
May 6	Cash: dishonoured cheque				6,000		6,000 Dr
	Cash: transfer	6,000		6,000 Dr		6,000	—

CASH ACCOUNT

Date	Details	Office account			Client account		
		Dr £	Cr £	Balance £	Dr £	Cr £	Balance £
May 1	A: moneys received				6,000		
May 2	A: deposit paid					6,000	
May 6	A: dishonoured cheque					6,000	
	A: transfer		6,000		6,000		

5 (a) ANN

Date	Details	Office account			Client account		
		Dr £	Cr £	Balance £	Dr £	Cr £	Balance £
Jan 20	Costs	200					
	VAT	35		235 Dr			
Jan 27	Costs abatement		40				
	VAT abatement		7	188 Dr			

(b) GAMMA INSURANCE CO. ACCOUNT

Date	Details	Office account			Client account		
		Dr £	Cr £	Balance £	Dr £	Cr £	Balance £
Jan 20	Cash: premium (Louise)					100	100 Cr
	Commission	5		5 Dr			
	Cash: transfer		5	—	5		95 Cr
	Cash: you				95		—

(c) ADAM ACCOUNT

Date	Details	Office account			Client account		
		Dr £	Cr £	Balance £	Dr £	Cr £	Balance £
Jan 20	Balance			117.50 Dr			
	Cash: you		117.50	—		382.50	382.50 Cr
Jan 21	Cash: Wilshire county court				382.50		—
Jan 22	Cash: dishonoured cheque	117.50		117.50 Dr	382.50		382.50 Dr
	Cash: transfer	382.50		500 Dr		382.50	—
Jan 28	Cash: you		500	—			

(d) DEBRA ACCOUNT

Date	Details	Office account			Client account		
		Dr £	Cr £	Balance £	Dr £	Cr £	Balance £
Jan 20	Balance					2,000	2,000 Cr
	Cash: interest payable					35	2,035 Cr
	Cash: you				2,035		—

FURTHER TRANSACTIONS

CASH ACCOUNT

Date	Details	Office account Dr £	Cr £	Balance £	Client account Dr £	Cr £	Balance £
Jan 20	Gamma insurance: premium					100	
	Gamma insurance: transfer commission	5				5	
	Gamma insurance: balance of premium					95	
	Adam	117.50			382.50		
	Interest payable re Debra		35				
	Debra: in lieu of interest				35		
	Debra					2,035	
Jan 21	Adam: Wilshire county court					382.50	
Jan 22	Adam: dishonoured cheque		117.50			382.50	
	Adam: transfer		382.50		382.50		
Jan 28	Adam:		500				

6

DONALD ACCOUNT

Date	Details	Office account Dr £	Cr £	Balance £	Client account Dr £	Cr £	Balance £
2001							
Mar 3	Cash: deposit					3,000	3,000 Cr
Mar 28	Cash: completion					27,000	30,000 Cr
	Cash: High Rate Building Society				7,221		22,779 Cr
	Costs	200					
	VAT	35		235 Dr			
	Cash: estate agent				352.50		22,426.50 Cr
Mar 31	Cash: transfer to Neville				395		22,031.50 Cr
	Cash: transfer costs		235	—	235		21,796.50 Cr
	Cash: you				21,796.50		

NEVILLE ACCOUNT

Date	Details	Office account Dr £	Cr £	Balance £	Client account Dr £	Cr £	Balance £
2001							
Mar 4	Balance					100	100 Cr
	Costs	400					
	VAT	70		470 Dr			
Mar 7	Cash: agents disbursements	25		495 Dr			
Mar 11	Cash: you		395	100 Dr			
	Cash: transfer		100	—	100		—
Mar 13	Cash: dishonoured cheque	395		395 Dr			
Mar 31	Cash: Donald		395	—			

FURTHER TRANSACTIONS

MARIA ACCOUNT

Date	Details	Office account			Client account		
		Dr £	Cr £	Balance £	Dr £	Cr £	Balance £
2001				117.50 Dr			
Mar 5	Balance						
	Bad debts		100				
	Customs & Excise		17.50	—			

BETA INSURANCE CO. ACCOUNT

Date	Details	Office account			Client account		
		Dr £	Cr £	Balance £	Dr £	Cr £	Balance £
2001							
Mar 10	Commission due	20		20 Dr			
	Cash: premium					90	90 Cr
Mar 14	Commission	5		25 Dr			
	Cash: transfer commission		25	—	25		65 Cr
	Cash: you				65		—

JOHN ACCOUNT

Designated deposit account
Opened: ....
Closed: 12 March 2001

Date	Details	Office account			Client account		
		Dr £	Cr £	Balance £	Dr £	Cr £	Balance £
2001	Balance					5,000	5,000 Cr
Mar 12	Deposit cash interest					200	5,200 Cr
	Cash: you				5,200		—

DAPHNE ACCOUNT

Date	Details	Office account			Client account		
		Dr £	Cr £	Balance £	Dr £	Cr £	Balance £
2001	Costs: agreed fee	100					
	VAT	17.50		117.50 Dr			
Mar 20	Cash: debtor					18,000	18,000 Cr
	Cash: transfer		117.50	—	117.50		17,882.50 Cr
	Cash: you				17,882.50		

Note: the cheque for £18,000 payable to Daphne could have been shown on the account by way of a memorandum entry.

FURTHER TRANSACTIONS

7 Teepot, Cupp & Saucer

MILKO

Date	Details	Office account			Client account		
		Dr £	Cr £	Balance £	Dr £	Cr £	Balance £
2001 Nov 1	Petty cash: disbursement	6		6 Dr			
Nov 25	Costs	300					
	VAT	52.50		358.50 Dr			
Nov 29	Cash: sale proceeds					36,000	36,000 Cr
	Stakeholder: transfer: deposit					4,000	40,000 Cr
	Cash: transfer: costs from client to office account		358.50	—	358.50		39,641.50 Cr
	Cash: you				39,641.50		—

LEMON

Date	Details	Office account			Client account		
		Dr £	Cr £	Balance £	Dr £	Cr £	Balance £
2001 Nov 4	Cash: sale proceeds					54,000	54,000 Cr
	Stakeholder: transfer: deposit					6,000	60,000 Cr
	Alexander: transfer: redemption				9,675		50,325 Cr
	Alexander: transfer: redemption costs	47		47 Dr			
Nov 5	Cash: Cupp				10,000		40,325 Cr
	Cash: estate agent	1,200		1,247 Dr			
	Costs	800					
	VAT	350		2,397 Dr			
Nov 14	Cash: in lieu of interest					124	40,449 Cr
	Cash: transfer: costs		2,397	—	2,397		38,052 Cr
	Cash: you				38,052		—

ALEXANDER

Date	Details	Office account			Client account		
		Dr £	Cr £	Balance £	Dr £	Cr £	Balance £
2001 Nov 4	Costs	40					
	VAT	7		47 Dr			
	Lemon: transfer: redemption					9,675	9,675 Cr
	Lemon: transfer: redemption costs		47	—			
Nov 5	Cash: you				9,675		—

SUCROSE

Date	Details	Office account			Client account		
		Dr £	Cr £	Balance £	Dr £	Cr £	Balance £
2001							
Nov 8	Cash: you					500	500 Cr
Nov 21	Cash:						
	disbursements	80		80 Dr			
	Costs	400					
	VAT	70		550 Dr			
Nov 26	Cash: you		50	500 Dr			
	Cash: transfer: costs		500	—	500		—

SMITH

Date	Details	Office account			Client account		
		Dr £	Cr £	Balance £	Dr £	Cr £	Balance £
2001	Balance			70.50 Dr			
Nov 8	Bad debt		60				
	Customs and Excise		10.50	—			

ORANGE

Designated deposit account
Opened May 2001
Closed 11 November 2001

Date	Details	Office account			Client account		
		Dr £	Cr £	Balance £	Dr £	Cr £	Balance £
2001	Balance						10,000 Cr
Nov 11	Deposit cash: interest					450	10,450 Cr
	Cash: you				10,450		—

STAKEHOLDER ACCOUNT

Date	Details	Office account			Client account		
		Dr £	Cr £	Balance £	Dr £	Cr £	Balance £
2001	Balance					6,000	6,000 Cr
Nov 1	Cash: Milko					4,000	10,000 Cr
Nov 4	Lemon: transfer				6,000		4,000 Cr
Nov 29	Milko: transfer				4,000		—

FURTHER TRANSACTIONS

10.9 Test on Further Transactions

Allow approximately 1 hour to complete this test.

Harriet, Peter and Alex are solicitors, and they deal with the following events:

2001

2 January	Brown pays cash (£104) to the firm, who act as agents for the Nonpay Insurance Co. Ltd. Commission currently due to the firm on that agency amounts to £43. The firm is not liable to account to any client for the commission.
3 January	Paid by cheque the sum of £2,000 on behalf of Black, and received later the same day from Black, a cheque for £1,500 in partial satisfaction. The balance is to be paid from the proceeds of the sale of his house, which will be received within a few days' time.
6 January	Cheque for the agreed fee (£40 plus VAT) received from White in respect of debt collection work.
7 January	Received cheque, in respect of the sale of Black's house, amounting to £22,634, being the balance of purchase money. The sum of £2,500 is transferred from stakeholder account the same day. The firm also acts for the mortgagees of Black, the Savall Building Society, and £7,436 is sent to that company to redeem the mortgage. Requisite bill of costs rendered to building society. The costs of redemption of Black's mortgage (£20 plus VAT) are to be borne by Black.
10 January	Cheque received drawn in favour of White, for £1,250 (which is indorsed over to the firm). Bill of costs is sent to White in respect of debt collection, showing the agreed fee (£40 plus VAT) less abatement of fee £20 plus VAT.
10 January	Bill of costs sent to Black (£240 plus VAT).
13 January	Pink repays a personal loan of £1,000 made by Peter, a partner in the firm.
14 January	Black requests that the amount due to him should be retained by the firm for the time being, as he will not require payment for some months. The amount due to the firm is transferred to office account.
15 January	The amount due to White is paid by cheque, and the account is then closed.
15 January	The firm acts for Yellow in a court action, having already paid the counsel's fee of £100 plus VAT (the principal method was used). The firm had appointed local agents, and their bill showed profit costs of £120, less agency commission £20, plus VAT. Agency disbursements consisted of court fees of £12. Bill of costs is sent to Yellow, showing profit costs of £100 (excuding agents' profit costs) plus VAT and the disbursements.
16 January	Grey pays £200 on account of her pending divorce action costs, and cash disbursements of £16 are paid in respect thereof on the same day.
17 January	The net amount due to the Nonpay Insurance Co. Ltd is paid, being the gross premium received (£104) less commission of £15 and prior commission due (£43).
20 January	Received amount due from Yellow, and paid the amount due to the local agents who acted in his court action.
22 January	Paid enquiry agent, on behalf of Grey, the sum of £40 (no VAT), the cheque being drawn on client account.
24 January	The bank notifies the firm that the cheque from Grey has been returned unpaid by the paying bankers.
29 January	The sum of £1,000, which has been held on behalf of Blue for some three months, is repaid to Blue, together with agreed interest of £40. The payment is made by means of a cheque drawn on client account. The money has not been deposited in a designated deposit account.

FURTHER TRANSACTIONS

Write up the client's ledger accounts, showing all relevant entries. All accounts are to be balanced. The rate of VAT is to be taken as 17.5%.

(Law Society Final Examination, updated.)

10.10 Suggested Answer to Test on Further Transactions

NONPAY INSURANCE CO. LTD

Date	Details	Office account			Client account		
		Dr £	Cr £	Balance £	Dr £	Cr £	Balance £
2001 Jan 2	Balance	43		43 Dr			
	Cash: Brown					104	104 Cr
Jan 17	Commission	15		58 Dr			
	Cash: you				46		58 Cr
	Cash: transfer: commission					58	—
	Cash: transfer: commission		58	—			

BLACK

Designated deposit account
Opened 14 January 2001

Date	Details	Office account			Client account		
		Dr £	Cr £	Balance £	Dr £	Cr £	Balance £
2001 Jan 3	Cash	2,000		2,000 Dr			
Jan 3	Cash: you		1,500	500 Dr			
Jan 7	Cash: purchaser's solicitors					22,634	22,634 Cr
	Stakeholder: transfer					2,500	25,134 Cr
	Cash: Savall Building Society: redemption				7,436		17,698 Cr
Jan 10	Costs	240					
	VAT	42					
	Costs (mortgage redemption)	20					
	VAT	3.50		805.50 Dr			
Jan 13	Cash: transfer: costs				805.50		16,892.50 Cr
	Cash: transfer: costs		805.50	—			

WHITE

Date	Details	Office account			Client account		
		Dr £	Cr £	Balance £	Dr £	Cr £	Balance £
2001 Jan 6	Costs (agreed fee)	40					
	VAT	7		47 Dr			
	Cash: you		47				
Jan 10	Cash: you					1,250	1,250 Cr
	Costs: abatement		20				
	VAT: abatement		3.50	23.50 Cr			
Jan 14	Cash: you	23.50		—	1,250		—

283

FURTHER TRANSACTIONS

YELLOW

Date	Details	Office account			Client account		
		Dr £	Cr £	Balance £	Dr £	Cr £	Balance £
2001							
Jan 15	Balance			100 Dr			
	Costs	220					
	VAT	56		376 Dr			
Jan 20	Cash (agent disbursement)	12		388 Dr			
	Cash: you		388	—			

GREY

Date	Details	Office account			Client account		
		Dr £	Cr £	Balance £	Dr £	Cr £	Balance £
2001							
Jan 16	Cash: you					200	200 Cr
	Petty cash: disbursements	16		16 Dr			
Jan 22	Cash: enquiry agent				40		160 Cr
Jan 24	Cash: returned cheque				200		40 Dr
	Cash: transfer	40		56 Dr			
	Cash: transfer					40	—

BLUE

Date	Details	Office account			Client account		
		Dr £	Cr £	Balance £	Dr £	Cr £	Balance £
2001							
Jan 29	Balance					1,000	1,000 Cr
	Cash: interest					40	1,040 Cr
	Cash: you				1,040		—

Note: an account is not opened for Peter as he is a partner in the firm and it would be in breach of the Solicitors' Accounts Rules 1998 to pay the money received from Pink into client account.

10.11 Test on Ledger Accounts Including VAT

Allow approximately 1 hour to complete this test.

Except where specifically referred to in the questions, taxation (including VAT) should be ignored.

FURTHER TRANSACTIONS

Bread, Butter and Honey are solicitors, and they deal with the following events:

2001

3 April	Paid £23.50 (including VAT £3.50) by cheque drawn on office account, in respect of the reproduction of documents. The invoice is made out to the client, Phantasia, for whom the firm are acting in a tax matter before the special commissioners.
4 April	Received banker's draft for £49,500 from the purchaser's solicitors, being the balance of purchase money re the sale by Smith of his house 'Figleaf'. On the same day the sum of £19,500 is sent by cheque to the mortgagees of the property, in full payment of the amount due to them.
7 April	Logger, Hedd and Co., the estate agents acting for Smith, send cheque to firm for £4,235, being the deposit on 'Figleaf' less their commission.
8 April	Received the sum of £300 from Phantasia on account of costs generally.
11 April	The firm acts for Jones in the collection of a debt due to her, amounting to £5,000. The debtor sends two cheques for the debt, each cheque being for the sum of £2,500 and dated 16 May 2001 and 16 June 2001, respectively.
14 April	Sent cheque for £587.50 (including VAT £87.50) to A. Builder in respect of pre-sale repairs to 'Figleaf'. The invoice was addressed to the firm.
28 April	Paid fee of £235 (including VAT £35) to E. X. Pert, a witness who appeared on behalf of Phantasia. The payment was made out of client account.
29 April	Bill of costs sent to Smith (£300 plus VAT).
5 May	Paid from client account £94 (including VAT) in respect of transcripts obtained on behalf of Phantasia.
9 May	Smith requests that the amount due to him should be retained by the firm for the time being, and the sum is transferred to a designated deposit account; profit costs and disbursements are transferred to office account on the same day.
20 May	Bill of costs in respect of tax matter is rendered to Phantasia, showing profit costs of £700 plus VAT.
16 June	Received cheque in settlement of Phantasia's account with the firm.
17 June	Bill of costs for £60 plus VAT delivered to Jones.
20 June	Both cheques from the debtor of Jones, having been presented and met, the total amount due, after deduction of costs but inclusive of interest allowed by the firm (£22), was paid over to Jones. It is the practice of the firm to record all interest payments made by the firm on the client's ledger account. The amount due to the firm is transferred from client to office account.
30 June	The bank credits the designated deposit account of Smith with interest of £375 and the firm allows interest of £250 for the period before the designated deposit account was opened for Smith.

You are required to show the ledger accounts of Phantasia, Smith and Jones, recording all the above transactions. The rate of VAT is to be taken as 17.5%.

(Law Society Final Examination, updated.)

FURTHER TRANSACTIONS

10.12 Suggested Answer to Test on Ledger Accounts Including VAT

PHANTASIA

Date	Details	Office account			Client account		
		Dr £	Cr £	Balance £	Dr £	Cr £	Balance £
2001							
Apr 3	Cash: production of documents	23.50		23.50 Dr			
Apr 8	Cash: you					300	300 Cr
Apr 28	Cash: E. X. Pert				235		65 Cr
May 5	Cash: transcripts				94		29 Dr
	Cash: transfer	29		52.50 Dr			
	Cash: transfer					29	—
May 20	Costs	700					
	VAT	122.50		875 Dr			
June 16	Cash: you		875	—			

SMITH

Designated deposit account
Opened 9 May 2001
Closed 30 June 2001

Date	Details	Office account			Client account		
		Dr £	Cr £	Balance £	Dr £	Cr £	Balance £
2001							
Apr 4	Cash: purchaser's solicitors					49,500	49,500 Cr
	Cash: redemption				19,500		30,000 Cr
Apr 7	Cash: estate agent (less commission)					4,235	34,235 Cr
Apr 14	Cash: A. Builder	500		500 Dr			
Apr 29	Costs	300					
	VAT	140		940 Dr			
May 9	Cash: transfer: costs				940		33,295 Cr
	Cash: transfer costs		940	—			
June 30	Deposit cash: interest					375	33,670 Cr
	Cash: interest					250	33,920 Cr

JONES

Date	Details	Office account			Client account		
		Dr £	Cr £	Balance £	Dr £	Cr £	Balance £
2001							
May 16	Cash: debtor					2,500	2,500 Cr
June 16	Cash: debtor					2,500	5,000 Cr
June 17	Costs	60					
	VAT	10.50		70.50 Dr			
June 20	Cash: interest					22	5,022 Cr
	Cash: transfer				70.50		4,951.50 Cr
	Cash: transfer		70.50	—			
	Cash: you				4,951.50		—

10.13 Revision Questions

Explain how a firm of solicitors should deal with the following. You should state the principles/rules involved. There is no need to state the debit and credit entries involved.

1   The firm is dealing with a probate matter and the deceased's bank agrees to advance £20,500 to the executors in respect of inheritance tax. A loan account is opened by the bank for the executors and a cheque for £20,500 is drawn by the executors, payable to the Inland Revenue, and handed to the firm of solicitors.

2   The firm has held the net proceeds of sale of a house on behalf of its client David for the past two months. David now asks for the net proceeds, totalling £10,000, to be sent to him.

3   The firm has referred investment business work for its client Fred through a stockbroker, who splits the commission on sales and purchases of shares with the firm of solicitors. Can the firm retain the commission?

4   Jane, a client, owes the firm £940, being £800 re costs and £140 re VAT. Jane has just been declared bankrupt, and the firm writes off the debt.

5   The firm receives cash of £600 on behalf of its client Clarke. Clarke has asked that the firm pay this cash over to Boswell in payment of a debt due from Clarke to Boswell.

6   The firm acts for Ruby, a partner in the firm, and her friend John, who is a legal executive in the firm. They are selling a cottage and purchasing a larger house in town. The firm receives a cheque for £30,000 to hold as agent for the seller.

7   The firm has received commission from the Welsh Widowers' Insurance Company in the sum of £320. This is in respect of £20 commission due re a premium collected from Albert, one of the firm's clients, £150 in respect of commission payable for collection of a premium from a non client, and £150 payable in respect of commission received in respect of another client, Susan.

8   The firm receives a cheque for £400 on general account of costs from their client Ian. A disbursement of £415 (no VAT payable) is paid by the firm on behalf of Ian.

9   The firm receives a cheque for £770 from their client Lisa. This is in respect of the firm's bill for £400 plus VAT, which had been sent to Lisa, and counsel's fees of £300 (no VAT) which have not yet been paid.

10.14 Suggested Answers to Revision Questions

1   No entries need be shown on the solicitors' accounts at all, as the loan account at the bank belongs to the executors and not the firm. The cheque is made out to the Inland Revenue, so it does not belong to the firm and it should merely be forwarded to the Inland Revenue.

2   As £10,000 has been held for two weeks or more, here two months, then the money should have been placed on a designated deposit account to earn interest for David. The proceeds plus the interest should be paid to him. If the money has not been placed on a designated deposit account for David then the firm should pay an amount at least equivalent to the amount that would have been earned. Interest in lieu will come from the firm's office account.

3   Under the Solicitors' Practice Rules, r. 10, solicitors must account to their clients for any commission received of more than £20 unless the client has been told of the amount of commission in writing and has agreed that the firm retain the commission.

FURTHER TRANSACTIONS

4 As Jane has been declared bankrupt the firm may claim bad debt relief. Thus the amount of £800 will be recorded as a bad debt, and the VAT of £140 can be debited to the Customs and Excise account, thus reducing the VAT payable to Customs and Excise.

5 Although normally a firm of solicitors must pay money received on behalf of a client into a client bank account, under r. 17 of the Solicitors' Accounts Rules 1998, where money is received in cash and is without delay paid in cash in the ordinary course of business to the client or on the client's behalf there is no need to pay into the client bank account. The firm can therefore pay the money to Boswell. However, entries must be made on the accounts showing the receipt and payment out of client money.

6 Although money received on behalf of partners in the firm is not client money, where the money is received on behalf of a partner together with a non partner then the money will be client money and as this is held as agent for the seller, it can be recorded on a client ledger card for Ruby and John.

7 See Practice Rule 10 as stated in **Answer 3** above. As the commission of £20 is not more than £20 the firm may retain the commission. It may also retain the commission of £150 in respect of the non client. It must account to Susan, however, for the £150, unless she has been advised in writing and has agreed that the firm may retain the commission.

8 The £400 on general account of costs should have been paid into client account. The firm cannot pay the total disbursement of £415 from client account. Although it would be technically possible for the firm to pay two cheques, one for £400 from client account and one for £15 from office account, this would seem odd, and the better course would be to pay £415 from office account, and then transfer £400 from client account. It is also possible for the firm to advance money to fund the payment under r. 15. It may be necessary to ask the client for further funds if these are needed for other disbursements.

9 This is mixed office/client money. The sum of £470, being £400 plus VAT £70, is office account money. The remaining £300 should be held on client account until counsel's fees are paid. The cheque may be split or, more usually, the whole amount paid into client account, and then £470 transferred to office account within 14 days. Alternatively the entire sum may be paid into office account and counsel's fees paid or the money transferred to client account by the end of the second working day following receipt (Rule 19).

10.15 Self Assessment Questions on the Solicitors' Accounts Rules 1998

Decide whether the following transactions should be dealt with through client account or office account, and show the entries that would be made on the accounts.

1 A solicitor receives £400 on general account of costs from Janet.

2 A solicitor receives £470 as an agreed fee in respect of work to be done for Harold. The firm has not yet sent a bill to Harold.

3 The solicitor holds £200 on general account of costs from Ethel. An enquiry agent is paid £150 (no VAT is payable).

4 The firm is acting for one of the partners, John, in respect of his sale of a flat in Mersey Quays. The sale price of £54,000 is received on completion from the purchaser's solicitors.

5 The firm is acting on behalf of one of its employees, Patsy, in respect of the sale of a house. Sale proceeds are received in the sum of £90,000.

FURTHER TRANSACTIONS

6   The firm is acting for one of its partners, Jane, together with her husband in respect of the sale of a house. Sale proceeds are received in the sum of £150,000.

7   The firm has £80,000 on general client account. The office account is overdrawn at the bank. A disbursement of £50 has to be paid on behalf of their client Brian, who has not yet sent any money on account of costs.

8   The firm sent out a bill to Anthony for £800 plus VAT £140. Counsel's fees are due but not yet paid in the sum of £600. Anthony sends a cheque for £1,540.

9   The firm receives £5,000 in respect of Derek's sale of 'The Gables', to hold as stakeholder.

10   The firm receives £6,000 in respect of Mary's sale of 8, Beaumont Square, to hold as agent for the seller. The sum of £5,000 is paid out in respect of her purchase of 10, Bloxham Road.

11   A cheque made out to client James for £300 is received by the firm.

12   The firm receives £60 cash on behalf of their client Cecil. Later that day the cash is handed to Cecil who has called into the office.

13   The firm receives a cheque for £450 on behalf of Barbara which is then endorsed over to her.

14   The firm receives a cheque for £70 made out to Andrew, on 17 January. On 21 January Andrew endorses the cheque over to the firm, on general account of costs.

15   A cheque is received made out to the firm for £9,000 in respect of a debt due from Agnes to their client Joe.

10.16   Suggested Answers to Self Assessment Questions

1   Money on general account of costs is client money and must be paid into client account (see r. 13).

JANET

Date	Details	Office account			Client account		
		Dr £	Cr £	Balance £	Dr £	Cr £	Balance £
	Cash: you on account of costs					400	400 Cr

CASH BOOK

Date	Details	Office account			Client account		
		Dr £	Cr £	Balance £	Dr £	Cr £	Balance £
	Janet: on account costs				400		

289

FURTHER TRANSACTIONS

2   An agreed fee is office money and must be paid into office account (r. 19(5)).

So:

(a) Credit Harold client ledger card office account.

(b) Debit the cash book office account.

3   The £200 on general account of costs would have been paid into client account. As this money is available, and VAT is not involved, the enquiry agent can be paid from client account.

ETHEL

Date	Details	Office account			Client account		
		Dr £	Cr £	Balance £	Dr £	Cr £	Balance £
	Cash: you on account of costs					200	200 Cr
	Cash: enquiry agent				150		50 Cr

CASH BOOK

Date	Details	Office account			Client account		
		Dr £	Cr £	Balance £	Dr £	Cr £	Balance £
	Ethel on a/c costs				200		
	Ethel enquiry agent					150	

4   Client's money does not include money to which the only person entitled is the solicitor himself or herself or, in the case of a firm of solicitors, one or more of the partners in the firm: see the notes to r. 13. The money cannot be paid into client account; it must be held on an office account in the name of John.

JOHN

Date	Details	Office account			Client account		
		Dr £	Cr £	Balance £	Dr £	Cr £	Balance £
	Cash: sale proceeds		54,000	54,000 Cr			

CASH BOOK

Date	Details	Office account			Client account		
		Dr £	Cr £	Balance £	Dr £	Cr £	Balance £
	John: re sale	54,000					

FURTHER TRANSACTIONS

5 Patsy does not fall within the exception in **Answer 4** above: she is a client and the money will be paid into client account on her behalf. So:

(a) Credit Patsy client ledger card client account.

(b) Debit the cash book client account.

6 Provided Jane's husband is not a partner in the firm, the money is again client money: see **Answer 4** above, i.e., Jane is not the only person entitled. So:

(a) Credit Jane and husband client ledger card client account.

(b) Debit the cash book client account.

7 Although there are sufficient funds on client account to pay the disbursement, as the firm is not holding any money on behalf of Brian, the payment cannot be made out of client account, it must be made out of office account. See r. 22(8), which makes it clear that money drawn cannot exceed the total held on account of the client. So:

(a) Debit Brian client ledger card office account.

(b) Credit the cash book office account.

8 A solicitor may only pay money into office account in respect of, *inter alia*, 'costs', which excludes counsel's fees which have not yet been paid. On the assumption that no VAT is payable in respect of counsel's fees in this case then £940 is office money, and £600 is client money. The cheque may be split, i.e., £940 paid into office account and £600 into client account, or all the money may be paid into client account, and then £940 transferred to office account within 14 days or all the money may be paid into office account and then either counsel's fees paid or transferred to client account, within 2 working days see r. 19.

Entries where the money is split:

ANTHONY

Date	Details	Office account			Client account		
		Dr £	Cr £	Balance £	Dr £	Cr £	Balance £
	Costs	800		800 Dr			
	VAT	140		940 Dr			
	Cash: you		940	—		600	600 Cr

The cash book would be debited £940 on office account, and debited £600 on client account.

Entries where the money is paid into client account and then transferred:

ANTHONY

Date	Details	Office account			Client account		
		Dr £	Cr £	Balance £	Dr £	Cr £	Balance £
	Balance re costs and VAT			940 Dr			
	Cash: you					1,540	1,540 Cr
	Cash: transfer costs		940		940		600 Cr

FURTHER TRANSACTIONS

CASH BOOK

Date	Details	Office account			Client account		
		Dr £	Cr £	Balance £	Dr £	Cr £	Balance £
	Anthony				1,540		
	Anthony: transfer costs	940				940	

9 The money does not belong to Derek until completion of the sale. It must be paid into stakeholder account, a client ledger card, client account. So:

(a) Credit the stakeholder account client ledger card client account.

(b) Debit the cash book client account.

10 As this money is held for Mary it may be paid into her client ledger card, client account and used in respect of the deposit payable on the purchase.

MARY: SALE 8, BEAUMONT SQUARE
PURCHASE 10, BLOXHAM ROAD

Date	Details	Office account			Client account		
		Dr £	Cr £	Balance £	Dr £	Cr £	Balance £
	Cash deposit: agent for vendor					6,000	6,000 Cr
	Cash deposit on purchase				5,000		1,000 Cr

The other entries would have been to debit the cash book client account with £6,000, and to credit the cash book client account in respect of the deposit paid on purchase, i.e., £5,000.

11 As the cheque is made out to the client, it cannot be paid into the solicitor's bank accounts, whether office account or client account. No entries need be made on the accounts, although a note may be made if required.

12 Although the rules do not require this money to be paid into client account at the bank, client's money has still been received and then paid out.

Receipt:

(a) Credit the client ledger card of Cecil client account.

(b) Debit the cash book client account.

Payment out:

(a) Debit the client ledger card of Cecil client account.

(b) Credit the cash book client account.

FURTHER TRANSACTIONS

13 Again this money need not be paid into the firm's client bank account. However, the receipt of client money, and payment out of client money, should be recorded on the accounts. The entries would be as in **Answer 12** above, on Barbara's client ledger card and the cash book re £450.

14 The firm cannot pay this cheque into a bank account until 21 January, when it is endorsed over to the firm. When this is done, as it is on general account of costs, it is client money. So:

(a) Credit Andrew's client ledger card client account.

(b) Debit the cash book client account.

15 As the cheque is made out to the firm it can be paid into the firm's bank account. The money is received on behalf of Joe and is client money. So:

(a) Credit Joe's client ledger card client account.

(b) Debit the cash book client account.

INDEX

Abatements 268
Accountants, inspections by 175
Accountants' Report Rules (1991)
   inspection by accountant 175
   report to Law Society 175
Accounting bases 104–5
Accounting concepts
   accruals 104
   business entity 103
   consistency 104
   cost 103
   going-concern 104
   materiality 104
   money measurement 103
   prudence 104
Accounting policies 104
Accounts
   classification *see* Classification of accounts
   consolidated *see* Consolidated accounts
   double-entry bookkeeping *see* Double-entry bookkeeping
   duty to keep 175
   final *see* Final accounts
   interpretation *see* Interpretation of accounts; Ratio analysis
   layout 2
   presentation *see* Presentation of accounts
   purpose 1
   types to be kept 1–2
   see also individual accounts eg Client account; Personal accounts
Accruals concept 104
Acid test 159–60
Adjustments
   exercises 59–69
   expenses 38–40
   need for 38
Agency
   acting as agent 265–6
   instructing an agent 266–7
   receipt of deposit as agent 209
Assets
   balance sheet 32–3, 34, 36
   current assets ratio 159
   disposal of part of group 58–9
   final accounts
      disposal of part of group 58–9
      sale of assets 55–9
   revaluation 83–4
   sale 55–9

Assumptions *see* Accounting concepts
Attorney, power of 181
Auditors' report, Companies Acts requirements 128
Authorities, retention of copies 175

Bad debts *see* Debts
Balance sheet 30
   adjustments 39–40
   assets 32–3, 34, 36
   capital 33
   Companies Acts requirements 128
   company accounts 129–32
   consolidated accounts 142–7
   current assets 32, 34
   definitions 32–4
   depreciation 53–4
   exercise 36–7
   fixed assets 32, 34
   liabilities 33–5
   long-term liabilities 33
   partnership 80
   vertical format 36, 129–31
Balance, trial *see* Trial balance
Bases 104–5
Bill of costs, abatement 268
Bonus issue 126
Business entity concept 103

Capital
   balance sheet 33
   gearing ratios 164–5
   redemption reserves 125
   return on capital employed 162, 166
   working capital ratio 161
Capital account
   business proprietor 9–10
   partnerships 76–7
Cash account 186–7
   double-entry bookkeeping 5–8
Cheques
   dishonoured
      into client account 269–70
      into office account 269
   endorsed 184–5
   retention time 175
   split between office and client account 192–3
   third parties 185
   uncleared, drawing against 270–1

INDEX

Classification of accounts
  nominal accounts 11–15
  personal accounts 8
    of business proprietor 9–10
  real accounts 10–11
Client account
  balance sheet 36
  cash at bank 36
  cheques
    dishonoured, paid into 269–70
    split 192–3
    uncleared, drawing against 270–1
  controlled trusts 180–1, 241–2
  credit balances 36
  definition of client money 177
  designated deposit 242–5
  earned interest 247–9
  payments into 177–9, 183
    from Legal Aid Board 179
    from third party 179
  power of attorney 181
  receipt of 183
  separation from office money 176
  transfers
    between accounts 190–2
    from office account 189
    to office account 188–9
  withdrawals from 179–80, 184
  see also Interest payment
Client money 35
Clients, financial statements to 207
Closing stocks 42–3
Commissions 261–4
Company accounts
  balance sheet
    example 131–2
    vertical form 129–31
  bonus issue of shares 126
  Companies Acts requirements 128–32
  consolidated *see* Consolidated accounts
  debentures 116–17
  deferred taxation 120–1
  dividends 122–3
  exercises 132–41
  group companies *see* Consolidated accounts
  liabilities 124–5
  limited companies 113–41
  medium size companies 128–9
  preference shares 115–16
  premium shares 114–15
  profit and loss account 118–27
  profits, retained 124
  provisions 124–5
  public companies 131
  records required 128
  reports required 128
  reserves 124–5
    capital reserves 125
    capitalisation 126
    revenue reserves 125
  retained profits 124
  share capital 113–16
  sinking funds 127
  small companies 128–9
  taxation 119–20
    deferred 120–1

Computerised systems, hardcopy and reproduction capability 175
Consistency concept 104
Consolidated accounts 141–55
  acquisition of shares
    for less than book value 146–7
    for more than book value 145–6
  balance sheet 142–7, 149–50
  exercises 152–5
  holding majority interest in subsidiary 149–51
  profit and loss account 147–9, 151
Controlled trusts 180–1, 241–2
Conveyancing transactions 207–8
  completion
    financial statement 216–18
    purchase completion 222–4
    sale completion 218–21
    simultaneous sale and purchase 225–7
  exercises 227–40
  mortgage advances
    acting for buyer/borrower only 214
    acting for mortgagee only 213
    acting for mortgagee and purchaser 210–13
  mortgage redemption, acting for seller and private lender 214–16
  receipt of deposit
    as agent 209
    as stakeholder 209–10
Corporation tax 119–20
Cost account 11
Cost concept 103
Costs, abatement 268
Court of Protection receivers, Solicitors' Accounts Rules (1998) 181
Current accounts, partnerships 77–8
Current assets ratio 159

Debentures 116–17
Debts
  bad
    in final accounts
      effect 49–52
      recovery of written off debt 48
      writing off 46–7
    VAT relief 47–8, 271
  collection 160
  doubtful 49
Deferred taxation 120–1
Deposit interest *see* Interest payment
Depreciation
  calculation 52–3
  final accounts 52–4
  recording in accounts 53–4
Directors' report, Companies Acts requirements 128
Dividends
  appropriation 122
  cover 166–7
  interim 123
  payment 122, 123
  yield 166
Double-entry bookkeeping 2–3
  cash account 5–8
  exercises 20–6
  principle 3–5
  test 26–8
  worked example 15–18

INDEX

Drawings
  business proprietor 9–10
  partnerships 75
    cash 75
    end of year 76
    in kind 75–6
  profit and loss account 33
Duty to keep 175

Earnings per share 166
Efficiency ratio 163–4
Errors
  of commission 19
  compensating 19
  of entry 19
  not revealed by trial balance 19–20
  of omission 19
  of principle 20
Exercises
  adjustments 59–69
  balance sheet 36–7
  company accounts 132–41
  consolidated accounts 152–5
  conveyancing transactions 227–40
  double-entry bookkeeping 20–6
  final accounts 36–7, 59–69
    partnerships 84–96
  further transactions 272–81
  ledger entries 194–200
  manufacturing accounts 110–12
  partnership final accounts 84–96
  probate transactions 250–5
  profit and loss account 36–7
  ratio analysis 171–4
  trial balances 20–6
  value added tax 205–6
Expenses, partnership 74

Final accounts
  assets
    disposal of part of group 58–9
    sale 55–9
  balance sheet 30, 36–7
  closing accounts 30–1
  closing stocks 42–3
  debts
    doubtful, provisions 49
    effect of bad debts 49–52
    recovery of written off debt 48
    writing off bad debts 46–7
  depreciation 52–4
  exercises 59–69
  partnerships *see* Partnerships
  payment in advance 40–2
  presentation 31–2
  profit and loss 29, 32, 36–7
  sale of assets 55–9
  work in progress 44–5
Final balances, adjustments 39–40
Financial accounting concepts *see* Accounting concepts
Financial statements
  conveyancing transactions 216–18
  to clients 207
  see also individual statements
Format *see* Presentation of accounts

Gearing 164–5

Going-concern concept 104
Interest payment
  clients' money 247–9
  deposit interest 241–50
  designated deposit 242–5
  example 249–50
  money in lieu 245–7
  payment to client 241–7
  Rules 241–2
  trust money 241–2
Interest receivable account 11
Interpretation of accounts
  efficiency ratio 163–4
  factors outside the accounts 157–8
  gearing 164–5
  investment ratios 166–8
  liquidity ratios 159–60
  overtrading 161
  past years 158
  profitability ratios 162–3
  ratio analysis *see* Ratio analysis
  trends 158
Investment ratios 166–8

Law Society, accountant's report to 175
Layout of accounts 2, 31–2, 118–19, 129–31
Ledger entries
  exercise 194–200
  including VAT, test 284–6
Letters of administration 250
Limited companies *see* Company accounts
Liquidators, Solicitors' Accounts Rules (1998) 181
Liquidity ratios 159–60
Loan accounts, partnerships 78–9
Long-term liabilities 33

Manufacturing accounts 105–6, 108–9
  example 109
  exercise 110–12
  stock 108
  work in progress 108
Materiality concept 104
Medium size companies, Companies Acts requirements 128–9
Money measurement concept 103
Mortgages
  advances
    acting for buyer/borrower only 214
    acting for mortgagee only 213
    acting for mortgagee and purchaser 210–13
  redemption, acting for seller and private lender 214–16

Nominal accounts 11–15
  cost account 11
  interest receivable account 11
  rent receivable account 11

Office account
  dishonoured cheque paid into 269
  payments into 181–2, 189
  payments out of 182–3, 190
  receipt of office money 182
  split cheques 192–3
  transfer from client account 189
  transfer to client account 190

INDEX

Overtrading 161

Partnerships
    appropriation account 71–2, 82
    asset revaluation 83–4
    balance sheet 80
    capital accounts 76–7
    changes in constitution 82–3
        revaluation of assets 83–4
    current accounts 77–8
    drawings 75
        cash 75
        end of year 76
        in kind 75–6
    expenses 74
    final accounts 71–4
        balance sheet 80
        example 80–1
        exercises 84–96
        expenses 74
        profit and loss account 71–3
        test 96–102
    general 71
    loan accounts 78–9
    profit and loss account 71–3
    revaluation of assets 83–4
    sole practitioner taking in partner 82
Payment in advance, final accounts 40–2
Personal accounts 8
Personal accounts of business proprietor 9–10
    capital account 9
    drawings account 9–10
Petty cash 186–7
Policies 104
Power of attorney 181
Preference shares
    cumulative 115
    non-cumulative 115
    participating 115
    redeemable 115
Presentation of accounts 2
    balance sheet 33, 129–31
    final accounts 31–2
    profit and loss account 32, 118–19
    vertical format 31, 118–19, 129–31
Preservation period 175
Price earnings ratio 167–8
Probate transactions
    advertisement payments 250
    collection of assets 250
    costs 250
    distribution of estate 250
    exercises 250–5
    grant of letters of administration 250
    grant of probate 250
    property 250
    tests 255–60
Profit
    gross profit percentage 162–3
    net profit percentage 163
    retained 124
Profit and loss account 29
    comments on 32
    Companies Acts requirements 128
    consolidated 147–9
    depreciation 53–4
    drawings 33

Profit and loss account — *continued*
    exercise 36–7
    limited companies 118–27
    partnership 71–3
    vertical format 31, 118–19
    work in progress 44–5
Profitability ratios 162–3
Provisions
    company accounts 124–5
    doubtful debts 49
Prudence concept 104

Ratio analysis 157–8
    acid test 159–60
    capital gearing ratios 164–5
    collection period 160
    current assets ratio 159
    debtors to creditors ratio 161
    dividend cover 166–7
    dividend yield 166
    earnings per share 166
    efficiency ratio 163–4
    example 168–71
    exercise 171–4
    gross profit percentage 162–3
    investment ratios 166–8
    liquidity ratios 159–60
    net profit percentage 163
    payment period 160–1
    price earnings ratio 167–8
    profitability ratios 162–3
    rate of stock turnover 163–4
    return on capital employed 162, 166
    return on ordinary shareholders interest 166
    trade creditors to purchases ratio 160–1
    trade debtors to sales ratio 160
    working capital ratio 161
Real accounts 10–11
Receivers (Court of Protection), Solicitors' Accounts
    Rules (1998) 181
Rent receivable account 11
Reserves 124–5
    capital reserves 125
    capitalisation of 126
    revaluation reserve 125
    revenue reserves 125
Retained profits 124
Retention time
    accounts 175
    authorities 175
    paid cheques 175
Return on capital employed 162, 166
Return on ordinary shareholders interest 166
Revaluation reserve 125

Sale of assets, final accounts 55–9
Share capital 113–16
Share premium account 125
Shares
    acquisition
        for less than book value 146–7
        for more than book value 145–6
    bonus issue 126
    earnings per share 166
    preference 115–16
    premium 114–15
    Stock Exchange 131

INDEX

Sinking funds 127
Small companies, Companies Acts requirements 128–9
Small transactions 271
Solicitors' accounts
   abatements 268
   agreed fees 188
   cash account 186–7
   cheques
      dishonoured
         into client account 269–70
         into office account 269
      endorsed 184–5
      split between office and client account 192–3
      third parties 185
   client account *see* Client account
   commissions 261–4
   controlled trusts 180–1, 241–2
   costs 187–8
   delivery of bills of costs 187–8
   duty to keep accounts 175
   further transactions 261–93
      exercises 272–81
      tests 282–4
   ledger entries exercise 194–200
   office account *see* Office account
   petty cash 186–7
   trustees 180–1
   value added tax
      accounting to Customs and Excise 202
      agency method 203, 205
      charging output tax 201
      disbursements 203–5
      exercises 205–6
      paying input tax 201–2
      principal method 203–5
      registering for 200
Solicitors' Accounts Rules (1998) 175–81
   liquidator, trustees in bankruptcy and receivers 181
Stakeholder 209–10

Stock
   closing 42–3
   manufacturing accounts 108
Stock Exchange, sale of shares on 131
Stock turnover rate 163–4

Taxation
   companies 119–21
   corporation tax 119–20
   deferred 120–1
   value added tax *see* Value added tax
Trading accounts 105–8
Transactions *see individual transactions eg* Conveyancing transactions
Trial balance
   errors not revealed by 19–20
   exercises 20–6
   preparation 18–19
   purpose 18
   test on 26–8
Trustees, solicitors as 180–1
Trustees in bankruptcy, Solicitors' Accounts Rules (1998) 181
Types to be kept 1–2

Value added tax
   accounting to Customs and Excise 202
   agency method 203, 205
   bad debt relief 47–8, 271
   disbursements 203–5
   exercises 205–6
   input tax 201–2
   ledger accounts 284–6
   output tax 201
   registering for 200
   solicitors' accounts 200–6

Work in progress
   closing 45–6
   manufacturing accounts 108
   profit and loss account 44–5
   worked example 45–6
Working capital ratio 161